A SEA FULL OF TURTLES

A
SEA FULL
OF
TURTLES

THE SEARCH FOR OPTIMISM
IN AN EPOCH OF EXTINCTION

BILL STREEVER

PEGASUS BOOKS
NEW YORK LONDON

A SEA FULL OF TURTLES

Pegasus Books, Ltd.
148 West 37th Street, 13th Floor
New York, NY 10018

Copyright © 2024 by Bill Streever

First Pegasus Books cloth edition July 2024

Interior design by Maria Fernandez

Library of Congress Cataloging-in-Publication Data is available.

ISBN: 978-1-63936-669-9

10 9 8 7 6 5 4 3 2 1

Printed in the United States of America
Distributed by Simon & Schuster
www.pegasusbooks.com

This book is for the legions of volunteers and professionals in all nations and cultures working to protect and promote our planet's biodiversity.

"We have the dubious distinction of being the
deadliest species in the annals of biology."
—Yuval Noah Harari, in *Sapiens*

"I have great faith in optimism as a guiding
principle, if only because it offers us the opportunity
of creating a self-fulfilling prophecy."
—Arthur C. Clarke, 2007, in a farewell video
recorded on his ninetieth birthday

"Humans have the potential not only to create happy
lives for themselves, but also to help other beings."
—The Dalai Lama, in *The Dalai Lama's Little Book of Wisdom*

"May your children swim in an ocean full of turtles."
—Osha Gray Davidson, in *Fire in the Turtle House*

Contents

Preface

I am a biologist, but first and foremost, I am a lover of nature. It is a tragic moment to be so, as I behold an extinction event comparable to those which took from us the once ubiquitous trilobites, the nautilus-like ammonoids, and the dinosaurs.

I am hardly alone in this role. You, too, are a witness. As is everyone you know. As is every person alive today. But we are more than mere spectators. We watch the tragedy of the Anthropocene unfold, the epoch during which our kind shapes the planet, and by virtue of being alive, we participate.

It is perfectly natural to look at our situation with disgust, anger, and pessimism. But I do not want bitterness to define what is left of my life. I want, somewhat desperately and unreasonably, to live with hope and optimism.

I set out in search of something resembling good news with a sense of dread, with a nagging knowledge that I might encounter little in the way of promise and much along the lines of anguish. Or that all I might find would be something akin to a group of concerned citizens applying self-adhesive bandages to the still-warm but pulseless victim of a drive-by shooting. I might be chasing something that cannot exist, something as impossible as a flying mermaid or a diving unicorn.

But I also set out thinking of sailors confronted with catastrophic sinkings, trapped on lifeboats for weeks on end far out at sea, the food supply long gone and drinking water maddeningly rationed. The best predictor of their survival, of their success, has never been physical fitness or past experience or an ability to swim. The best predictor has always been their faith in a better future. "For if any of them had despaired," wrote William Bligh in 1790, "he would most probably have died before we reached New Holland." The "them" to which he referred were the eighteen men cast away by the *Bounty* mutineers, the men who sailed with Bligh for 3,618 desperate miles in a 23-foot-long open boat before reaching a safe harbor.

I wrote this book while weathering the COVID pandemic in Mexico's Gulf of California (still known to many as the Sea of Cortez, although that name is falling out of favor with some in Mexico today), having sailed northwest from Nicaragua just as Central America closed its ports. Had protective measures not rendered the crossing of borders so difficult, I might have taken a wider-ranging, more peripatetic approach to this book. I might have sought out firsthand experiences and stories of turtle conservation in Australia, Asia, Africa, and the United States. But before long, I realized the story of turtles in Mexico, and specifically in the Gulf of California, was exactly what I was after.

In parts of Mexico, people face problems that many in the wealthy world have little hope of understanding—problems with poverty, with education, with frequent power outages, with cartel violence, with the tenuous nature of the rule of law, with a lack of opportunity even for the talented and hardworking. For people living on the shores of the Gulf of California, add to these challenges the scarcity of freshwater and, in many areas, the absence of anything resembling a serviceable road.

And yet, sea turtle populations here are bouncing back, or seem to be. If sea turtles can recover in the Gulf, why not other species in other places? Mexico taught me that there may be room for hope even as we face the seemingly overwhelming wave of extinctions that we caused. But at the same time, hope does not assure positive outcomes. Could what I saw as conservation successes be sustained? Was there room not only for hope, but for optimism?

While writing this book I became so depressed at times that I had to put everything aside. I would spend a day, three days, a week, a whole month feeling terribly sad and deeply troubled. I would walk the rocky hills surrounding the Gulf of California. I would paddle my kayak around islands. I would swim and dive. I would sail forty miles north or twenty miles south to a new anchorage, a new place, the grandeur of even the diminished nature around me always holding my attention, distracting me as I attempted to reject despair in the face of biological catastrophe. But always I stumbled upon signs of the disappearance of organic wealth which is everywhere apparent. To anyone unfortunate enough to be trained and experienced in field biology, the evidence is abundant, in plain and glaring sight.

Occasionally, I simply refused to think of that horrible phrase, that most obscene combination of words, "human-caused extinction."

But I would return to the work, to my search for optimism with regard to this living planet and our role, the role of humanity, in its future. Without optimism failure is all but assured. Without optimism there is no compelling case for change. Why even try to fight the enemy if that enemy has already won?

I am by my nature an optimist, at least in the long-term. But realize this: I am no fool. I know humans are capable of notorious transgressions, that they have and will continue to commit crimes not only against humanity but against life itself. I see daily evidence of stupidity, misunderstanding, ignorance beyond belief, and relentless selfishness. Even so, I also see promise. I see examples of decency, wisdom, and self-sacrifice. Because I am no fool, I see the good despite the bad. I see the ability of our own flawed species to grow over time, to change our ways, and maybe, before it is over, to do more good than harm.

It was thoughts like these that drove away despair and allowed me to return to my words. And it is thoughts like these that continue to guide me in my life.

My hope is that this book will in some way allow others to see what I have come to see: This extinction crisis can and must end, and we can all be part of its demise. I am far from perfect, and I know I can be better. I can do better by my fellow species. And maybe, sometimes, I can motivate other people to do a better job of protecting their fellow species.

With all this in mind, I will know that the effort I have put into this book is worthwhile if its existence somehow results in the protection of a single reproductive female turtle. And even more so if that success cascades, spawning through the magic of inspiration additional victories not only for sea turtles, but for the magnificent spectrum of other species who share our world.

ONE

The Sexual Turtle

Truth be told, long-distance sailing at its best can and should be boring. The wind should be from the right direction, slightly abaft of the beam, and of the right strength, neither too strong nor too weak, a Goldilocks wind. The captain and crew should be content and well-fed, reasonably sober and out of the sun. Few things on the boat, or at least few things of importance, should be broken or breaking. The bilge should be dry, signifying a boat not faced with the immediate risk of sinking. Nothing should be on fire.

When boredom sets in, the helmsman stares at the waves. A form of meditation transforms the day. The boat moves, the mind wanders, the eyes take in an ever-changing sea.

I was the helmsman on such a day, sailing with my wife some few miles off the Pacific coast of Mexico, when there they were. Turtles screwing, specifically olive ridley sea turtles, *Lepidochelys olivacea* to the overly educated. One clung to the top of the other, flippers of the uppermost clasping the shell of the undermost, the lower of the two seeming to swim for both of them, keeping them on or near the surface and in view under a blazing sun.

Male on top, for those who are curious about such things.

There are of course other ways to describe this sighting. A biologist might choose a word like copulation. Or coupling. Or mating. But despite my habit of sailing from place to place with no visible means of support, I am a biologist. I have spent my career studying animals and plants, and while I no longer draw a regular paycheck I remain an observer of all things living. In my experience the best biologists save the more polite words for polite company, for reports to funders, and for papers in scholarly journals. A biologist in the field, stumbling upon such a sight as the one before me, is as likely as not to rely on the vernacular. Screwing works well, as does bonking, or, as a friend often says with regard to paired caribou and bears, humping. And even, in cruder moments, simply fucking.

So this is where it starts—my interest in turtles, my sea turtle story. With screwing. With reptilian marine sex. With turtle erotica. With wildlife porn.

And yet, in the here and now of the helmsman on watch, I do not know that what I am seeing will become a story. I do not understand that on this day, at this moment, I have set out on a quest for optimism in a world in which humans have become by far the single greatest force behind the annihilation of life on Earth, the exterminators of myriad and diverse species large, small, and all sizes in between.

I have embarked on a search for optimism when the reality of the situation has progressed far beyond the realm of pessimism to what might fairly be described as calamitous and catastrophic. Doomsday lies faintly visible on the horizon, but these two turtles, one on top of the other, full of lust in clear water under a bright sun, offer hope. They are a living sign that optimism may not yet be entirely naïve.

A digression, by way of explanation, and only the first of several.

It is simple, really. We are just the two of us, man and wife, captain and captain. We are both biologists—specifically, I am an aquatic ecologist and Lisanne is a marine biologist, at one time specializing in corals and sponges but later branching out to work with gray whales in eastern Russia.

Some years ago, we decided to trade our mainstream habits for the life afloat, for the opportunity to spend time closer to nature. Since then we have been on a slow voyage to no place in particular.

Now we have sailed into the coronavirus years. We crossed through the Panama Canal from the Caribbean to the Pacific just as the pandemic was beginning to make regular headlines. We made our way up the coast as the news worsened. By luck, we left Nicaragua the day before the nation's authorities closed its ports, declaring, without warning, that no one would leave and no one would enter. We sailed offshore past Guatemala and Honduras and El Salvador to Mexico, not knowing what to expect. But the Mexican authorities welcomed us. We cleared into the country, wearing masks and maintaining distance, in Chiapas, the first harbor north of the country's southern border. Two months later, despite the confusion that reigned throughout the world, we continued north, eager to escape the worst of the hurricane zone before summer set in. We sailed toward the Gulf of California, toward Steinbeck's Sea of Cortez.

As to our boat, *Rocinante*, she is a mostly restored 1965 ketch, meaning she has two masts, the shorter one standing just forward of the rudder post. By modern standards she sails somewhat inefficiently, clumsily, and slowly, but she is solid and safe, a John Alden design with classic wine-glass lines.

As sailors, we have been and will remain on the learn-as-you-go program, thankful for a forgiving boat. As biologists, too, we remain on the learn-as-you-go program, working on whatever strikes our fancies, on whatever we might happen to see as we sail from place to place with no definite schedule and no clear destination.

Rocinante, the name of the boat that we call home, comes from the novel *Don Quixote*. Specifically, Rocinante was Don Quixote's horse, a weathered farm animal that became a noble steed in the mind of its delusional master.

For the record, Lisanne would probably not choose to apply the word "screwing" in reference to copulating turtles. But neither would she object to such a term, which in her view would likely appear not so much crude as simply direct.

People like sex. Well, I cannot speak for all people, but I can speak for myself and most people I know well enough to discuss such matters. The same can and has been said of most animals.

Jonathan Balcombe, a biologist specializing in animal behavior and author of books with titles like *What a Fish Knows*, *Pleasurable Kingdom*, and, most recently, *Super Fly*, told me that turtles probably enjoy sex.

"It's not a stretch to think that turtles enjoy sex," he said, "at least not in my book. Or any of my books. I always try to include something about enjoyment of sex in my writing. Even in my new book about flies. Fruit fly studies in Israel show that the flies enjoy ejaculation. They sense 'reward'—you'll hear the word 'reward' in the sciences more than 'pleasure.' If one can make the case that flies enjoy sex one can make the argument that turtles enjoy sex. Not sure what the science says. One way to see how they are feeling is to sample their blood. Look at their dopamine levels. I would really be surprised if it turns out that turtles don't get some pleasure out of sex."

Why am I dwelling on sex? Obviously, it is a great topic in and of itself, but here its importance lies with the connection it makes between us and them, between we humans and a host of other living organisms.

It is not the only thing we have in common with other organisms. It is just one example of many.

No one should be surprised by this. All living organisms on Earth can be traced to a single common ancestor, to the Last Universal Common Ancestor, or LUCA.

In 1859, Charles Darwin wrote, in *On the Origin of Species*, "Therefore I should infer from analogy that probably all the organic beings which have ever lived on this earth have descended from some one primordial form, into which life was first breathed."

This was not quite the LUCA. The LUCA probably lived among other organisms. It was not the first to ever live but rather the earliest to live whose descendants remain with us today. The LUCA is the one whose genetic hoofprint was lucky enough to succeed for something close to four billion years in an ever-changing world, taking the form of species beyond counting, hanging on in no small part because of the diversity it facilitated.

This is not crackpot stuff. This version of reality is brought to us by modern science. It is surrounded by discussions that only molecular geneticists can love, by debates over the role of horizontal gene transfer, by sentences along the lines of this one: "We analyzed this LUCA gene (LG) group, and a random sample of 500 genes from the gnomAD database (RG group)."

Laugh if you like, poke fun at scientists and the sciences, at their perpetual chasing of grant money and their publishing of papers in erudite though seldom-read journals. But think it through and it is not at all surprising that we—the greater We, the We that includes us and turtles and amoebas and pine trees, among others—are clearly related to one another. Cousins. Not first or second or even third cousins, but still cousins.

The LUCA probably used RNA as a means of copying itself, of reproducing itself. Although DNA gets most of the press today, in fact we too use RNA in our reproductive cycle. The LUCA manufactured proteins—that is, it built itself, it grew—just as we do. The LUCA used adenosine triphosphate—ATP, which some might remember from high school biology classes—as a means of storing and moving energy from place to place. The

LUCA had genes that can still be found today, widely distributed, the ultimate family heirloom passed down through billions of years.

It is hard to believe that the LUCA enjoyed sex. The LUCA was an early microbe that, in all likelihood, reproduced primarily asexually. Occasional forays into sexual reproduction, into the endlessly fascinating exchange of bodily fluids or at least genetic material, may not have resulted in anything that we humans would have recognized as pleasurable. It may well be that enjoyment of sex arose far later in the history of life. This is the sort of thing that remains impossible to prove or disprove. I know of no credible, or for that matter frivolous, research on this topic, and so will leave further consideration to the imagination.

So there I was, at the helm off the Pacific coast of Mexico, continuing our sail northwestward, occasionally watching turtles and thinking about sex and LUCA, and about just how closely the man at the helm and the turtles in the sea are related. Which led me to think about all of the sea turtles I had seen before. In the Atlantic, in the Mediterranean, in the Adriatic, the South China Sea, the Caribbean, the Gulf of Mexico.

I have had the good fortune, over many years, to see greens, hawksbills, olive ridleys, and loggerheads. I have probably seen, from a distance and fleetingly, a leatherback. That leaves only two existing species out of sight, the Kemp's ridley of the Caribbean, which is similar enough to the olive ridley that I may have seen one without realizing it, and the flatback, which frequents the areas surrounding the northern coast of Australia.

Which in turn led me to remember that, as a boy, I had once worried that sea turtles would disappear forever. That they would go extinct. Poof. Gone. Never to be seen again. And at that time I was a turtle virgin. I had never had the privilege of seeing a sea turtle in the wild, of watching one of these strange armored beasts swim or feed or breathe or copulate.

Thanks to humanity, sea turtles, after more than a hundred million years on Earth, were on their way over the finish line. They were on their way out. They might disappear, I thought, before I ever had a chance to see them.

At the time it was a legitimate worry.

But then, poof, sea turtles were listed as endangered, protected by law in the United States and throughout most of the world. Now they are so common that I can watch them having sex. At least, one species of them is so common in this one region that I can watch them having sex.

But that second poof, the one of protection, was less of a poof and more of a long, quiet sigh that continues to this day, a somewhat but not entirely successful sigh that is an important part of the current leg of the sea turtle story.

Those are among the things that went through my wandering mind as we sailed up the coast, stopping at places like Puerto Vallarta, where we could buy boat parts; at San Blas, where we could go upriver to see hundreds of crocodiles and thousands of black-bellied whistling ducks; at Isla Isabela, where we could walk quietly among nesting blue-footed boobies and spend Christmas with fishermen; at Mazatlán, where we could ride bicycles along the clifftop shoreline. After each stop, back underway, more turtles popped up, some alone and some paired, coupled, occasionally so abundant and absorbed in their own thoughts and deeds that we had to change course to avoid running them down.

Extinct. We toss that word about casually for everything from dinosaurs to mastodons, from dodos to passenger pigeons, from Java Man to Neanderthals. And, well, for turtles and tortoises.

Take, as examples, two species of freshwater turtles, Viesca mud turtles, last seen in 1961, and Nubian flapshell turtles, last seen in 2000. Or take this dire sentence from a 2018 article in the academic journal *Bioscience*: "As of 2017, 356 turtle species were recognized worldwide, of which approximately 61% are threatened or have become extinct in modern times."

But the word extinct was not so long ago used only to convey the putting out of a candle flame and the wiping out of debt. Application of the word to living beings, to organisms, was rare before 1800. The possibility that a species could go extinct resided somewhere between the not-considered and the unthinkable.

Early applications of the word to life and death were cautious, guarded. Look at the 1753 paper breathlessly titled, "A Discourse Concerning the Large Horns Frequently Found under Ground in Ireland, Concluding from Them That the Great American Deer, Call'd a Moose, Was Formerly Common in That Island: With Remarks on Some Other Things Natural to That Country," by Thomas Molyneux. "That no real species of living creatures is so utterly extinct," wrote Molyneux, "as to be left entirely out of the world, since it was first created, is the opinion of many naturalists, and is grounded on so good a principle of providence taking care in general of all its animal productions, that it deserves our assent."

No, Molyneux argued, animals could not go entirely extinct. Even if a species might be wiped out in one part of the world, so decimated "as to become there utterly unknown," it would persist elsewhere. As he put it, "It cannot be denied but the kind has been carefully preserved in some other part of the world."

Regarding the animal referenced in his title, the supposed moose, the grand creature responsible for the giant horns found buried in Irish soils: It could no longer be found in Ireland, he claimed, but it still roamed free in America.

He was, of course, dead wrong. The creature he called a moose was something else entirely. Moose grazed happily enough in North America, but the last lonely majestic *Megaloceros giganteus*, with its moose-like antlers that could stretch more than ten feet wide, had died, or more specifically had been killed by Molyneux's ancestors, seven thousand years before he himself had been born.

Or look at the words of none other than Thomas Jefferson, from 1797, when he was serving as vice president of the young United States under John Adams. "The animal species which has once been put into a train of motion," he wrote, "is still probably moving in that train."

Enter Georges Cuvier, born in 1769. Looking at the record found buried beneath Paris, Cuvier saw layers of saltwater and freshwater inundation and the appearance and disappearance of species unknown to humanity. He put his faith in the evidence he found rather than in the opinions of men like Molyneux and Jefferson. While Napoleon and his thugs wreaked havoc across Europe, Cuvier wrote of global changes that ended lives not only of individuals but of lineages, giving us wonderful insights as well as delightful sentences. Such as this: "All these facts, consistent among themselves, seem to me to prove the existence of a world previous to ours."

He would eventually tell the existing world that fossilized mammoth and mastodon jaws were not at all the same as those found in living elephants. Seven decades after Thomas Molyneux's strange moose paper and two decades after Jefferson's rant, in the 1818 English version of his 296-page *Essay on the Theory of the Earth*, Cuvier was using the words "extinct" and "extinction" somewhat casually, as in "the ancient and now extinct species were as permanent in their forms and characters as those which exist at present" and "their races even have become extinct, and have left no memorial of them except some small fragment which the naturalist can scarcely recognize." He would go on to catalog forty-nine species found nowhere but in the fossil record.

This is how "extinction" came into the lexicon as we know it today. The term and the concept can be used unapologetically, without flinching. Thanks to this change in the language I can write, with no need for much explanation, that more than five hundred species have gone extinct in the last hundred years. Five hundred species. That is more species than the average person can name or recognize. This does not count the legions of species with limited habitats that go extinct before they are even recognized as species, the tiny beetles and spiders and ferns, not to mention nematodes and tardigrades and mushrooms, all falling victim to axes and bulldozers and agricultural poisons before being cataloged, before being appreciated by their cousins, the humans. Include these, and we go from five hundred species in a hundred years to eight thousand species in a single year. Or more. Maybe, as the United Nations Convention on Biological Diversity concluded, more than fifty thousand species per year.

The numbers are debatable and are in fact debated. But even at the low end, the numbers are high.

Consider this: The background extinction rate, the number of species lost per year during typical periods in the history of our planet, is something like 0.00143. That is, in more typical times, we might expect to see one extinction every seven hundred years, not even close to five hundred in one hundred years, and far, far fewer than eight thousand in a single year.

For now, for just a few minutes, forget about the numbers. Ignore the unknown species found only in small areas and perhaps never seen or at least seldom noticed by people. Cast all that aside and take a moment to remember our more well-known and charismatic cousins. Pause long enough to say goodbye to the Tasmanian tiger and the Caspian tiger, farewell to the Carolina parakeet and the heath hen, so long to the Caribbean monk seal and the Japanese sea lion. Not see you later, but see you never again. No more sex for any of you.

Charles Darwin, well before he wrote his landmark *On the Origin of Species*, well before he penned *The Voyage of the Beagle*, discovered what turned out to be a new genus of frog, one which would be called *Rhinoderma*. This was when he was in Chile, taking a break from his chronically seasick life aboard the *Beagle*. He was twenty-five years old.

There are two species in the genus, *Rhinoderma darwinii* and *Rhinoderma rufum*, the southern Darwin's frog and the northern Darwin's frog. South or north, the two species look similar and in fact were considered one and the same until 1975. They have in common inch-long bodies sporting arrow shaped heads, spindly limbs, and brown or green backs. But on closer examination the northern frog has a membrane between its toes that is more or less absent in its southern cousin, and their calls differ to the well-trained ear. Neither species stands out. In fact both are frogs that could be easily overlooked in the leaf litter that they call home.

Weirdly, they, along with the sea horse, are alone among living or recently living vertebrates in which the males internally brood their young. After mating, male Darwin's frogs pick up developing eggs with their mouths, dropping them into their swollen vocal sacs where the eggs hatch to become tiny tadpoles. In the south, the tadpoles live in the male's vocal sac for up to ten weeks before finally changing into tiny frogs, which then hop their way out into the world. In the north, the tadpoles are released into the wild before metamorphosis. To make a peculiar story even stranger, whether south or north, the eggs ingested may have been fertilized by the brooding male or by some other male that is no longer on the scene.

Why is *Rhinoderma* relevant? Why care about Darwin's frogs? Only because the animals appear, at this time, to be in trouble. The southern Darwin's frog is endangered, hanging on in lonely groups restricted to isolated patches of habitat. Its close cousin, the northern Darwin's frog, is almost certainly already gone, last seen in 1981, one of the unfortunate many that have made a mockery of the background extinction rate in our times. What happened to the curious little frog? No one can say for sure, but probably *Rhinoderma rufum* has fallen victim to an amphibian-skin-infecting fungus that not long ago had a limited range but that today, probably thanks to jet-setting humans with sticky boots, can be found pretty much everywhere.

One might say turtle sex is where the sea turtle story starts, with the joining of sperm and egg on a sun-scorched sea. One might, but I would not. To me, this would be a short-sighted vision of the sea turtle's long slow swim.

To me, the starting line lies in the distant past, some four billion years ago, long before the first turtles joined together in reptilian matrimony, long before even the rise of the reptiles, or for that matter the appearance of the first of the vertebrates. The starting line lies on a very young Earth.

One could place the starting line even earlier, at something just shy of fourteen billion years ago, at the birth of the universe, when the precursors to the stuff that would eventually become sea turtles came into being. As astrophysicist Carl Sagan once said, "If you wish to make an apple pie from scratch, you must first invent the universe." But that view might be on the extremist side.

But what about the finish line? Where will this story end?

Extinction, whenever that might be. Extinction of sea turtles or extinction of humanity, whichever of these two inevitabilities may come first. Extinction of sea turtles because, aside from some epilogue about their legacy, once the last one is gone the story of sea turtles has come to an end. And extinction of humanity because without us, as far as we know, there are no storytellers, or at least no storytellers capable of managing a story as complex as that of the sea turtle.

Wait a minute, one might say. This book, so says its subtitle, is supposed to portray a search for optimism. Yet here the extinction of sea turtles or the extinction of humanity are thrown out right from the start as inevitabilities. What kind of positive outlook is that?

It is the kind that does not define extinction itself as a problem. Extinction is perfectly natural and a necessary part of life. On average—a weird sort of average, to be sure—any one invertebrate species will last about eleven million years, while vertebrate species are less long-lived. The average mammal species might be good for a mere million years, give or take.

The numbers themselves are not so important, and they are, after all, just estimated averages. The point is that species go extinct in the normal course of events.

No, the problem is not extinction. The problem is premature extinction caused by humans—by human exploitation in some cases, by human apathy and carelessness in others.

Wait a minute, one might say again. This is supposed to be a book about sea turtles. At this point one might be a bit suspicious about where all these words are going. One might be concerned that this book is about more than just sea turtles.

If so, one would be correct, because this is a story more complex than that of sea turtles, more complex than that of any single species or group of animals or plants or fungi. One might even suspect that a book subtitled *The Search for Optimism in an Epoch of Extinction* might have something to say about how we strange creatures that call ourselves human beings interact with our distant cousins a million times removed.

All true, but this is still a book about sea turtles.

When I was a boy, my father had a motivational poster tacked to the wall of his basement workshop. The poster showed a box turtle or a tortoise and the words, "Behold the turtle: It makes progress only when it sticks its neck out."

Sea turtles, unlike the 350 or so other named and still living or recently extinct species of turtles and tortoises, have no ability whatsoever to withdrawal into their shells. Their necks, as long as they live, are out. As is mine, I sometimes think, for having the audacity to attempt to search for optimism in the midst of this extinction crisis.

It is my hope that the story conveyed here will not one day unfold as the worst of all tragedies, a collection of horrible events ending unhappily in the untimely expiration of one of its protagonists. What humans have done to sea turtles in the past few centuries is without a doubt terribly shameful, in the sense of something about which we should feel collective shame. But still, I cling to the belief that in the end, the story of the sea turtle will not be unmanageably sad. It will not be tragic. I know turtles will eventually go extinct through natural causes, maybe before or maybe after the extinction of our own kind, but their extinction will not be our fault. At least I hope not.

Take this as evidence of my bias toward optimism.

Note that I write these words understanding that there exist among us those who will not agree with anything resembling an upbeat outlook when it comes to the extinction crisis. Optimistic environmentalism has been called an oxymoron, and at least one writer has suggested that optimistic environmentalists may be not so much oxymorons as just plain morons.

Let the naysayers cast stones as they please. For myself, I will search for optimism. Within limits and with caveats, and knowing that things will get worse before they get better, I see optimism as the only path to success when it comes to ending the biodiversity crisis. That is why I spent two years sailing in the Gulf of California on what amounted to an uncertain quest for good news.

As we sail northwest along the coast, we continue to see paired turtles, more screwing, usually a mile or more from the coast, but occasionally in anchorages and once at the mouth of an estuary, within a boat's length of rocks placed to protect a channel leading shoreward into dense mangroves. Ashore, along the beach that stretched in either direction from the channel and its protective rocks, people sat under palm trees and swam in the shallows. Children dug in the sand. Fishermen cast lines from the rocks or waded out onto sandbars.

We watched the turtles and the people for half an hour. As far as we could tell, no one but us noticed the turtles. Likewise, the turtles did not appear to notice the people. But the turtles, of course, were preoccupied.

So how about more on the sex life of sea turtles? It seems to me that few of us know much about the topic. It is not that humanity does not know a great deal about turtle sex, but that the average human does not devote much time to thinking about it. Perhaps no time at all before reading the next few paragraphs.

Here is how it works.

All turtles, of course, start as hatchlings. To contribute to the long-term conservation of the species, a turtle must at the very least live long enough to become sexually mature. The animals, male and female, must survive long enough to dispense with virginity for the common good.

Age of consent varies among species, from as little as seven or eight years for leatherbacks to as much as forty years for greens. A frequently offered and disturbing estimate: Something like one out of every one thousand sea turtle hatchlings survive to maturity.

The survivors, both males and females, lead solitary lives for the most part. But when mating season arrives, they make their way toward established nesting beaches. Males arrive first, lurking around offshore, waiting for females. There is little in the way of obvious or even subtle courtship or selection. A male sees a female and climbs aboard, mounting her from above and behind, using long claws on his front flippers to hang on to the leading edge of her shell. His claws often leave marks.

Turtle anatomy is generally similar to human anatomy, but with some differences. The shell, for example. But also, turtles—like other reptiles, birds, amphibians, and a handful of mammals—possess a cloaca, a single opening to the urinary tract, the downstream end of the digestive tract, and the reproductive tract.

In sea turtles, the cloaca sits at the base of the tail.

Atop the female, the male twists his tail forward under the female's shell. His penis emerges from his cloaca. It is a penis, incidentally, that can be half as long as his shell. He slides it into her cloaca. Then he maintains his grip.

Under normal circumstances, sea turtles use their front flippers for propulsion and their rear flippers for steering. The male, with his front flippers occupied, relies on the female to keep the pair afloat, to carry them to the surface now and then for a breath of air.

Other males may show up. They may nip and bite at the male in place. But he has no interest in letting go.

Copulation may continue for twenty-four hours. Or longer.

With the deed completed, the male slips away without ceremony. He will rest for a while before finding another female, and perhaps another. Or not.

The female also mates again, and perhaps again. Or not. She has the ability to store sperm, and can use the sperm from a single copious donation to fertilize her eggs throughout an entire nesting season.

Why do I twice throw in the caveat, "Or not?" Because some evidence suggests that sea turtles mate repeatedly in a season, while other evidence suggests sea turtles mate once and call it good. Looking at the genetics of hawksbill turtles in the Seychelles, researchers found that 90 percent of all females laid eggs fertilized by just one mate. An additional 9 percent laid eggs fertilized by two different mates. No males were found to have fertilized more than a single female. In short, neither sex appeared to be especially promiscuous.

In any case, with the act or acts behind them the males wander away, never to set foot ashore, while the females crawl ashore to lay eggs that may grow into new turtles. I use the word "may" because eggs do not always produce hatchlings. Some are not fertile. Some are lost to flooding, others to drought and overheating, still others to bacterial infections. And some are eaten by raccoons or coyotes or dogs. Or humans.

A typical nest will have from fifty to two hundred eggs, and a typical female will nest between two and eight times in a season.

The math behind that magical aforementioned one-in-one-thousand ratio becomes discouraging. Only the luckiest of couples will see even one of their season's progenies grow into an adult.

Well, none will see their young grow into adults, since the fathers are long gone and the mother's duties are complete once her eggs are laid and buried, but the point remains: Turtle survival rates are low.

Nonetheless, sea turtles, unlike so many of their cousins, counter to the predictions made when I was a child, have not gone extinct. This in itself is nothing less than miraculous. This is why I can sail along toward the Gulf of California watching waves in a meditative state until turtles screwing ends the helmsman's boredom. This is why I can at least consider the possibility of sailing on a quest for optimism with regard to the extinction crisis.

TWO
Walking Beaches

Along the coast, authorities close ports to fight the spread of the virus. Economic conditions deteriorate and authorities reverse closure orders, and then, at times, reinstate them. Port Captains appear to work more or less independently from one another and from central mandates. Businesses react to changing rules coming from federal and municipal authorities. People stay home from work and try to survive without income. In places, uniformed men patrol beaches. In scattered urban areas, criminal gangs pass out care packages bearing their own logos, a less than subtle narcomensaje, a message from the crime cartels to the government, saying, in effect, "we own this neighborhood and we take care of its people."

Information is spotty and uncertain. Many people we talk to ask us what we think about the virus. The Mexican fishermen we meet express what can only be described as a fatalistic view of the whole affair. Some seem to think the virus is not real. Through masks, and from a distance, we answer their questions as best we can. But really, we know little more than they do. Despite an atmosphere of confusion, tinged or sometimes deeply colored with fear, the people we meet are without exception friendly, welcoming, and as concerned about our well-being as they are about their own.

Even within the prevailing fog of uncertainty, under a barrage of dire reports from around the globe, the crew of two aboard *Rocinante* are in fact well-off, isolated but barely inconvenienced, grateful beyond measure. We move when weather and the virus and legal restrictions allow, enjoying coastlines devoid of cruise ships and anchorages that are empty except for us. We do what we can to help through fundraising drives and by supporting local economies. After many months—now more than ever before there is no need for haste—our sailing brings us into the Gulf of California. We cross from the mainland side to the Baja side. We hide from strong northerly winds. We stroll through forests of cardón cactus, the tallest cactus in the world. We pass our time constructively, that is, with nature.

We lose count of the number of times we have seen sea turtles, but it is fair to say that we have seen them most days. Along with them, we have often seen humpback whales, several species of dolphins, and acrobatic rays, either actual manta rays or the closely related mobula rays. Anticipating hurricane season, we again cross the Gulf of California, sailing back over to the mainland side.

After covering hundreds of miles since our first encounter with sexual turtles and weathering numerous pandemic restrictions, we find ourselves in San Carlos. It is a small community on the mainland edge of the Gulf of California, in the state of Sonora, founded in the 1950s to attract retirees from Canada and the United States. Within a week of arriving our boat sits on stands in a boatyard, no longer for the moment in the company of turtles, but instead spending her time undergoing maintenance, much of it deferred after several years on the move and in ports where parts were nonexistent or in short supply.

When I am not in the boatyard with tools in my hands, I spend time trying to figure out why sea turtles remain extant. How can an animal requiring decades to mature before making babies that will almost certainly perish before they themselves can reproduce still be around? More puzzling still, how can many sea turtle populations be at least seemingly recovering from overhunting and rampant egg harvesting even in the presence of ongoing poaching, not to mention all the other natural and human-made hazards still in place?

Fortunately for me, figuring this out involves walking on beaches.

It is 5:40 on an early August morning. I share the sand, clear dawn sky, and already pervasive heat of the Sonoran Desert summer with Judith Moore, a turtle volunteer, an American retiree and artist now based in San Carlos, a woman who, before volunteering here, never worked in conservation or biology. Judith, although seventy-one years old, swims laps and paddles her racing outrigger kayak on a regular basis. She has the walking pace and carriage of an athlete. She sports a stylized turtle tattoo, a Hawaiian iconic image, around her left wrist. If I were to describe her in a single word, I would choose "upbeat."

Judith and her fellow volunteers call this beach San Francisco Central, as opposed to San Francisco West or San Francisco East. Turtlers like Judith divide almost all the beaches around San Carlos in this manner, allowing individual volunteers to walk stretches of beach that are similar in length. During "the season"—that is, nesting season, which runs from about June until November—each stretch of beach is walked every morning. Or at least every morning that volunteers are available.

Most of these beaches could be fairly categorized as party beaches. In the absence of COVID closures—especially in the hot months, most of the nesting months—weekends find them full of cheerful beer-drinking families. On weekdays, they are somewhat less full.

I referred to Judith and her colleagues as "turtlers." A note on the word: A "turtler," according to Merriam-Webster, is "one who hunts turtles or their eggs." In general, and especially in the past, a turtler hunted turtles and eggs as a source of food, whether for personal consumption or for the market. This sort of turtling continues, mostly illegally.

But as a counterexample, on the beaches of Ostional, Costa Rica, turtlers can legally harvest and sell the first wave of eggs to be laid. Why? Because locals and scientists know that, at this particular stretch of beach, the first turtles of the season to lay eggs are for the most part wasting their time. The beach at Ostional is so heavily used by nesting turtles that these first eggs would be dug up or crushed by other turtles as more and more of them crawl ashore to lay more and more eggs. There is some thought that the legal harvest might reduce demand for black-market eggs taken by poachers later in the season. The local community, including its sea turtle conservation program, benefits financially.

The situation at Ostional is anything but normal, but what happens to the eggs at Ostional suggests what has happened to eggs in the past from beaches all over the world and to illegally collected eggs today. At least some wind up in bars where they are mixed with catsup and beer to become one of the many variations of the drink called sangrita. Some go into cookies and cakes, making them fluffy and light; there was a time when bakeries bought truckloads of turtle eggs. Others are scrambled or fried, although by most accounts scrambled and fried sea turtle eggs are a slimy affront to the palate.

But now, a turtler might not be hunting turtles or their eggs as food. In this confused world of ours, a turtler might also be a volunteer like Judith, a person hunting turtles or eggs for the purpose of saving them, protecting them, helping them.

At the far end of San Francisco East, a condominium development abuts a protected estuary. At the far end of San Francisco West, restaurants and hotels rise up from the sand. Well within San Francisco Central, we walk past a massive palapa, someone's business dream, reputedly approved by an outgoing political faction and then, after construction was all but complete, disallowed by the incoming political faction. This sort of thing, this starting and stopping of projects, is not at all atypical in Mexico.

Right now, this beach and all of the beaches near here may be at least nominally closed, shut down in an effort to control the pandemic. But enforcement hovers between nonexistent and inconsistent. Over the past week conflicting information about closures has circulated. Whether the beach is open or closed is anyone's guess.

"If any officials show up," Judith says, "we will leave immediately."

This is something I learn quickly about conservation turtlers in Mexico: Caution is the watchword when dealing with officials. The regulations regarding conservation may or may not be straightforward, depending on one's viewpoint, and the intertwined agency hierarchies make as little sense as they do in any other government bureaucracy. Regardless, officials patrolling beaches have the ability to arrest the innocent and guilty alike. And some of the officials have guns. When turtling, even if turtling for conservation, even if operating in complete compliance and with all required permits in place as is the case for the turtlers of San Carlos, discretion remains important.

Where the surf breaks on this possibly closed beach, the sand is smooth and damp. A few feet above the tide line, tire tracks crisscross the ground. Seashells of various sizes and shapes share space with empty beer bottles. We step around a dead pelican.

Our job in walking here, in patrolling under the red sky of the rising sun, is to find turtle tracks, to find the plowed-up, rutted sand that marks the path of a mature female crawling out of the ocean, pausing to dig a pit and deposit eggs, then crawling back into the ocean.

Judith tells me about the program. Most of the volunteers are retired Americans with an average age that Judith identifies as "senior." Most of the younger volunteers are Mexicans, and the program is supervised by a Mexican veterinarian named Elsa Coria Galindo.

Volunteers, old and young, come and go. A core group, seniors all, tends to do most of the work. For others, daily beach walks become a burden.

Illness, jobs, children, parents, and spouses demand time. The beach, even early in the morning, is hot. Bugs abound. Life gets in the way.

This is Judith's fourth year as a turtler. By her own description, she is a "worker bee," just one of the many working these beaches.

"There are general volunteers, second responders, and first responders," Judith says. General volunteers are essentially helpers. Second responders do beach patrols. First responders also do beach patrols, but when a nest is found they are trained and authorized to assess and, if necessary, move the nest.

"If necessary" is, in the context of San Francisco beach, an almost meaningless phrase. Nest relocation is virtually always necessary. Eggs that are not moved will be driven over by cars and all-terrain vehicles, partied on top of by beer drinkers, destroyed. The abundance of tire tracks makes this beach unacceptably dangerous for turtle nests.

The nests, Judith explains, can be relocated to a safer place on the beach, out of the main traffic zone, and then cordoned off with poles and signs saying ¡NO MOLESTA!—DO NOT DISTURB!

This works, sometimes. But in at least one case someone drove right over a set of poles and signs. There is the possibility that the other kind of turtler, the kind that eats eggs or sells them as food, might see a marked nest as an easy target. Eggs have been seen for sale in a nearby community market for the equivalent of one dollar each, twenty pesos. A nest can hold more than a hundred eggs, a windfall in an area where many people earn less than a few hundred dollars a month.

So most of the nests are moved into an incubation room, a discretely placed trailer in a weedy lot on a sand road well-removed from the beach. A few are moved to a roped-off safety zone in front of a condominium building on the beach, well within the perimeter of the community's security patrols.

What keeps Judith walking these beaches day after day?

"Sea turtles," she answers, "are special." And there are release days, days when eggs found by the turtlers have hatched, when young turtles crawl into the sea. "Every release day is like the first time," she tells me. "Magical. Surreal. A new awakening."

Her answers to my questions come during our sweat-inducing walk. It is possible, it turns out, to search for turtle tracks quickly while conversing. They are not, if one knows what to look for, difficult to spot.

But luck fails us today. We reach the end of San Francisco Central, and the only tracks we have seen are those of tires, great blue herons, a raccoon, and our own feet.

My first turtle nest will have to wait for another day.

A brief but important interlude for a few more words on the evolution of sea turtles, on the timeline that joins Judith and her colleagues to the very beginning of this story.

I have said already that I would not start with the birth of the universe, despite the sage words of Carl Sagan. I am tempted to fast-forward to a starting line that lies with the birth of the world's first turtle, some 260 million years ago. That birth means turtles predated such beasts as *Tyrannosaurus rex* by well over a hundred and fifty million years. But even so, it is far too recent to capture the story of turtles in its fullness.

So where is the fair starting line, a beginning to the sea turtle story, the sea turtle marathon, that will offer the needed perspective? Why not start with the birth of the Earth? There will be other starting lines later, each with its own perspective, but for now, for this first foray, we embark upon a newborn Earth.

Our planet came into being 4.54 billion years ago. But few of us can think meaningfully about numbers in the billions, or even for that matter in the millions. It has become fashionable to condense the history of Earth into a day to give a sense of the relative passing of time. I am hardly the first to rely on such an explanatory crutch as this.

Leaning upon this crutch, think of 4.54 billion years ago as midnight last night, and think of the present as midnight tonight, so those billions of years are compressed into twenty-four hours.

It is midnight last night. A bunch of rocks and ice circling around the sun collide, one with the other with the other, becoming a planet. All that colliding leaves the young Earth rather warm. So warm, in fact, that liquid water cannot exist.

But the clock ticks and events unfold. The planet cools. Sometime around one or two in the morning, or maybe a bit later—the exact timing remains a matter of debate—water condenses. An ocean forms. In all likelihood, it comes and goes as the planet cools and warms. It is sterile, devoid of life.

But not for long. Within anywhere from seconds to an hour or so of the oceans forming, something seemingly very unlikely happens: Life springs up on early Earth. It is unicellular stuff. No nucleus. Not the LUCA, our Last Universal Common Ancestor, which comes later, but perhaps something superficially resembling the LUCA.

The LUCA, by the way, comes into the world as a thermophile, a heat-loving single-celled organism that had no immediate use for oxygen. It is the sort of life one might find today in a deep-sea thermal vent. On this early Earth, free oxygen—that is, the sort of oxygen that turtles breathe, the kind that we breathe, as opposed to the oxygen tied up in molecules of water and iron oxide and quartz—is only somewhat less rare than, say, diamonds.

Not much else happens until midmorning or early lunchtime, when some of that unicellular, nucleus-free but living stuff goes wildly photosynthetic. Life puts sunlight to work, manufacturing food for itself and spitting out oxygen. The oxygen is no friend of most of the life forms then present. In fact it kills them off, poisons them, drives them to extinction. But the oxygenation of the atmosphere moved slowly, in part because much of the newly released free oxygen immediately bound with minerals like iron. During that period, new life forms emerged from the old. These new forms thrive on oxygen.

At about the same time, or maybe just after lunch, say around the time that many writers and biologists typically pause for an early afternoon nap, eukaryotic life emerges. That is, cells with nuclei and other internal organelles, cells like the cells that make up our bodies and turtle bodies, but unicellular, single-celled, free living.

Oxygen becomes increasingly abundant.

Dinnertime passes without remark. Over a leisurely dessert, free oxygen becomes as abundant as it is today. Humans would not exist for quite some time, but had they existed they would have been able to breathe the air.

Between eight and nine in the evening, multicellular life gains ground. It comes late in the day but with a vengeance. In no more than a few minutes on our twenty-four hour clock, what we would recognize today as animals begin swimming around, or crawling on the seabed, or floating on the sea surface.

Unicellular life had found its way ashore earlier in the day, but it is close to ten o'clock at night before terrestrial ecosystems as we would recognize them today gain a toehold. Half an hour later, reptiles crawl and slither into the wilderness. Twenty or thirty minutes more pass, and behold, the first turtle walks the Earth. Another twenty minutes passes and some of those turtles slip back into the sea. These are the ancestral species of today's sea turtles. They are, of course, long gone, replaced by the turtles of today.

Of the seven species of sea turtles now with us, the leatherback came first, at around fifteen minutes before midnight, and not much changed from its immediate ancestors. But the first Kemp's ridley, the turtle that started this book off the coast of Mexico, did not breathe its first breath until just before midnight, after the Isthmus of Panama had emerged from the sea to form a barrier between the Atlantic and the Pacific.

The evolutionary fluke that would eventually call itself human, *Homo sapiens*, shows up a mere few seconds before midnight. But within those few seconds, this upright walking supposedly brainy oddity becomes remarkably deadly. Within a fraction of a second before midnight, its penchant for carving the last of the world's remaining sea turtles into steaks, to packaging their flesh in cans, to hanging their shells on walls, and to eating their eggs comes dangerously close to wiping out its sea turtle cousins.

But then, realizing the error in its ways, with the tiniest fraction of a second to spare, these strange hulking beasts decide that wiping out their cousins is just not the right thing to do. Or, more cynically but with a similar effect, they decide that once the last turtle is gone no amount of money will ever again buy a bowl of turtle soup. The turtle conservation movement is born. The conservation movement as a whole is born.

On a more personal note: I divide and multiply to determine at what time in a twenty-four hour clock I came onto the scene, and it turns out that, at the age of sixty in actual years, I have been around for a total of slightly more than one one-thousandth of a second.

A lot has happened, good and bad, in that one one-thousandth of a second.

Yet another digression, this one for the religiously inclined: It is possible that God created the Earth and the sea and everything that we mortals think of as biodiversity, including sea turtles, with the wave of a divine hand. Or several waves of a divine hand during what most would consider to be a very busy week.

Or it is possible that the version espoused by scientists and outlined in the last few paragraphs is more or less correct.

Or perhaps God's waving hands guided the physics and chemistry that gave rise to life. There is room for science even within religion.

In any case, something difficult to explain occurred, a miracle, with or without the implication of divine intervention.

Strike that. Not a miracle, but miracles.

Miracles occurred.

Leaving the beach behind I follow Judith west, back into town, and then over some wash-boarded sand roads. We park in front of a chain-link fence. Behind the fence, a once-white trailer with rusting wheel hubs sits in a weedy lot. On the side, someone has strung up a fabric banner: INVESTIGACIÓN EN PROCESO, RESEARCH IN PROGRESS, with both the Spanish and English in red letters. Beneath those letters are two logos. On the right, a logo shows a dolphin, a pelican, a sea lion, and a fox along with the words "CR²IFS, Centro de Rescate, Rehabilitación, e Investigación de Fauna Silvestre, AC," the superscripted two emphasizing Rescate and Rehabilitación. On the left a logo shows silhouettes of five of the world's seven species of sea turtles—the five species that occur along this coast. It also shows a mermaid, and the words, "Grupo de Tortuguero de las Californias."

The words, for those who struggle with Spanish, bear translation. On the left, "The Center for the Rescue, Rehabilitation, and Investigation of Wild Fauna," which represents the local organization that owns and operates the trailer and manages the turtle patrols in and around San Carlos. On the right, "Group of Turtle Workers of the Californias," or, less literally, "Group of People and Organizations Devoted to Turtles in the Californias." Californias refers not to the state north of the border, but to the two Mexican states of the Baja peninsula, Baja California and Baja California Sur, the northern and southern halves of the long string of mountainous land that forms the western boundary of the Gulf of California.

It seems strange to me to see two names on the same banner, the titles of two separate organizations. Even more difficult to understand is why an organization of the people of the Californias appears here, on the mainland, in the state of Sonora. But, as is often necessary in Mexico, I let the mystery pass for the moment, unmolested.

Judith unlocks the door to the trailer and disables an alarm. "We don't want anyone to steal our eggs," she says without a hint of a smile.

Inside, the front half of the trailer houses a small desk and metal shelves holding boots, nets, and other paraphernalia for working in and around water. In the back half, through another door, Styrofoam boxes partly fill a few of what is mostly an empty rack of shelves. The boxes are labeled 24, 47, 25, 105, 108, 133, 1, and 3. These numbers, Judith tells me, are egg counts. These boxes hold, in total, 446 turtle eggs.

"Those two," Judith says, indicating the boxes labeled 1 and 3, "hold eggs that might be damaged. Maybe something happened when we brought them in." They are separated because they may not be viable. They may rot, and their rotting could hurt their sibling eggs.

She opens the lids of the boxes, one after the other, checking the sand in each for moisture and any signs of trouble.

Inside, there is nothing to see but sand from the very nests that provided the eggs. The eggs themselves are buried.

"In gravelly sand," Judith says, "the hatch rate is lower than in finer sand. In finer sand, something like 85 percent of the eggs should hatch."

She shows me a photograph of neatly lined up empty eggshells taken the previous season. There are eighty shells that hatched and nine unhatched shells that, she says, were probably not fertilized.

High season for incubation is September and October, when the incubation room will be stacked high with boxes.

After fifty or sixty days lying together in the Styrofoam box full of sand, almost all eggs in a nest will hatch within hours of one another. The first to hatch starts moving, stimulating his or her siblings.

After hatching, they will remain quiet for a day or two as their tiny bodies consume what is left of their yolk sacs. When they become more active, they are checked, each individual inspected. Is the yolk fully absorbed? Is the plastron—the underside of the shell—sufficiently closed? Those that pass inspection are moved from the Styrofoam box that has been their home into another box for transport. In this new box, they are carried to the beach where the eggs were found. There, the young turtles are set free.

If the survival rate estimate of one in one thousand is correct, it is not only possible but somewhat likely that none of the turtle eggs in the incubation room will survive to fertilize or lay eggs of their own.

This sort of math could be discouraging.

But here is another way to look at it: If these eggs had been left in place, if Judith and her fellow volunteers did not move them and care for them and take them back to a beach for release, the probability of surviving to hatch on beaches overrun with cars, all-terrain vehicles, beer-swilling tourists, dogs, and raccoons would be approximately zero.

One in one thousand might seem like vanishingly small odds, but one in one thousand is infinitely greater than zero.

When thinking about evolution and extinction, about conservation of biodiversity, it is worth considering just how many species exist today. Not species of sea turtles, which we know to be seven, but all species.

The short answer: Nobody knows.

How can this be?

For starters, what we actually mean by the word "species" can be more than a little confusing. A typical but deeply flawed definition goes something like this: A species is a group of organisms that can breed with one another (again with the sex) to produce offspring that can breed with one another to produce more offspring, just as their parents had done. Why flawed? Because not all species reproduce sexually. Also, individuals and groups of some would-be species are isolated on, say, islands, or in caves, or in oases, or in different ocean basins, and by virtue of isolation they are sometimes but not always considered to be separate species. And some obviously different species, like polar bears and grizzlies, very occasionally get together to produce offspring that can themselves produce more offspring.

Further complicating all of this, many species have to be identified not by what they do—not by their mating habits and reproductive success—but by their appearance. As an example, differences and similarities in mouthparts of certain flies can be important species identifiers even though those doing the identifying have no idea about the importance or lack thereof of these mouthparts when it comes to choosing mates.

Attempts to refine the exact meaning of "species" have led to claims that at least twenty-seven definitions are in play.

We can turn here to a letter from Charles Darwin to his friend and colleague Joseph Hooker. "It is really laughable," Darwin wrote, "to see what different ideas are prominent in various naturalists' minds, when they speak of 'species;' in some, resemblance is everything and descent of little weight—in some, resemblance seems to go for nothing, and Creation the reigning idea—in some, sterility an unfailing test, with others it is not worth a farthing. It all comes, I believe, from trying to define the indefinable."

Set the academic nuances aside and assume we have at least a somewhat functional definition that works most of the time, at least for multicellular life. Accepting this, why not just count the number of species that have been identified? Just go through the scientific literature dating back to 1735, when Carl Linnaeus published his *Systema Naturae*, setting more or less in stone the general manner in which species are named and cataloged. Just go through the literature and count the named species.

But attempt this mother of all reviews and immediately problems arise. For one thing, there is the sheer number of species. Linnaeus himself accounted for twenty thousand species. By 2009, according to at least one effort, the number had blossomed to just shy of two million.

Keep in mind that this is not a simple matter of counting. Some species, it turns out, have more than one name. Other species, as fate would have it, are not one species but many.

New species, for anyone interested in looking, pop up everywhere. My wife and cocaptain, for example, discovered a species of sponge later named in her honor. It was a matter of such small importance to her that, twenty years later, she cannot remember exactly what the creature is called.

The renowned and only recently deceased biologist Edward O. Wilson, in his book *Half-Earth*, said, "I've described about 450 new species of ants." Although he had every right to brag, he was not bragging. He was instead illustrating what he calls taxonomic overload, the idea that there are more species around than one might imagine, and certainly more than we can conveniently count. Potentially new species, Wilson pointed out, pile up in museums awaiting scrutiny by experts.

How many more species have yet to be described is by its nature unknown. One could simply make up a number, and no one could prove it wrong. Or one might supplement a guess by looking at how many new species are discovered each year, plotting a line of new species by years, and projecting this line forward. Or by estimating the number of new species found per square mile in various well-studied sites and multiplying that by the number of similar sites that have yet to be examined.

A number that is as good as any, a number often suggested as an estimate of the undescribed species still roaming the Earth, is just shy of nine million.

That number, by the way, only includes eukaryotes—the creatures that arrived just after lunchtime in the 4.54-million-year day whose cells hold a nucleus and other organelles, creatures that include plants and animals, fungi and amoebas. Among these eukaryotes, those willing to make predictions have suggested such values as five million insects, a half a million arachnids, and a hundred thousand crustaceans.

If one were crazy enough to include bacteria, the number would explode. Instead of nine million, the number might be something like a trillion.

Returning again to extinction rates: So what if we lost five hundred species in the last hundred years? Or maybe the higher estimates are right and we are losing fifty thousand a year. Either way, the cynic might suggest, there are plenty more where those came from. Extinction is perfectly normal. This is nature doing what nature does, nothing to lose any sleep over.

But consider again the degree to which extinction rates vary. At times, species counts remain reasonably stable for long periods. But other times present greater challenges. During big extinction events—five are widely recognized, not including the one occurring right now—the majority of species might disappear over a million or two million years. The first, at the end of the Ordovician period, sent 85 percent of the world's species to oblivion about 440 million years ago. The third and worst so far, at the end of the Permian period, wiped out 95 percent of all species about 250 million years ago. The trilobites, the ammonites, the dinosaurs, and hosts of others were, in one mass extinction or another, wiped out. The causes were probably complicated and are not well understood, but none of them involved humans. Humans were not around for the first five mass extinctions. Think instead about collisions with asteroids, about volcanic outbursts, about the effect of continental drift on climate.

But we are around now. While five hundred extinctions in a hundred years may not sound like so much, it is a number that tells us that we have landed squarely in the planet's sixth mass extinction. The current extinction rate is somewhere between 100 and 1,000 times higher than would be expected during a normal period, during an era between mass extinctions. Even worse than that, the rate of extinctions today may be between ten and a hundred times higher than the rate of extinction during the previous five mass extinction events.

Edward O. Wilson, the same aforementioned discoverer of ants by the hundred, suggested in his 2002 book *The Future of Life* that half of Earth's species would be extinct by 2100.

We are the cause. We are worse than asteroids, than volcanic outbursts, than the impact of continental drift on climate.

How is that for optimism?

Incidentally, sea turtles are not exempt from the vagaries associated with species definitions. We say there are seven sea turtle species in the world today, but within the last twenty years there was an eighth.

The eighth did not go extinct. It was simply recategorized. What had been two species became one.

Linnaeus himself recognized and named the green turtle in the tenth edition of his *Systema Naturae* in 1758, which, after some name changes, became known as *Chelonia mydas*. *Chelonia* designated the genus and *mydas* designated the species, in keeping with Linnaeus's binomial naming scheme. In the time of Linnaeus, *Chelonia mydas* was a very common turtle in what were then the Caribbean colonies and elsewhere.

A century later, the French naturalist Marie Firmin Bocourt looked at what was commonly called the black turtle from the Pacific and assigned it a genus and species name. The genus was *Chelonia*, the same as that of the green turtle. The species was *agassizii*, after the famous Swiss-American zoologist Louis Agassiz. Sure the green and the black looked similar, but one might expect that from two species in the same genus, and they were, after all, separated by the American continents.

Flash forward a century and a half. Scientists applied genetic methods. Two of them, writing in the academic journal *Conservation Biology* in a paper titled "Evolutionary significant units versus geopolitical taxonomy: Molecular systematics of an endangered sea turtle (genus *Chelonia*)," argued almost apologetically that their results did not justify separate species designations for green and black turtles. The two turtles were in fact a single species. *Chelonia agassizii* would henceforth be known as *Chelonia mydas*.

So it is, mostly. Although some persist in using the old name, even in print. Others refer to the black as *Chelonia mydas agassizii*, suggesting under the rules of nomenclature that it should have a subspecies status. Still others, those who tend not to read technical articles about molecular genetics, those who reside on the west coast of Mexico and on the shores of the Gulf of California, remain loyal to the common name, referring to the black green turtle as the black, or, more often, since Spanish prevails, the tortuga negra. To confuse things still further, they might call it the prieta, a word sometimes used in Spanish slang to refer to someone with dark skin, eyes, and hair.

By the way, when green and black sea turtles were officially combined to become one species, no one reduced the estimated number of species worldwide by one. No one, for example, argued that the Earth no longer supported 9,000,000 species. Nobody suggested that, based on the name change, there were only 8,999,999 species left.

No, that would have been ridiculous.

Two weeks pass, and I am on the beach again with Judith very early in the morning. This time my wife Lisanne is along.

We walk east in the morning twilight, toward a rising sun that has yet to emerge. Behind us, an almost full moon approaches the western horizon. Surf breaks against the beach in two-second intervals, each wave bringing with it the crashing sound of its own demise followed by the pleasant tumbling of pebbles against sand.

This year, Judith tells us, the beach seems less rocky than it was in previous years.

A sandpiper forages in front of us. Yellow-footed gulls lounge on the ground and in the water just beyond the surf, issuing occasional squawks. We offer a casual passing greeting to a gringo couple walking three dogs. Judith sees them here on many mornings, out early, like her, to avoid the daily onslaught of August heat from the Sonoran Desert.

Today's sunrise illuminates the remains of two dead pelicans, clumps of green algae, a cluster of whelk eggs, discarded beer cans occasionally in small piles, a diaper, a few feet of rusting barbed wire, scattered clamshells, innumerable crab burrows, two fully inflated and entirely deceased blowfish with gray-green spines, a Styrofoam cup, a great blue heron, meandering raccoon tracks, and ruts left by various kinds of vehicles.

Judith explains that olive ridleys—by far the most commonly encountered nesters in this area—leave lateral flipper prints in the sand while other species leave flipper prints spaced more or less diagonally from one another.

We reach the end of San Francisco Central. "Lots of tracks," Lisanne says, "but the wrong kind."

"Not the kind that lead to eggs," Judith says.

In the shadow of a condominium we meet another turtler, an American named Jim Straw. He is on watch, babysitting a nest relocated here under the protection of the condominium. The nest is surrounded by yellow tape and plastic fencing.

Some of the young turtles have become active. Jim expects to see youngsters on top of the sand very soon. Maybe today or tomorrow, or certainly by the next day.

Jim retired from a career as a pilot. Before becoming a turtler, he had no experience with wildlife. But he does have fond memories of seeing turtle conservation efforts in Oman, in what he remembers to have been a government funded effort. Now he typically volunteers for about an hour and a half each day, but today he will be on watch for six hours. The organization is short on help and someone has to keep an eye on the nest.

"Sometimes baby turtles might hatch but then stay underground for a day or two or three," he says. "We have no idea. And then in batches they might make a run for the surf, maybe three or four or five at a time. They seem to come out in small groups, not always all at once."

Recently, a couple of hatchlings unexpectedly made a run for it, tunneling under the protective fencing around their nest. By following their tracks—two-inch-wide trails in the sand—turtlers found them stuck in a tire rut. They had been heading down the beach toward the lights of San Carlos rather than heading out to sea. If they had not been found they would have been eaten by gulls or broiled alive in the heat of the day. As things worked out, they were returned to the nest to mature a while longer.

"It is in the category of its our job to protect them," Jim says.

We stand together watching the nest. Watching a turtle nest before the turtles emerge is synonymous with watching sand. It is neither more nor less interesting than watching paint dry and grass grow.

He talks about volunteering. When he started working with turtles, he realized the biggest obstacle was resources. Mexico is not, after all, awash in money. "A group of us started looking for solutions," he says. These solutions involved organizational work and funding. With others he started a nonprofit organization. He explains the difficulties of getting nonprofit status, "donativo status," in Mexico. Apparently, he says, the crime syndicates, the cartels, realized long ago that nonprofit organizations offered excellent fronts for money laundering. Nonprofits, along with hotels and restaurants, bars and surf shops, could clean money made from narcotics, kidnapping, arms trade, prostitution, smuggling, human trafficking, and even the killing and selling of endangered species. Despite this Jim and his colleagues moved forward. They hope to raise $65,000 to support infrastructure development this year. This is, for perspective, more than enough money to buy a house in this part of Mexico.

"What we've decided to do is to facilitate," he explains. "Mexicans need to make this their own."

He explains that Elsa Galindo, the Mexican veterinarian whose name I have heard several times by now, directs the program. She holds the permits. She offers training to the volunteers. She manages relationships with government offices. In this sense, this is already and has always been a Mexican program. But as I have heard before, it so happens that on this stretch of coast most of the people who have both time and money on their hands as well as an interest in turtle conservation are retirees from the United States and Canada. The boss is one hundred percent Mexican, but the volunteers are not.

The conversation jumps from topic to topic, as might be expected to happen when the participants are staring at an unmoving patch of sand.

"A nest," Jim tells me, "especially the third nest of the season, may not even be fertile, or it might be say 50 percent fertile. The rotting infertile eggs will kill the viable eggs. They'll ruin the nest." If a nest is late in hatching, turtlers might dig it up to check for rotting eggs. This is true even for a nest like this one, a nest that has been relocated for its own protection. If rotting eggs are found, still-viable sibling eggs will be separated or even moved to the incubation room.

When hatchlings start to break out of the sand, the first thing a turtler might see is a beak. But it could also be the end of a flipper or the top of a shell. They squirm around in the sand, pushing their way out.

"This is the first year that the sand has been too hot for the newly hatched turtles," he says. "But it will get worse." Climate change. Warming. Turtles emerging in the heat of the day, without help, will die before they reach the sea.

"Our job is to protect and if necessary rescue," he says, repeating in a slightly modified form his earlier statement, giving it the tone of a slogan.

We watch a boat pass offshore, shiny white fiberglass gleaming in the sun, propelled by a big black outboard. Almost certainly, it is the boat of a retired gringo.

"Every year," Jim says, "boats run into turtles out here."

When onlookers pass by, Jim encourages them to talk. "Part of our job is to explain and educate," he says. "Sometimes explaining and educating results in new volunteers. Sometimes people we talk to might report seeing a turtle laying eggs. Just getting the word out about who to call is important. People need to understand that turtle eggs might be good to eat but live turtles are good for ecotourism, and ecotourism is cash."

A Mexican couple stops to talk. They are middle-aged and perhaps overly well-fed for their bathing suits, but they are fluent in English. They look closely at the nest as Jim explains what he and his colleagues are doing. They are openly delighted. But what they really want to see, they say, is turtle hatchlings swimming out to sea.

Me too, I think to myself. Me too.

THREE

The Veterinarian

A few days later I meet Dr. Galindo at the incubation center. I expect someone right out of veterinary college, a young idealist, but she looks as though she might be in her forties. We talk through COVID masks, mostly in English, which she speaks with a delightful accent—calling me Beal instead of Bill, for example—and with occasional pauses to search for words. Her eyes smile above her mask, signaling what I take to be cheerfulness, an enthusiasm for her topic, a love of her path in life.

Within minutes it is clear that Elsa is a veterinarian not only by training but by avocation. Her love for animals would allow her to be nothing else.

She is the mastermind behind CR²IFS. Her organization, she explains, was conceived of as early as 2007. At that time her work focused on sea lions. More specifically, she freed sea lions who had become tangled in the same kind of fishing nets that kill turtles. This work continues today as part of a larger and growing program.

"It is sometimes hard to convince fishermen that sea lions should be protected," she says. "After all, the sea lions destroy their nets. But even so, some of the fishermen help." The process involves darting large animals with a tranquilizer that leaves them conscious enough to float and breathe, but not active enough to harm Samaritans cutting away nets. An adult male sea lion in the Gulf of California can weigh more than a thousand pounds. Even the young pups are big enough to intimidate a human in the water. Elsa, in contrast, is slender, slight of build, no one's idea of a sea lion wrangler.

From conception to launch took ten years, so it was not until 2017 that CR²IFS was really going, initially with a small group of volunteers. That group grew to almost fifty active volunteers, of which four or five are Mexican and the rest are retired Americans and Canadians. "The Mexican volunteers are busy working and raising families," she says, echoing comments from Judith. She goes on to explain that CR²IFS is a member of a larger group, of the network called Grupo Tortuguero de las Californias, which explains why I had seen both names on the banner outside. Grupo Tortuguero is a mother organization. Despite its name, its reach has spread across the Gulf of California to the mainland and extended down the west coast of Mexico. They are headquartered, Elsa says, in La Paz, and I make a note to myself that we will have to sail the 230 miles to La Paz in the coming season.

"The same fishermen that help with the sea lions help with the turtles," she explains. "They know that the sea is no longer giving enough food. There is overfishing. The big boats that fish sardines are out eleven months of the year."

The big boats she refers to are purse seiners, work boats typically exceeding a hundred feet in length. A purse seiner's net is lowered from a boom and pulled into a circle that surrounds an entire school of fish. Other boats, smaller boats, fish with longlines—that is, lines that can stretch a mile or more in length, carrying thousands of hooks. Still others use gillnets, which are typically shorter, perhaps five hundred feet in length, sometimes less. Gillnets capture fish not so much by surrounding them as a seine would do but by entangling them in a monofilament mesh. And there are shrimpers pulling dredges over the bottom, small boats that deploy traps for fish and octopus, other small boats that support divers who take scallops, clams, lobster, sea cucumbers, and, well, anything they can catch and sell.

"The fish hardly get a break," Elsa says.

She mentions, too, the illegal trade in sea lion testicles and swim bladders from massive endangered totoabas, a kind of drum fish similar in appearance to the white sea bass, found only in the Gulf of California. And the illegal trade in both sea turtle eggs and meat.

In the past, she worked in pet clinics. It was a way to earn a living. Saving sea lions was a sideline. But in Mexico, veterinarians are poorly compensated, so much so that donations to support wildlife care could replace the income she brought in from pet clinics.

I ask if she is willing to tell me what a veterinarian might earn in this part of Mexico. She tells me that it varies, but sixteen thousand pesos would be a good salary. This is the equivalent of about $800.

"Per week?" I ask. No, it is per month. This is in a reasonably well-paid part of Mexico, relatively close to the northern border and in the vicinity of large urban areas.

"Now I have no salary," she adds. "I had a salary last year, from donors, but not this year." The donations, for the moment, have thinned out, so she still sometimes works on pets, waiting for funds to come in, for more grant applications to bear fruit. This is a financial sacrifice that impacts her family, but her husband and children know that the program will fall apart without her or someone like her in place. Sea lions will remain entangled. Turtles will die unnecessarily.

A great thrashing and scraping at the door disturbs our interview. "That is our pelican," Elsa says. "This is his exercise time."

The pelican was found injured and is now under her care.

Elsa, over the years, has helped blue-footed boobies, brown boobies, red-tailed hawks, great horned owls, several species of gulls, chipmunks, skunks, raccoons, and various kinds of snakes. All in addition to sea lions and turtles.

As an example, she describes a green turtle, a prieta, she helped in 2019. The animal had been brought to her with a flipper almost severed by the monofilament line of a gillnet. She saved the flipper and nursed its owner back to health. She released the turtle, which now, she thinks and hopes, swims free.

In a rambling discussion about the turtlers—Judith and the cadre of volunteers—she explains the permitting process. No one in Mexico can handle sea turtles or their eggs without a permit. The regulatory process involves agencies within agencies. The details are specific to Mexico, but the agencies go by acronyms, collectively becoming the alphabet soup familiar to conservationists working in many nations, perhaps in all nations. While the roles of each agency undoubtedly make perfect sense to the well-initiated, there is, as is often the case, an appearance of overlap and confusion.

Law enforcement, she points out, is handled by one of the agencies, but they sometimes have the help of the army and the navy.

"Some people still like the meat of the black turtle," she says, referring to the black green turtle. "They are habituated to turtle meat."

It must be said that turtle eaters in Mexico do not have permits. The laws surrounding the protection of sea turtles have a complex history, but consumption of turtle meat, turtle eggs, or any product made with parts of turtles or turtle eggs has been a federal crime in Mexico since May 31, 1990.

She does not remember seeing turtle meat or eggs routinely on sale in grocery stores, but people talk to her about cooking and eating turtles. She knows of a policeman who served turtle at a party.

"Many people wonder when they will be able to eat turtle again," she says.

She continues: "At least one nest of eggs is stolen each year, probably by someone from the south, from Oaxaca."

What she means is that at least one nest marked by her volunteers is raided each year. Oaxaca is one of the poorest states in Mexico. People from Oaxaca travel north as seasonal migrant laborers, working on farms scattered in the irrigated desert around San Carlos. She suspects that the same person or the same family might have figured out how to spot marked nests and may be responsible for the thefts. "It is in this hope of tricking poachers that we sometimes set up decoy nests," she says.

Her organization relocated twenty-three nests in 2018, forty-four in 2019, and forty-seven in 2020. She knows these figures without checking her notes. The numbers increase with the number of volunteers walking the beaches.

For a time, on and off, pandemic closures put many beaches in Mexico off-limits. "Closures helped the turtles by protecting the beaches," Elsa says, "but the reopenings were crazy. Everyone came to the beach at once." They drove their trucks and their all-terrain vehicles on the beaches. "There were tire tracks everywhere."

Her volunteers had marked one nest with plastic posts and signs. Someone used the posts to frame an impromptu palapa, a bit of shade from under which they could drink beer and watch the waves. When diplomatically confronted the person said he was going to put the posts back as soon as the sun was low enough in the sky.

"These beaches around San Carlos are no longer safe for turtles. Not only because of poachers, but because of holiday makers, four wheelers. So we move most nests to the incubation room."

No one knows how many turtles nest in the Gulf of California, she tells me. Many of the beaches are remote, at least for people who do not earn a living by fishing.

As to the survival rate of hatchlings, she repeats the one-in-one-thousand odds that I had by now heard from several sources. But this, she says, is for unassisted hatchlings. She thinks the help of organizations like CR²IFS may double or triple survival rates. The youngsters are, to the extent possible, shielded from predators as they make their way from nest to beach. They are protected from their own ineptitude, their inability to march from the nest to the sea without getting lost. If she is right, the odds are good that at least some of the eggs in the incubation center will survive long enough to reproduce, to save their species from extinction.

But here is a reality check: Youngsters cannot be tagged and followed as they grow, so the one-in-one-thousand number is more of a guess than an estimate. Elsa's belief that protection of eggs and young might double or triple survival rates seems reasonable but is purely speculative. The only fact is that hatchlings will be released and they will swim away, and many years later some of them, some small minority of them, may come back. Her efforts and the efforts of her volunteers improve the odds from some unknown but tiny fraction to some indefinite but probably slightly larger fraction.

And that is enough.

"I think there are more sea turtles because of human help," she says. Although she says, "I think," she is clearly convinced.

Her eyes smile more widely than normal when she talks of turtles.

Sea turtles have rather obviously not gone extinct. Less obviously, they are nowhere near as abundant as they once were.

No one made serious attempts to count turtles hundreds of years ago, but information survives. Take, for example, this description of sea turtles from a Spanish Priest who sailed with Christopher Columbus in 1494, somewhere off the coast of Cuba: "The sea was all thick with them, and they were of the very largest, so numerous that it seemed that the ships would run aground on them and were as if bathing in them."

Or this, from Ferdinand Columbus, second son of Christopher Columbus, writing in 1503 regarding his father's naming of the Tortugas, later renamed the Caymans: "On Wednesday May 10 we were in sight of two very small and low islands, full of tortoises, as was all the sea about, in so much that they looked like little rocks; whence these Islands were called Las Tortugas."

Sea turtles were abundant, but do not for a moment think that they were not exploited in the Caribbean before Columbus arrived. For that matter, do not think for a moment that they were not exploited by humans for thousands of years pretty much everywhere the two species coexisted. It is not unusual to find the remains of slaughtered sea turtles in five-thousand-year-old archaeological sites.

Then as now, humans ate turtles. At times in both the distant and recent past and for that matter through today, turtles were and are sometimes cooked in their own shells. But our ancestors found other uses for turtles, including uses for many of their more than two hundred bones, so much so that at least one archaeologist has referred to the turtle as "the ultimate tool kit." In the time before humans invented writing, turtle parts became ornaments, knives, weaving tablets, scrapers, combs, pins, fishing hooks, weights for fishing nets, cooking pots, jewelry, adzes, shovels, shavers, and war shields. In at least one region, people used the largest of shells for shelters and boats. In many cultures, people buried deceased relatives with remnants of a hunting and gathering life, including turtle bones and shells in abundance.

Early written records describe a trade in sea turtles in the ancient Sumerian city of Ur; their goddess Ningal was offered thirty "finger-shaped" pieces of turtle. In ancient Mesopotamia, both commoners and rulers ate turtles and used various parts medicinally. The *Periplus Maris Erythraei*, written two thousand years ago as a handbook for Indian Ocean traders, features sea turtle shells.

Even in those ancient times humans could and did cross the line between exploitation and decimation, wiping out local and regional sea turtle populations. Stone age sites show evidence of "overkill," archaeological code for localized extinction or near extinction. Written evidence also documents the ability of humans to wipe out sea turtle populations well before the modern age. Refer back to the Cayman Islands, where turtles were so abundant in 1504. When Columbus's followers were not busy spreading infection, raping, pillaging, fighting among themselves, and forcing native people to dig for silver and gold, they hunted turtles. By

1790, green sea turtles—almost universally considered to be the best eating of the sea turtles—were so scarce around the Cayman Islands that turtle hunters made the then somewhat perilous trip to the south coast of Cuba in search of untapped stocks. By 1830, the Cuban stocks were depleted, so the hunters moved on to the Miskito Banks, off present-day Nicaragua and Honduras. By 1890 concerns over turtle scarcity on the Miskito Banks— "diminution in the supply," as it was referred to—led to calls for artificial nurseries, places where turtles could be hatched and reared before being sent back to sea.

Or take Bermuda, out in the middle of the Atlantic Ocean, discovered possibly as early as 1498, famously used by victims of a shipwreck for nine months beginning in July 1609, and officially colonized in 1612.

A survivor of the 1609 shipwreck wrote of the island: "There are also great store of Tortoses (which some call Turtles) and those so great, that I haue seene a bushel of egges in one of their bellies, which are sweeter then any Henne egge and the Tortose it selfe is all very good meate, and yeeldeth great store of oyle, which is as sweete as any butter; and one of them will suffice fifty men a meale, at the least and of these hath beene taken great store, with two boates, at the least forty in one day."

But only ten years would pass before the still-wet-behind-the-ears Bermuda Assembly passed what is sometimes called the world's first wildlife conservation legislation, "An Act agaynst the killinge of ouer younge Tortoyses." Its words, although awkward to modern ears and eyes, are telling:

> In regard that much waste and abuse hath been offered and
> yet is by sundrye lewd and impvident psons inhabitinge wthin
> these Islands who in there continuall goinges out to sea for fish
> doe upon all occasions, And at all tymes as they can meete with
> them, snatch & catch up indifferentlye all kinds of Tortoyses
> both yonge & old little and greate and soe kill carrye awaye
> and devoure them to the much decay of the breed of so excel-

lent a fishe the daylye skarringe of them from of our shores and the danger of an utter distroyinge and losse of them.

It is therefore enacted by the Authoritie of this present Assembly That from hence forward noe manner of pson or psons of what degree or condition soeuer he be inhabitinge or remaining at any time wthin these Islands shall pesume to kill or cause to be killed in any Bay Sound Harbor or any other place out to Sea being wthin five leagues round about of those Islands any young Tortoyses that are or shall not be found to be Eighteen inches in the Breadth or Dyameter and that upon the penaltye for euerye such offence of the fforfeyture of fifteen pounds of Tobacco whereof the one half is to be bestowed in publique uses the other upon the Informer.

The Act might slow down the waste and abuse offered by sundry lewd and improvident persons, but hunting of the larger animals would continue. Likewise for those found more than five leagues—fifteen miles—offshore, and also for those taken by people whose friends and acquaintances would not turn them in for a few pounds of tobacco.

More discussion will come later about a modern age of waste and abuse offered by sundry lewd and improvident persons that goes far beyond mere hunting. For now, consider estimates of turtle populations from the days entirely before exploitation, that is, long before Columbus. Consider how many sea turtles might have been around before large numbers of human beings showed up on the scene.

In "Roles of Sea Turtles in Marine Ecosystems: Reconstructing the Past," researchers Karen Bjorndal and Jeremy Jackson wrote of such times, saying, "sea turtles occurred in massive numbers that are now difficult to imagine." But they did not leave the numbers entirely to the imagination, at least for one region. Instead, they offered estimates for two species in the Caribbean. There were, they suggest, at least sixteen million and maybe more than six hundred million adult green turtles and half a million adult hawksbill turtles in that one region alone.

Today, fewer than two million adult greens and eighty thousand hawks-bills exist worldwide. For the bigger picture, estimates of the worldwide population of adult sea turtles, including all seven species, suggest at most about six-and-a-half million animals.

Sixteen paragraphs ago I wrote that sea turtles are nowhere near as abundant as they once were, and I meant it.

Regarding fishermen, Elsa has more to say: "I am convinced that our close relationship with fisherman is having a good result."

Some time ago, when she suspected that some of the fishermen in nearby Guaymas were illegally taking sea turtles, she started a dialogue. She encouraged them to tell stories about sea turtles. Most of them talked about people they knew, or had heard of, who illegally took turtles. Of course one might presume that the people in the stories were surrogates for themselves. The stories involved intentionally hunted turtles but also turtles that came up dead in nets. The animals, however caught, were sold.

The men, in telling their stories to someone like Elsa, could not help but feel some level of shame. She believes this helped some of them change their ways, and that each one who changes the way in which he thinks about turtles might influence several others, a reality strengthened by the family ties characteristic of the fishing community, where grandfathers and fathers and sons and uncles and nephews and brothers and cousins fish together, learning from one another.

"So this is about changing the culture of turtle hunting," she says. "It is a chain reaction resulting in fewer turtles killed."

I tell Elsa a story about a British conservationist named Tom Harrison. Harrison had, in the 1930s, been involved with early efforts to assess public opinions about various issues in Britain. It was his view that attitudes could be changed through media campaigns. In June 1964, he wrote an article titled, "Must the Turtle Die?"

Harrison's article was picked up by the *Sunday Times of London* and the German magazine *Die Umschau*.

At this time, many different companies sold turtle products in Europe. Turtle meat and turtle skins were widely accepted consumer products, available essentially everywhere. One of many enterprises trading in turtles, a single firm in Germany, sold more than a million cans of turtle soup each year.

While it might be easy to scoff at the importance of media campaigns, to shrug them off as meaningless and useless, the German soup canner did not see it that way. The soup canner objected to Harrison's suggestion that the industry might be contributing to the extinction of a species. They saw what was coming. They could see as well as Harrison that attitudes could indeed be changed, influenced, manipulated. Clearly, Harrison's article worked, or at least it contributed to a greater movement that worked. Neither turtle soup nor turtle leather are readily available throughout the world today. Where products are available—in certain Caribbean nations, for example—they are widely shunned by visiting tourists.

Elsa continued talking about her fishermen. With grant money, she pays some of them to help her capture turtles, as allowed by her permit, for monitoring purposes. The captured turtles are measured, weighed, and sometimes tagged before they are released. This kind of monitoring is used globally as a means of determining whether or not turtle numbers are increasing or decreasing. By participating, fishermen can earn more than 1,200 pesos in six hours or less, more than they would earn by selling a turtle.

"We need to respect each other," Elsa says. "The fishermen are not bad people. They are not evil people. We need to find a way to live together."

But also, she points out, "We are not the owners of the planet."

Turtles mating off the coast of Mexico. *Photo by Lisanne Aerts.*

ABOVE: *Rocinante*, a mostly restored Pearson Countess ketch designed by John Alden and built in 1965. *Photo by S/V Crystal Blue.* BELOW: Relocated turtle nests in front of a condominium, where they can be protected at all hours by security guards. *Photo by Bill Streever.*

The ancestors of modern sea turtles appeared about 120 million years ago in the Cretaceous period. *Photo by Lisanne Aerts.*

ABOVE: The incubation center in San Carlos. *Photo by Bill Streever.*
BELOW: A shrimper in the Gulf of California. *Photo by Lisanne Aerts.*

A turtle hatchling release. *Photo by Lisanne Aerts.*

The last of the turtle hatchlings to reach the water. *Photo by Lisanne Aerts.*

Hatchling releases educate the public and encourage popular support of turtle conservation. *Photo by Lisanne Aerts.*

ABOVE: The first step in the necropsy is the removal of the dead turtle's plastron.
BELOW: The final resting place of the necropsied turtle. *Both photos by Bill Streever.*

Luis Martín Castro Romero (Martin) releasing turtle
hatchlings at San Basilio. *Photo by Lisanne Aerts.*

Hatchlings swimming for the first time in the shallow waters of San Basilio.
Both photos by Lisanne Aerts.

ABOVE: *Rocinante* anchored near Punta Púlpito.
BELOW: What at first looked like a sleeping turtle sadly turned out to be dead.
Both photos by Lisanne Aerts.

The Gulf of California, like all oceans and seas, has suffered from overfishing and other insults, and yet it still teems with life. *Photo by Lisanne Aerts.*

ABOVE: Gillnets stacked on a beach, a common sight on the shores of the Baja peninsula.
BELOW: The sign at the headquarters of Grupo Tortuguero de las Californias.
Both photos by Lisanne Aerts.

Sea turtles sometimes suffer from buoyancy disorders, preventing them from diving. *Photo by Lisanne Aerts.*

ABOVE: Eared grebes near Bahía de los Ángeles.
BELOW: One of many guitar fish in an anchorage near Isla Ángel de la Guarda's northern tip.
Both photos by Lisanne Aerts.

ABOVE: A highly endangered vaquita porpoise meets a Day of the Dead mermaid in a Puerto Peñasco wall painting. BELOW: A purse seiner. *Both photos by Lisanne Aerts.*

A few words about legally hunting sea turtles.

One might think, as I once did, that turtle hunting is universally banned by international treaties, such as the Convention on International Trade in Endangered Species of Wild Fauna and Flora, or CITES, which has protected sea turtles since 1975. Even after learning of the legal hunts that occur in some circumstances, such as the legal egg harvest in Ostional, in Costa Rica, one might cling to the belief that this sort of thing is very closely monitored and allowed only with conservation objectives in mind. Or, discovering that some turtle hunting continues, one might think as I once did that it occurs in no more than five or six pariah nations. Ten at the most.

One would be wrong. As of January 2013, sea turtles could be legally hunted in forty-two countries. In Papua New Guinea more than fifteen thousand turtles are legally taken per year. In Nicaragua, more than nine thousand. In Australia, more than six thousand. In all, more than forty-two thousand sea turtles are legally taken—where "taken" is the standard euphemism that in this context simply means killed—each year.

Claims of regional abundance combined with cultural significance justify the slaughter. The argument goes something like this: "We see lots of sea turtles here, and we have always eaten sea turtles, so we should be allowed to keep eating sea turtles."

It is, in other words, the kind of argument that could drive a sane man mad.

A few pages ago I promised more on the modern age of turtle slaughter, on the ongoing waste and abuse offered by sundry lewd and improvident persons, and by that I was not referring only to legal and illegal hunting.

I was referring to seining, gillnetting, longlining, shrimp trawling, beach development, dredging, plastic pollution, boat strikes, dogs digging up nests, beach buggies running over nests, and water pollution of various kinds.

It is difficult to assign anything more than rough estimates to the number of sea turtles killed by legal hunting each year. Because so few criminals are willing to fill out survey forms, offering up a number for those killed by illegal hunting is even more challenging. In the still harder basket lies assessment of an approximate number put to death every year by human carelessness.

But we might get some idea. We can find clues that offer insights.

A single abandoned fishing net found adrift off the coast of Brazil held seventeen dead turtles. Such ghost nets are common. In the Atlantic Ocean alone, an astounding seven thousand kilometers of nets are lost each year. Because the nets are made from plastic, they could last hundreds of years. And it is not just the ghost nets that catch and kill turtles. Turtles breathe air. Any net left in the water for more than an hour or so, which is to say most nets, can drown turtles.

Of course fishers also use hooks. Longliners tie dozens to hundreds or even thousands of hooks spaced at intervals along a stretch of strong rope that may be well over a mile long, and they catch turtles whether they want to or not. One researcher suggested that long-liners kill two hundred thousand loggerhead turtles a year worldwide.

And do not forget shrimpers. Shrimpers often drag nets across the seabed. Turtles often rest on the seabed. Other turtles might be swept up in midwater as the nets are hauled back aboard. More than fifty thousand turtles a year may die on the shrimping grounds of the United States, despite regulations and modifications to trawls intended to limit bycatch.

The numbers are dodgy. Fishing advocates argue that estimates lean toward the high side of reality. They also point to changes in fishing practices that decrease bycatch levels. Net mesh size can be changed to avoid the capture of turtles, hooks that are less likely to catch turtles can be used, and shrimp trawls can be outfitted with turtle exclusion devices. To be fair, if the numbers of turtles killed are as high as is often claimed, and if the estimates for the total number of sea turtles in the world are even in the right ballpark, we would have no sea turtles left today.

But still, any argument claiming that commercial fishing does not hurt sea turtle populations simply does not hold water. It cannot be reasonably denied that innumerable, countless, too many sea turtles die every year, killed by fishers not on purpose but incidentally.

That does not even consider the number of turtles swept up in dredges, choked by ingested plastic, whacked in the head by passing ships and boats, or poisoned—slowly or quickly—by various kinds of water pollution. Nor does it consider the beaches destroyed by development, the condominium lighting schemes that prevent even the most capable of hatchlings from finding the sea, the beach buggies and dogs that crisscross the nesting grounds.

Set aside the vain but necessary attempts to assign numbers. Instead, think about what it is to be a turtle today. To live, you must survive about two months as an egg, buried under a couple of feet of beach sand. If the nest is not dug up—that is, if you are not eaten before you hatch—you have to make it to the water. At this stage, you are virtually defenseless against birds and raccoons and dogs, and while you have some sense of direction, some idea of where the water might be, you can easily go astray, heading into the dunes, or you can become stranded behind driftwood or in a tire rut, or if your timing is off you might overheat under the sun. But you are not alone. Your siblings surround you. In the mad scramble away from the nest, you crawl over some of them and some of them crawl over you. If you are lucky enough to make it to the water, you face a year or longer developing a shell hard enough to ward off fish and sharks and sea birds.

Then comes a decade to several decades of swimming about, trying to avoid nets and hooks and shrimp trawls, dodging oil spills, resisting the temptation to wolf down bits of plastic no matter how much they may resemble tasty jellyfish or sea grass, diving at the sound of every approaching vessel. If you are a male, you will never return to shore. But if you are a female, you will go back ashore, probably to the beach where you were born. If the beach remains intact, not covered by condominiums, you will scamper through the surf-washed shallows to belly crawl on dry sand. Although you may look clumsy ashore, you know how to use your front flippers to scoop out a body pit. Settling into this shallow depression, your hind flippers come into play. They are surprisingly adept in the art of digging. With them, you excavate a vertical shaft and expand it into a chamber at the bottom. You lay your hundred eggs, ping pong balls in shape and size, leathery rather than hard, each containing the beginnings of a single child. Perhaps you rest a bit. Then you fill in your diggings, crawl back to the surf, and swim away. Maybe you return after a few days or a week, perhaps you return several times, but only to bury new eggs, and never to visit your earlier eggs, never to take care of a previous nest. Your young, like you, are on their own.

The first time I heard that survival rates of turtles might be as low as one in one thousand, I was somewhat doubtful. It seemed too low a number to be realistic. But when I thought about what it takes for a turtle to survive to adulthood, to do its job as a reproductive unit, my skepticism grew. Only then, the number seemed too high to be realistic.

A very brief digression with regard to fishing nets, ship traffic, and other turtle-killing obstacles at sea, from a sailor's perspective.

It is impossible to sail coastal waters in most of the world's oceans without making abrupt course changes to avoid nets and other vessels. Ask any sailor who has put more than a few thousand miles beneath the keel, and you will hear stories of entanglements and near collisions. You will learn that sailing through polluted waters, waters so foul as to be unswimmable, so grungy as to leave tarry stains on hulls, is just part of the lifestyle.

Turtles do not sit on bar stools telling sea stories. But if they did, they too would have stories of entanglements and near collisions and water nasty beyond belief.

When I first walked a beach looking for but not finding nests, there were 446 eggs in the incubation room. A little less than a month has passed.

"Now we have about 2,000 eggs in the incubation room," Elsa tells me from behind her ever-present COVID mask. "And another 200 on the beach."

She compares her organization to that of others working along this coast and on the coast of Baja, on the other side of the Gulf of California. "Some other groups might handle fewer nests, as few as five or six. But in some places groups manage a hundred thousand eggs! Sometimes in one night they might have one hundred nests!"

Olive ridley sea turtles come ashore more or less alone to lay eggs in at least thirty-two countries, ranging from India and Mozambique to Burma, Brazil, and, of course, Mexico. Some beaches are more active than others. But some beaches—at least thirteen are known around the globe—are phenomenally active. Olive ridley females, laden with eggs, swarm ashore by the hundreds and thousands in synchronized mass nesting events called arribadas, Spanish for something like "arrival" or "arrival by sea." Further south on Mexico's west coast, in Oaxaca and Michoacán states, where the coastline arcs gently eastward, two active arribadas remain, one supporting more than four hundred thousand nesting turtles and the other supporting about two thousand. On beaches such as these, a hundred nests in a night would be a small fraction of the total nests.

As a footnote, three arribadas in Mexico and one in Suriname are no longer active, having fallen victim to egg hunters and other pressures. As a second footnote, an arribada in Costa Rica's Ostional supports something like five hundred thousand nesters. This is the beach where egg hunters work legally and within limits, where eggs are sold for consumption in bars or as ingredients for cookies and cakes.

But on ordinary nesting beaches, where smaller numbers of turtles show up to lay eggs, turtlers routinely move nests to incubators. Or they cordon off nests in place, protecting them from people and their dogs, from raccoons, from foxes and armadillos. Or turtlers might do what they can to protect entire beaches.

We talk about bringing eggs to the incubation room. "We have a protocol and a score card to decide if a nest should be moved," Elsa says. "In other places it is more subjective. Volunteers make a guess at what will be best."

She thinks it is better to have a protocol, and she wants to share hers with others.

She continues, nodding as she talks. "Yes, of course there is a controversy about moving nests." When she started, volunteers were split between those who thought moving nests was best and those who thought that nests should be left where found. Feelings ran high. One or two volunteers quit over the to-move-or-not-to-move-the-nests debate. "But little by little the volunteers have seen that it is usually best to move nests away from beaches like San Francisco to incubators," she says.

Even before Elsa brought it up, I had heard and read about complaints regarding the moving of sea turtle nests. Some object on principle, on the basis that humans should not interfere with nature. As an extension of this theme, others point to concerns about unintended consequences. Still others believe that moving eggs leads to higher mortality rates than would occur if they were left in place, a position that rests entirely at odds with the experiences of those who have moved eggs in a responsible manner, those who only move nests doomed to total failure if left in place. The entire discussion tends to ignore history, to gloss over the fact that there is nothing new about moving nests. Turtle nests were relocated in Borneo as early as 1957.

It seems that the objection may have its roots in the widely held belief that birds abandon nests if eggs or chicks are handled by humans. As it turns out, this belief is more myth than reality. Most birds return to handled eggs and chicks. In any case, sea turtles are not birds. Whether or not eggs are handled, the father is long gone and the mother is not coming back.

None of which, of course, is an argument in favor of unnecessarily moving nests. Elsa and her volunteers do not move nests as a matter of sport or entertainment. They move nests to save and protect eggs, to tip the scales in favor of future hatchlings.

While no legitimate conservation argument can be made for leaving nests to die in unsuitable locations, I ask Elsa if her efforts might be better placed elsewhere. It might be more effective to protect those animals, those one-in-one-thousands, that are ready to lay eggs. Point blank, I ask if she might make more progress in terms of saving the species by fighting gill-netting than she is making by moving nests. Or she could fight longlining or shrimp trawling or any of the other deadly activities taking the lives of turtles that have already run the gauntlet to adulthood.

"That's a very good question," she replies. "We have many things in play here. But behind it all the main thing is to protect the population. You know we put in so much effort here, when there are so many more eggs moved at other locations. But what we are doing is also a form of education. We educate the fishermen. And it is a social program. It gives retired people a way to contribute. Some of the retired people go into schools to talk about turtles. So it goes beyond protecting turtles to help break down the wall between Mexicans and Americans."

The turtles are acting, in part, as ambassadors, bridging the fishing community and the conservation community, bringing together gringo retirees and local youths. She tells me of gringo guest appearances in the schools of the nearby community of La Manga. "The children are so happy to try out their English, just a word or two, but they are so happy." The English they try focuses on the protection of sea turtles.

She talks of releases. She tells me that people who see hatchlings swim to the sea will never think about sea turtles in quite the same way. That in itself is a means of fighting for turtles.

Refer back for a moment to numbers past and present. In the time of Columbus there were far fewer people than turtles in the world. Today there are more than a thousand people for each of the world's sea turtles. Is it any wonder that turtles face extinction?

When I was younger, when I thought it might be a matter of poof and sea turtles would be gone before I ever had a chance to see them in the wild, I was mistaken. It would never have been a matter of poof. To say so is to exaggerate. There has never been a time when the existing number of sea turtles has been so low that they were truly and irrefutably on the brink of extinction. Their situation, as desperate as it is, cannot be compared to that of, say, the baiji dolphins of the Yangtze River, which may exist even though none have been seen alive since 2002. Or the vaquita porpoise, of which fewer than twenty individuals remain alive today, with the term "fewer" including the possibility of zero. Or the Javan rhinoceros, with a population of less than one hundred.

Turtles are far less abundant than they were at the time of Columbus, shockingly and tragically less abundant, but they are in fact still abundant.

That is a problem with extinction. Simple abundance is no guarantee of long-term viability.

In the 1960s, the International Union for the Conservation of Nature, the IUCN, approached legendary turtle biologist Archie Carr. Founded in 1948, the IUCN now boasts well over a thousand member organizations, draws on the knowledge of nearly twenty thousand experts from around the globe, is recognized by the United Nations, and is known by millions of people around the world. The organization does many things, but it is known in large part because of its Red List. The Red List provides the world with an inventory of species and their conservation status. Each entry in the list is ranked, from "Extinct" to "Extinct in the Wild" to "Critically Endangered" and so on down to "Species of Least Concern."

The Red List is sometimes described as a comprehensive inventory, but this is not even remotely true if the word comprehensive is taken to mean complete or all-inclusive. The list contains only 147,500 species, which sounds and is impressive, but it is only a fraction of the two million or so species that biologists have described and an even smaller fraction of the total number of species on Earth. But it includes all seven species of sea turtles.

Back to the 1960s. It was then that the IUCN asked Archie Carr to determine which of the world's sea turtles were in danger of extinction. Carr ran into a few difficulties. For one thing, species identities were not completely clear in the 1960s. Were the black and the green turtle different species? There were some who doubted that the Kemp's ridley was anything more than a hybrid, the spawn of a loggerhead and a green, a crossbreed. The absence of information on populations posed an even greater problem. The handful of people around the world working on sea turtles had, at best, a very sketchy notion of the number of animals that were out there. There was, too, a third difficulty. There existed a feeling that population numbers had to be low for a species to be threatened with extinction. The original categories used to rank extinction risk relied on degrees of rarity. While no one knew how many turtles there were, everyone knew there were quite a few. They could hardly be considered rare.

On the other hand, anyone who was paying attention knew that fewer and fewer turtles survived from one year to the next. Breeding adults were hunted without mercy, their carcasses eaten or converted to leather or rendered into beauty creams, their shells hung on walls or turned into combs and cheap souvenirs. Their eggs were plucked from beaches as though infinitely abundant. Focus on rarity and struggle with absolute numbers all you like, but the trajectory was clear. What Carr saw was analogous to a boat headed full steam directly toward a rocky outcrop. Without a course correction, catastrophe was imminent.

"If it is the long run you think of," Carr wrote to the IUCN, "all sea turtles are endangered."

What do sea turtles, polar bears, whale sharks, various corals, and a number of other species have in common? All are reasonably abundant, but all are considered at risk of extinction, all are thought to be on a collision course with utter ruin and the ultimate demise.

Is it even possible to change this course?

FOUR

Releases

A week passes and I am back on the beach with Judith. In twenty minutes the sun will rise. For now, a red glow from the east lights low cumulus clouds in dead still air.

Within minutes, midges and occasional mosquitoes find us, hovering around our faces, wishing us good morning. We pass a group of young Mexicans finishing off a night of revelry with a swim.

Ten minutes into our walk, with Judith moving at her usual clip, progressing by virtue of her habitual short rapid paces, we find tracks. Actual turtle tracks.

The tracks form a V, one arm of which leads up from the very light surf to maybe two feet above the tide line, and the other arm of which leads back down. In dry sand at the apex of the V sits a nest depression, a divot four feet across, slightly larger than a mature olive ridley female.

Using a metal stick the length of a walking cane, Judith gently probes the sand. She works systematically, from the outside inward.

"It's probably not a nest," she says. "It is too close to the water, and the depression is too deep." Normally the mother would partly fill and obscure the body pit after backfilling the nest cavity, after burying her eggs, but here the edge of the depression remains sharp, a five-inch bluff of sand.

Judith also points out the spray from the digging, the sand flung up and out by the turtle's flippers, which shows that the animal was facing inland while she dug. This is not always the case. Sometimes a mother will turn back toward the sea before she starts digging.

Judith is in no way visibly excited. She has found two sets of tracks so far this year, one that turned out to be a nest that had already been found and excavated and one that turned out to be a test nest.

"Sometimes turtles will come up, dig a little to test the conditions, and turn around without laying eggs at all," she says.

Nevertheless, she continues working the probe in a grid pattern along the edges of the depression, gently poking at three-inch intervals.

"I'm looking for soft sand," she says. If this is a nest, the sand around the edges of the cavity holding the eggs will be very soft, so much so that the probe will push through as if pushing through air. Turtlers have been known to fall over face-first when their probes unexpectedly push from firm sand into the loose diggings at the edge of an egg-filled nest cavity.

In this case, Judith does not quite fall, but when she hits soft sand she stumbles a bit. Her face lights up. It is, after all, a nest. Or at least it is probably a nest.

She texts the team reporting her finding. When I ask who is up monitoring text messages so early in the morning, she says, "Everybody!" Including Elsa, who is up before dawn every day waiting to hear from volunteers.

Other turtlers respond within seconds.

Judith dons black surgical gloves, covering the turtle tattoo on her left wrist. As a first responder, she can unearth the eggs. Down on her knees, she scoops with the side of her right hand.

Seeing her, a passerby might wonder why a woman of her age wearing surgical gloves is starting a sandcastle at such an ungodly hour.

She digs from the outer edge of what might be a nest, working her way inward, just as she had probed. At a depth of eight inches she still finds hard, compacted sand. "I'm not feeling confident," she says. "Maybe just a test hole after all." Maybe the turtle moved some sand but decided not to drop eggs.

Using the back of a rubber-clad hand, Judith wipes sweat from her face. "Sorry to get your hopes up," she says. But she keeps pushing sand upward and outward.

Further in and ten inches down, she finds looser material. Her face brightens. "It's very soft," she says. "Now I am getting excited."

A moment later, "I think we have a nest here."

Uncovering the first of what turns out to be many eggs, she uses a technical term: "Woohoo!"

She snaps a photo and texts it to the group. The photo incudes our GPS location on the beach.

She refills her excavation. We return to her parked car at an only slightly curtailed trot to retrieve a cooler. We return to the nest without slowing. She wants to finish the job before it gets too hot. Already sweat drips down her cheeks, soaking her mask.

Still gloved, she scoops sand into the bottom of the cooler, spreading it loosely, then makes egg indents with her finger. With preparations complete she goes back to work on the nest, scooping away sand, flipping her hand sideways in a motion something like that of a mother turtle digging.

"We need to watch out for flies getting into the nest," she tells me.

The loose sand at the edge of Judith's growing crater intersects what can be best described as a chimney. This is the shoot into which the turtle would have deposited her eggs. The sand here is very loose. Judith scoops it out, ever so gently, to open the egg-filled cavern at the bottom. "It's amazing to see how these giant turtles with their giant flippers dig such delicate precise holes," Judith says. She is right. It is hard to imagine how a turtle can dig a hole in the form of an upside-down funnel, and yet that is what they do.

The top of the egg chamber and the shallow-most eggs sit just over a foot down. Within seconds of exposing the first egg, two others appear. They are white with the slightest orange tinge, yolk showing through thin shell.

She hands me a shiny new click counter. As she adds eggs to the cooler, along with occasional handfuls of loose sand, I click away. One egg, two, seven, ten, twenty, thirty-seven.

"This is very stressful for me," she says, though I would not have guessed it to see her, childlike in her delight.

She finds one broken egg and sets it aside, its yoke dripping into the sand, the leathery shell not so much cracked as torn. As Jim Straw had pointed out, one bad egg, rotting, can kill an entire nest.

I continue my role as lead clicker. Fifty-five, fifty-six, fifty-seven.

Before Judith is done, I have registered 105 clicks, 105 eggs. Plus one broken and dead, which goes back into the nest cavity to be buried, laid to rest.

We refill the hole and obscure the tracks.

Full sunlight casts sharp shadows of our bodies on the beach. Sandpipers scurry across tire ruts and around the usual selection of beer cans and bottles and plastic debris and yet another dead pelican. On the water, a gull and a cormorant argue over a fish.

Judith, though slight of form, insists on carrying the cooler, which must weigh more than thirty unergonomic pounds. Even so, her stride remains nothing less than fast, difficult to keep up with on this soft beach.

She tells me that driving back to the incubation center with a load of eggs makes her nervous. The roads are rough. Even where paved, there are potholes that would not be out of place on a weapons testing ground.

In the incubation center, she prepares a data sheet for the nest—the number of eggs, the location, the date, the expected date of hatch. While she works, I look over the data sheets on each of the coolers in the incubation center. The total, not including Judith's 105, is 2,549. A lot of eggs.

But on the other hand, not so many. Not so many at all if only one in one thousand live to be adults, or even if three in a thousand live to be adults. But on the other hand, well worth the effort. Fifteen or twenty years from now, if the survival rate estimates are about right, the number of adult sea turtles in the world will be up by at least two. And, since fractional turtles cannot exist in nature, it seems reasonable to round upward to three. If we accept the assumption that hatchlings helped to the sea have a better chance of survival than those coming from a natural nest, maybe as many as six or even seven of the eggs will grow into adults. Any of these numbers, whether two or three or four or seven, dwarf zero.

Eduardo Pérez, a young biologist interning with the program, joins us. He advises Judith to add a couple of inches of sand on top of the nest by scooping it in from the sides of the box rather than dropping it downward, directly on top of the eggs.

Finished, Judith pokes holes in the top of the box. She mentions that Eduardo has found more nests than anyone else this year. His record, per the labels in the incubation room, is four nests so far, 448 eggs. Or, by my upward rounding rules of turtle accounting, and by applying higher survival rates for hatchlings helped by turtlers, maybe as many as three or four adult turtles before Eduardo himself reaches late middle age.

We wrap up a fairly breathless morning at half past eight. Today, Judith has done more for turtles before breakfast than most people do in a lifetime.

Breaking news, released on September 29, 2021, from the U.S. Fish and Wildlife Service: They are calling for the removal of Endangered Species Act protection for twenty-three species, including eleven birds, eight freshwater mussels, two fishes, one bat, and one plant.

The proposed delistings do not reflect population recoveries. They do not convey a message of conservation success. They are not good news. In the words of the agency's press release: "The U.S. Fish and Wildlife Service is proposing to remove 23 species from the Endangered Species Act (ESA) due to extinction."

Officially extinguished are the ivory-billed woodpeckers, last seen in 1944. Officially gone are the Bachman's warblers, last seen in 1988. Lost forever are the Molokai creepers, the flat pigtoe mussels, the southern acornshell mussels, the Scioto madtoms, and the little Mariana fruit bats.

The agency, it seems, is tidying up paperwork, perhaps removing budgetary and regulatory requirements intended to protect species that no longer exist.

At least none of the species are sea turtles.

But still, for those of us keeping an eye on extinctions, for those enamored by biodiversity, news like this threatens anything resembling an optimistic outlook.

A rumor circulates among the turtlers. The nests near the condominiums on San Francisco beach, the same nests that the retired pilot Jim Straw had been guarding, may hatch soon. Any time now. Maybe today. Maybe this morning.

As soon as I hear the rumor, I drive out to the site. I arrive at seven-thirty in the morning, late by turtler standards.

The fences and signs are gone. Eduardo, the biologist who works with Elsa, has bad news. One of the nests, it turns out, was full of unfertilized eggs. As to the other nest, fly larva infested all but fifteen of the eggs. Only fifteen eggs hatched. Earlier that morning, he had taken the hatchlings to the incubation center.

There is really nothing more to be said. We stand around staring at the empty sand for a few minutes. Toward the end of those few minutes, Eduardo receives a call. Another potential nest has been discovered just down the beach. The turtler is a new volunteer, without the experience to probe the sand, so Eduardo will have to help. He invites me along.

The nest, if there is one, is above the tide line. It lies squarely in the path of a set of fresh tire tracks. The eggs, if there are any, definitely will have to be moved. He divides the nest depression—the cama, he calls it, Spanish for bed—into four sectors, and he begins the slow, systematic process of probing, all the while explaining his thoughts and actions to the volunteer. He turns the probe over to her and watches, now and then offering tips. In the still air, I can hear the probe working, the sand rolling and grinding against steel.

A hundred closely spaced probe marks turn up no clear signs of a nest. A passerby, a gringa in her early sixties, stops to gawk for a few minutes but says nothing, asks nothing, unmoved by the sight of two Mexicans with a metal probe working the sand while a gringo with a notebook looks on. She wanders away.

Elsa appears over the crest of a dune that separates the beach from a nearby marginally drivable dirt track. She wears a blue T-shirt printed with sketches of the five species of sea turtles known to occur in the Gulf of California. More importantly, she carries with her a cooler holding the fifteen surviving hatchlings from the fly-infested nest. She tells us they are ready to be released. But first she wants to see what is going on with this nest. She takes over probing. Her COVID mask, wet with sweat, puffs in and out with her breaths. It is already in the nineties under the sun.

"All of the sand here is soft," she says. Eduardo, also sweating, puts his now gloved hands to work scooping sand away from the edge of the depression. The volunteer slips on gloves and mimics Eduardo, tossing sand from the other side of the potential nest. All banter has for the moment stopped, but there are no signs of impatience, no hint of anything but cheerful endurance.

At first Eduardo and the volunteer remind me of archaeologists, bent over, knees in the sand, sending sand flying with scooping flicks of the wrist. But as their hands work deeper into the sand they remind me of turtles, just as Judith had done not long before.

Elsa continues to probe.

Another passerby stops, a slender Mexican woman wearing a fashionable bikini and dark glasses beneath a floppy broadbrimmed hat. She asks questions and take photographs. Elsa stops probing to talk to her. A few minutes pass, and the woman asks for a phone number. She may be a future volunteer.

When the woman leaves, everyone concludes in lockstep that the nest is a false alarm, a test nest. There was something here that the mother did not like. The quality of the sand, too much light from the restaurants down the beach, too much noise, a passing raccoon, something. Elsa explains all of this while smiling. She once saw a mom make fourteen test nests without once laying eggs. Some of the test nests were in the dunes, nestled among patches of salt grass.

"Maybe she will try again tonight," Elsa says.

Close to an hour has passed since Eduardo and I arrived at the test nest, an hour of probing and digging and standing in the full morning sun of a Sonoran Desert beach in summer.

"This is a perfect place to release the hatchlings," Elsa says. There are few birds around. No dogs are in sight. It is very close to where the eggs had been laid.

I ask if it is possible that the hatchlings came from the same mother that made the test nest. Sure. Why not? Who knows?

Elsa opens the cooler. The tiny turtles, seemingly all head and flipper, crawl over one another, trying to scale the walls of their Styrofoam box as if climbing out of a nest. But they just tumble back, sometimes landing upside down. With a few seconds of struggling effort, they right themselves and try again. Elsa checks each hatchling, holding them one at a time between thumb and forefinger. She points out that some of them have el leucismo, that is, leucism, or reduced pigmentation. They are far from albinos, but their shells shine with a lighter shade of gray than that which might be considered normal. Looking at their undersides, at their plastrons, she confirms that they have absorbed most of whatever yolk remained in their umbilicals, the final source of energy they will have to rely on until they are in the water, until they can feed.

Bottom line, these little guys seem ready to go.

We move to within twenty-five feet of the breaking waves and Eduardo gives the volunteer a new set of gloves. One at a time, she takes hatchlings from the box and puts them on the sand. And one at a time, in a dash that has been and should continue to be called a frenzy, they zig and they zag with a hobbling hatchling turtle sprint in the general direction of the water.

The first crosses the twenty-five feet of open sand in less than ninety seconds. At the water's edge, a wave carries the tiny squirming shell upward and seaward. Employing front flippers that function almost like wings, the hatchling flies through the water.

But the next wave, maybe a foot tall, throws the little turtle back onto the sand.

Without pause the animal rights itself and tries again. And once more. On the third try, swimming frantically, the hatchling sets off beyond the breaking waves, maybe fifteen feet out. The turtle is underway.

Over the next five minutes, all but two of the siblings are in the water and gone. These two are near the water's edge, wet and covered with sticky sand. They reached the water only to be tossed back ashore time and again, until now they seem too tired to persevere.

In fresh gloves, Eduardo picks up the sluggards and checks their plastrons. Are they really ready? One has some yolk left and if necessary could wait for another day. He puts her or him back onto the sand just above the breaking waves. The yolk on the other is fine. He holds the animal head down to drain water from flooded innards in an act of sea turtle pulmonary therapy. He puts her or him next to the other hatchling.

I say her or him because young turtles show no external sign of their sex, and I avoid the neuter form "it" because these creatures are alive and deserving of more than a label of "it."

The second of the two hatchlings dashes for the water, catching a wave within seconds. Swimming commences. The animal paddles clumsily and slowly compared to its more successful siblings. He or she tumbles in the surf and tries again. And again. And again. On try five the youngster is finally on the way, headed out to sea.

The other sluggard, the one with the hint of a remaining umbilical, just reaches the wet sand but then appears to give up once again, splayed out, immobile. Eduardo takes her or him back to the cooler. This exhausted hatchling will be given more time to build up strength, to completely digest what is left of the yolk.

Whatever else happens today, fourteen new turtle hatchlings swim free in the ocean. However many were here before, there are fourteen more now.

A cormorant swims offshore, fifty feet out. Cormorants are often considered to be the world's most efficient aquatic predators, capturing more prey per unit effort than any other species. I watch the bird's movements. Not finding our youngsters, the super predator swims east, turtleless.

A boat, large letters announcing its name as *Sun Shine*, passes just offshore. Our turtles are out there somewhere, ideally not being ground up by *Sun Shine*'s propellor.

The lone hatchling in the cooler remains quiet, legs and head relaxed, looking something like a tiny sunbather that has had way too much to drink.

I am an overly educated biologist, trained for better or worse not to identify with animals, not to see them as individuals, yet here I am worrying about my youngsters. Point of fact: I defy anyone to release a baby sea turtle without emotion. Admittedly, the sensation will be stronger for some than for others, but even Spock himself—of *Star Trek*—would be moved.

For myself, I resist feeling like a parent sending his five-year-old for the first day of kindergarten, hoping hoping hoping for the best, especially in this case, knowing the odds are highly stacked against the best. In fact, it is a good bet that none of our youngsters will reach adulthood.

But the fourteen youngsters are now well out of sight, and I feel undeniably great.

My thinking that afternoon falls under the influence of watching fourteen tiny turtles swimming out to sea. In such a state, I consult a dictionary. Merriam-Webster defines optimism in part as "an inclination to put the most favorable construction upon actions and events or to anticipate the best possible outcome."

But optimism can be relative.

When I say I am writing a book about the search for optimism with regard to the extinction crisis, I have to explain that my optimism can only be of the sort that grows from a fathoms-deep pit of despair, from a realization that we already live on a damaged planet, on a diminished Earth. If I find it at all, it will be an optimism borne from a starting point of, "My God, we are killing off the plants and the animals that I love, and there is no room for hope," a starting point that leaves me helpless and forlorn, that renders senseless any attempt to stem the deadly flow, that ends anything resembling personal responsibility. From there, this hypothetical optimism might mature to say, in effect, "My God, we are killing off the plants and animals that I love, but there is room for hope." It could become an optimism that believes not only that we can change, but that we have already begun to change, and that we will change even more before the direst of the extinction forecasts comes to pass. And that the change is not one I should expect from someone else, but rather from everyone else, including myself.

By the way, this realization of mine, this realization about the optimism I seek, includes as part of its envisioned maturing process the understanding that meaningful change does not happen overnight. Sadly, tragically, inevitably, more species will be needlessly lost before this extinction crisis ends.

But it is all the more vital, then, that we do not lose the will to fight.

Another rumor comes my way. Turtlers are saying that Elsa has a sick turtle in her care, an adult.

I find Elsa at the incubation center, but the turtle is not there. Elsa explains that she is caring for the turtle, a hawksbill, probably a female, at her home, where she and her husband can give it round-the-clock attention. It weighs seventy pounds and is twenty-nine inches long, just shy of the officially accepted adult length.

"Right now, we are giving her fluids once a day, with the amount based on her weight," Elsa says. She is getting 100 milliliters of fluids subcutaneously, injected through her leathery skin.

Elsa reaches into a black plastic tackle box, her black bag, to produce a stethoscope. To hear a turtle breathe, the stethoscope is applied to the upper side—"the dorsal side," Elsa says—of the shell. The turtle's lungs are just under the shell, which, after all, is a modified ribcage.

"Turtle lung infections are pretty common," she says. "And I could hear wheezing in her right lung. So I give her enrofloxacin once every two days."

Bayer makes enrofloxacin, and it is approved by the U.S. Food and Drug Administration for certain veterinary applications. It has been used to treat respiratory and other soft tissue infections in horses, and it is sanctioned for the treatment of swine and bovine respiratory diseases. Enrofloxacin is considered safe and effective against a variety of pathogens, and is additionally recommended for what are broadly classified as "exotic animals."

Within the world of veterinary medicine, it is safe to assume that sea turtles are considered to be exotic. Or at least more exotic than, say, dogs or cats.

The patient's lung congestion has improved after just four days of treatment.

"The infection could have started with a virus that opened the door for a bacterial infection," Elsa says. "And pollution increases the risk of infection." It occurs to me that I have heard something similar from my own doctor about my own body.

I ask if the turtle could have aspirated water during recent storms, but Elsa thinks her turtle was sick before that. "The barnacles and algae growing on her shell and skin tell me she has been sick for maybe six months."

This is not something I have ever heard from my own doctor.

I ask if she learned much about sea turtles in veterinary school. She laughs quietly for a second. "It was all about small animals and livestock. One semester on cows, one on goats, one on pigs. But I had a class on wildlife, from small mammals to crocodiles, and one day on marine mammals."

Of her own accord, she attended a semester-long class on marine mammals through her university's biology program. After graduating, she did a residency on marine mammals in the United States. Later, in Europe, she worked with river otters.

"Sea turtles are of course very different," she points out. "For example, we inject dogs in their limbs, but in reptiles we have to inject into their shoulders. The circulation in their limbs is too slow. And you know that reptiles and birds have nucleated red blood cells?"

I nod, although in fact I did not. The topic had never crossed my mind.

"So blood analyses have to be done by hand, under a microscope," she continues, "because machines that do blood work would count nucleated red blood cells as white blood cells."

There are several antibiotic treatments for reptiles, Elsa explains, including enrofloxacin, but dosages have to be much lower than in mammals because of the slower metabolism characteristic of reptiles.

To date, Elsa has worked on twelve sick sea turtles, mostly olive ridleys and greens. This one, she thinks, may need two months of care. Or more. The turtle needs to start eating. Then maybe she will recover her strength. If all goes well, she will be tagged and released. Elsa hopes to find a satellite tag that will transmit data, but if not a simple metal tag will have to suffice.

I ask Elsa about the turtle's chances, expecting to hear something along the lines of "excellent," or "pretty good," or "turtles are very tough, so she should be okay."

But no. Her answer: "About 50 percent."

Another digression, this time about Jains.

You might say, "What in God's name is a Jain?" Or if you know something about Jainism, anything at all, you might legitimately ask, "What in the world do Jains have to do with sea turtles?" Bear with me for a few hundred words to find out.

Jains follow the religion of Jainism. To some outsiders—to lots of outsiders—Jainism looks something like Hinduism. Some incorrectly think that Jainism is a Hindu sect. In fact Jainism probably arose well before Hinduism, and today's Jain is no more Hindu than a Hindu is a Jain.

The two religions have commonalities, foremost of which may be that both are practiced in India. But so are lots of other religions. From a ten-year-old census, about a billion Indians identify as Hindu, just under two hundred million as Muslim, a bit shy of thirty million as Christian, a little more than twenty million as Sikh, and so on. Jainism, prevalent mainly in western India, claims four-and-a-half million followers, or about the same number of followers as there are people in Los Angeles.

Enough statistics. The point is that Jains do not like to kill. Their dis-
taste for killing goes far beyond ordinary pacifism, far beyond their fellow
humans, which in fact can be killed under certain conditions. It is
nonhuman animals that they do not like to kill. They have no interest in
eating farm animals. Deer live without worries in forests inhabited by Jains.
Lobster, conch, and fish would be perfectly safe from human predators in
a sea visited only by Jains. As would sea turtles.

The swatting of flies and mosquitoes elicits feelings of guilt. Honey,
because its harvest exploits and leads to the death of bees, will not be found
on a Jain menu.

Their beliefs take them still further. Some Jains will not eat root crops
because of the risk to animals in the soil. Others avoid stepping in puddles
for fear of killing whatever might live there, down to and including
microbes. Car travel is out, or at least only used on a must-do basis, because
of its obviously murderous impacts, its tendency to splatter lives on wind-
shields and crush it under tires, and because of its deadly fumes. The support of animal hospitals is in, including some with stacked cages housing
convalescent doves, pigeons, chickens, song birds, and crows.

I do not think I have ever met a Jain, but I would like to. Jains give me
hope. They feed my optimism.

Meaning no disrespect, I am not especially interested in their dogma,
in the myths they have cultivated for thousands of years, in their spiritual
beliefs. My interest lies in the existence of a religion with millions of followers who think of life—not just the lives of turtles but the lives of all of
our fellow animals—as something fundamentally more than a commodity.
My interest lies in the realization that all of us do not see life as disposable,
that there are other paths than the one followed by the bulk of humanity
today.

I myself remain omnivorous, with no more than vegetarian leanings.
But I often like to think that I will change, and even more that coming
generations will change, that the killing of animals intentionally and

unintentionally will become if not unacceptable then something less than routine, that habitat now tied up in cattle pastures will return to nature, that one day sea turtles will not have to run a nonstop lifelong gauntlet of nets, hooks, trawls, oil spills, drifting plastic, and the other hazards of humanity.

If Jains can step over puddles to avoid slaughtering microbes, if they refrain from car travel because of the insects it kills, can the rest of us not figure out another way?

Evening approaches when I meet Eduardo on Algondones Beach, a few miles from the incubation center. He wears the same T-shirt that I have seen on Elsa, the uniform of CRRIFS with its outlines of five species of sea turtles. He has with him the familiar white plastic cooler. This one holds, he tells me, ninety-six hatchlings. We are here for an official turtle release, a planned public event.

Behind us, a line of luxury houses stretches away in both directions, most of them as white as the turtle cooler.

In front of us a two-foot swell breaks, the waves coming in on five second intervals, a light surf. Farther offshore a water skier passes. A catamaran sails parallel to the beach, taking advantage of the light sea breeze.

A half century ago Alan Arkin was here, starring in the movie *Catch-22*, pretending that this then-empty Mexican beach was in fact an allied air base on an Italian island in World War II. It is impossible to know whether there were more turtles here then, or fewer. There are no records.

Between Eduardo and the sea, a swath of beach sand fifteen feet wide and twenty-five feet long has been raked flat and roped off. A crowd of gawkers in beach attire hangs on the ropes, listening to Eduardo's rapid-fire Spanish, his practiced four-minute briefing on sea turtle life history, on sea turtle conservation, on please-don't-eat-turtle-eggs-or-turtle-meat.

The crowd ranges in age from babies in arms to well north of sixty years. Two children standing next to Eduardo, aged around five and six, sport surgical gloves. Their parents, also gloved and standing by their sides, have paid for the privilege of having their children release turtles into the wild. They have, in other words, adopted a nest. Their adoption fees pay for such things as Styrofoam coolers, rubber gloves, and other necessities.

At exactly six o'clock, right on schedule, the two very closely supervised children lift turtles one at a time from the cooler and place them on the beach. The turtles, once on the sand, head west in a dashing crawl, straight toward the setting sun, apparently more than a little eager to pass over the twenty-five feet of sand into the sea.

In less than a minute, the swath of cordoned-off beach is crowded with baby turtles, racing one another, in some cases stepping on top of one another. In places, they leave tiny turtle tracks. But elsewhere, where the sand is a little harder or a little drier, their tiny flippers leave no traces whatsoever.

With the low sun as their guide, exactly zero turtles stray off course.

The first of them hits the surf in less than two minutes.

A lingering myth beloved by sailors and surfers claims that waves come in sets of seven, that one can time waves to one's advantage. This is in fact not true. The turtles, wiser than humans in at least this regard, make no apparent attempt to time the waves. They merely press ahead. The sea, though full of predators, though full of risks of its own, is safer than the beach.

Turtles duck under what would be in human terms ten-story waves, gigantic roaring breakers crashing down upon their heads and shoulders. They ride the outbound surge underwater and surface a few feet offshore. Some, as I had seen before, are tossed back onto shore, tumbling, landing on the sand shell first, head first, tail first, akimbo, only to try their luck again. Others, successful on the first try or the second or the third, become tiny bobbing heads ten feet out, twenty feet out, and no longer in sight.

Children in the crowd call out, "¡Adios!"

The turtles do not look back.

Adios, of course, is Spanish for goodbye. But it is also a contracted version of "A Dios," or "To God," so a better translation might be something like "Go with God."

By eight minutes after six, the last of the ninety-six turtles is in the water. By fifteen minutes after six, the last of their bobbing heads is out of sight. The last "adios" is heard from a child's voice.

The crowd, cheerful, chattering in Spanish about turtles, disperses. Eduardo and his assistants remove the rope and the poles that held it above the sand.

By twenty minutes after six, this is just another swath of beach.

Walking away, I run into the family whose children released turtles. The younger of the two boys wears a dinosaur T-shirt. His father holds his hand.

I ask the child if he likes turtles. "¿Te gusta tortugas?"

His shy reply, as he looks down at his feet, smiling: "¡Si!" A simple but emphatic, "¡Si!"

FIVE

A Turtle Lost

The sick turtle is no longer sick. "She would not eat," Elsa says. "She grew weaker and weaker."

Her chance of survival diminished from 50 percent to zero. She is dead.

The death can in no way be linked to lack of effort. Elsa and her husband had taken turns through the night in their attempts to keep the turtle alive. They intubated her when her heart rate and breathing slowed, sliding a breathing tube through the animal's mouth and into her trachea. Elsa connected a self-inflating bulb, a version of the resuscitation bags used in ambulances and hospital emergency rooms to keep someone breathing. In the parlance of emergency medicine, the turtle had been bagged. Elsa, assisted by her husband, squeezed the bulb to force a breath into the turtle's lungs, then loosened her grip to let the bulb reinflate while the patient exhaled. She repeated this pumping as needed to move air into and out of failing lungs. She hoped for the best.

The procedure for turtles is of course not exactly the same as the procedure for humans. The bulb—the bag—is much smaller, and the respiration rate is slower. Another difference lies in the degree to which the procedure might be considered routine. Doctors intubate and mechanically ventilate well over a million patients a year in the United States alone. No one tracks that particular statistic for sea turtles, but it is safe to assume a very small number. Before this turtle, this now deceased female, Elsa had applied the procedure a total of two times. Neither attempt had resulted in survival. But she knows of other turtles whose lives had been saved by intubation and mechanical ventilation, some after twenty-four hours of assisted breathing.

"You cannot know," she tells me. "You can only try."

And this: "If you make the decision to give up, you think about what would have happened if you had pushed a little more, if you had tried a little harder."

Elsa and her husband took turns helping the turtle breathe for eighteen hours, one breath every three or four minutes. But early yesterday morning the turtle's heart stopped.

All that remains to be done is the necropsy and the burial. Elsa invites me to help with both.

Is it possible to understand the turtle story without understanding how the turtle is built? Maybe. Is it possible to embrace and internalize the turtle story without understanding at least the basics of how the turtle is built? Probably not.

First, more on turtle evolution through a second timeline that offers a different perspective, this one beginning with the earliest reptiles and ending today, with a dead hawksbill, an animal that has been called "the most beautiful of all sea turtle species" because of its lustrous shell. It is a shell that has been, in recent times, made into combs, sunglass frames, guitar picks, and souvenirs. It has been carved, sharpened, and strapped to the feet of fighting cocks. It is the shell that is most often—far too often—seen hanging on walls in bars and restaurants and even homes throughout the world. The hawksbill shell is, in short, a feature that has attracted hunters for millennia even though the meat of the hawksbill is generally considered inferior to that of the green.

In this case, illness, not a hunter, took this animal, this animal whose death marks the end of our second timeline, whose death we will call midnight tonight.

Midnight yesterday is set at just over three hundred million years ago, late in the Carboniferous period. It is the Age of the Amphibians, a time when flowerless trees that would become peat or coal prevail on land. But some of the amphibians are more robust than others, with stronger bones and thicker skins. It is right around midnight yesterday when they start laying a new kind of egg, a leathery egg entirely different from those of the other amphibians. This new kind of egg has specialized membranes, including an internal sack, an amnion, that keeps the embryo moist. Oxygen moves inward through the membranes and carbon dioxide and other wastes move outward, but moisture is retained. The egg, unlike that of amphibians, does not have to mature in water. It can be laid on dry land. It is the egg of a reptile, the class of animals that would give rise to dinosaurs, crocodiles, snakes, lizards, and, of course, turtles.

Early in the morning, that is to say about two hundred and twenty million years ago, the first turtle is born in what is now southern Africa. The exact time is unclear, and new discoveries, new fossils, confuse the issue, but around dawn or just after is vague enough to fit the changing facts.

This first turtle would not be recognizable as a turtle to the average person living today. At about a foot long it looks more like a flattened lizard than a turtle, shell-less on top but with a hardened underside.

Not much later, around breakfast time, ribs and spines fuse together to become shells. Turtles, at least some of them, now look like turtles.

A hundred million years pass before the first sea turtles appear, meaning breakfast is long gone and lunch is a fading memory. But have dinner on the beach and an ancestral leatherback might swim past. Be careful though, because not long after dusk a massive asteroid strikes the Earth, possibly wiping out the dinosaurs and almost certainly contributing to their demise.

If you are lucky a full moon rises, giving you at least a chance of seeing a green turtle, a flatback, a hawksbill, and a loggerhead. This is late in the evening, that is, thirty or forty million years ago.

Stretch, go for a short walk, and return to stare at the waves, now with some chance of spotting the ridley turtles, both Kemp's and olives.

During your vigils, especially early in the evening, you would, by the way, see other sea turtles out there. Lots of them. But all except our seven, those with which we share oceans today, would be lost, extinct through natural causes. It is a fact that most of the world's sea turtles and for that matter most of the world's animals and plants went extinct long ago, a reality that is not so much tragic as a reflection of the nature of evolution and of deep time, of the unfathomable years during which life has flourished and changed.

Sometime after eleven thirty at night, our hominin ancestors would be chipping stones and sharpening sticks, some of which would be used to kill sea turtles. But our own species, *Homo sapiens*, would not arrive until a minute or two before midnight.

Then, with milliseconds to spare before midnight, the conservation movement appears almost abruptly, suddenly doing what it can to encourage a measure of sanity.

I arrive early at the incubation center. While I wait for Elsa, her assistant, the recently graduated veterinarian Diana Barreto Luna, takes me to see an injured pelican that was brought in just yesterday.

The bird rests in a plastic dog kennel in the shade beneath the incubation center. The poor creature suffers from parasites, Diana tells me, and so far refuses to eat.

Diana also tells me that Elsa might be a little late, delayed because an injured osprey needs her care. A living osprey justifiably takes precedence over a dead turtle.

The necropsy table, two wooden pallets standing on a rusting metal frame in the yard behind the incubation center, is ready to go. On the weeds next to the pallets is a big black plastic box along with a large wide-necked jar of formalin, a bottle of ethanol, a roll of blue masking tape and a handful of markers for making labels, a box of rubber gloves, masks, face shields, and a collection of syringes, forceps, and knives. On the other side of the pallet lean two shovels of the sort sometimes favored by grave diggers.

In an old bathtub that sits beneath a nearby elephant tree, two bags of ice cover the thick green plastic bag that holds our dead turtle, our reptilian cadaver.

Thick clouds block the sun and a strong breeze grounds all insects, making the outdoor operating theater almost comfortable for the time being.

Elsa arrives. Without appearing hurried, radiating her usual calm but wasting no time, she dons a surgical apron. The apron in its current state, with half the waist strap missing, cannot be secured. Elsa picks up a knife suitable for cutting through a turtle's shell, a knife that would not be out of place in the hands of an eighteenth-century pirate, and cuts a hole through the apron. She loops the remaining strap through the hole and ties it off. Next come high rubber boots, a fresh mask, a face shield, and gloves. It is precautionary, she says, to protect against the small risk of cross infection.

I mention the coronavirus. "For sure there is a coronavirus in reptiles," she says. "It is a very widely seen virus, but it is not our coronavirus." She emphasizes again that cross infections, reptile to human or human to reptile, are rare, and all this safety equipment is a matter of precaution. And perhaps of protecting clothes.

Diana shows me a necropsy form, which includes a checklist of the samples needed: liver, skin, bladder, lung, heart, kidneys, adrenal glands, pancreas, stomach.

The two women struggle to lift the bagged turtle's dripping carcass onto the table. They cut away the plastic death shroud.

The carcass lies belly-up. Its plastron—the underside of its shell—is obviously deflated. It is yellowish and in places almost golden. "You can see that she was starving," Elsa says. She points out barnacle scars. While barnacles are not unusual on turtle shells, the abundance of barnacles on this animal marked it as being very sick, as being all but dead.

Intubation tubes still protrude from the animal's mouth. There are two. The larger tube is about a quarter of an inch in diameter, and the smaller maybe an eighth of an inch; the larger served to provide air to the turtle and the smaller to blow up a balloon that wedged the larger tube in place, that held it within the trachea.

With effort, Elsa pries the mouth open with her fingers to show Diana how the animal had been intubated. She deflates the balloon and removes the tube, which comes out covered in thick creamy paste. "The entire upper respiratory tract was full of mucus," she says. She shoots documentary photos of the plastron and the mucus.

The breeze has died. Right now, the smell comes mainly from the pelican in its kennel across the yard. From next door, a construction site, we hear the screech of a power saw.

Under Elsa's instruction Diana starts an incision at the left shoulder, cutting through the seam between the plastron and the carapace. She starts with a shallow slice. "It is cartilage," Elsa tells me as she sharpens a second knife. Then they are both cutting, one on each side, their foot-long blades sawing back and forth.

"This is the most difficult part of the necropsy," Elsa says. It is Diana's second necropsy, but Elsa has done more than she can readily remember. Certainly more than twenty, she suggests.

Their incisions grow and the underlying flesh becomes visible. It is subcutaneous tissue, grayish, ashen.

Encountering stubborn places, they hammer the handles of their knives with the palms of their hands.

Prying the plastron slightly at the right shoulder, Elsa points out a pool of clear liquid. It is from their attempts to hydrate the animal, where they had pushed fluids through syringes into the patient's flesh. She points out the blue skin on the turtle's neck. "It was blue like this when we intubated her, but it recovered to its natural yellowish with ventilation."

The dead turtle's eyes, partly open, are entirely lifeless, a terrible sight, the vista of death. For a painful passing moment, I imagine eyes like this in every turtle, everywhere. That would be the look of extinction.

The two women continue to cut at the seam, at what Elsa calls the suture line, as if trying to open an especially obstinate can.

The plastron is in fact akin to a large sternum. The carapace, what most people would think of as the turtle's shell, is for the most part fused ribs. Separating the plastron from the carapace, opening the turtle, is like separating a reinforced sternum from a fortified ribcage.

Now Elsa uses thick forceps to pull at the plastron, to pry it open, giving better access for her assistant's knife.

"When I was in school," Elsa says, "I tried to open every animal I could find."

"A crocodile?" I ask.

No, but she laughs in apparent delight at the thought.

The power saw that had been screeching next door has stopped. Now music comes from a car stereo.

There is surprisingly little blood so far, no more than a few small splatters.

Cutting at the bottom of the plastron, near the short tail, Elsa points out the cloaca at my request. She cheerfully pinches it between gloved fingers so that I can see the opening. The tail is maybe an inch long. A male this size, she says, would have a much longer tail.

"Because she is so skinny," Elsa explains, "it is very difficult to remove the plastron." She has her knife buried to the hilt, parallel to the underside of the plastron, carving through tissue.

Now I can smell the turtle, not a smell of death or decay or infection but merely of turtle innards, of raw meat and possibly digestive fluids. A few flies settle around the open suture line.

Elsa and Diana have been cutting for twenty-eight minutes. Disassembling a turtle is not quick work.

There is time, during the labor of cutting, to talk. We discuss conservation and personal behaviors. Elsa seldom eats shrimp—she loves them, but will only eat those caught from small boats, by fishermen whose methods do not kill turtles. She reuses and recycles plastics.

The talk turns to population.

"As humans we are changing the world," she says. "So it is our responsibility to help the environment. The oceans would be so different if we were fewer. We have a big responsibility."

I ask about family sizes in Mexico. "Yes," she says. "People in my generation here in Mexico have the children conversation." She knows couples who have decided against children. She and her husband made a conscious decision to stop at two.

Statistically, family sizes in Mexico have declined dramatically during Elsa's lifetime. Today many Mexicans do not have enough children to replace themselves. The nation's total fertility rate—the number of children per woman during childbearing years—stands at about 2.2, just high enough, on average, to slowly increase the population. But by 2065 Mexico's population will be in decline, just as it will be in the United States and most of the developed world. Even with immigration, projections show a decline in Mexico's population starting in about forty years.

Today, the world supports about eight billion humans. It is hard to argue that a world with more humans will be safer for sea turtles. Or for other endangered species. Or, for that matter, for us.

The clouds have cleared and the wind has died. The temperature is in the low nineties. Elsa sweats under her face shield. At her cheeks, moisture soaks her surgical mask.

At forty-one minutes into the necropsy, she pulls the plastron away from the carapace. The open carapace is now a tub of organs, blackened blood, muscle strands, and a smattering of yellowish-gray fat deposits.

Working together, Elsa and Diana tilt the carapace, pouring well over a gallon of pooled blood and other fluids into a white plastic bucket.

Opened, drained, the animal's jigsaw puzzle of anatomy stands exposed under bright sunlight. It is an anatomy familiar to anyone who has seen drawings of the innards of humans. No wonder. Compare genes from a turtle and a human and you will find about 90 percent similarity. We share the same general body plan of all vertebrates, an obvious result of shared ancestry.

Move further away on the intertwined entangled mass of vines that was once mistakenly thought of as the tree of life and genetic similarity remains striking. We share about 60 percent of our genome with certain flies, for example, and not much less, it turns out, with bananas.

Elsa points to the shoulder blades and their attached muscles, explaining that this is the main source of meat in the turtle.

This experience in no way makes me long for the forbidden taste of turtle soup.

A volunteer from the United States, a woman in her late sixties, wanders into the yard. Elsa greets her. The woman, moving closer, does not seem bothered by what she sees. I learn later that she had once worked as a nurse. She leaves after a few minutes.

Another woman, a Mexican, shows up. She is a friend but not a volunteer. She is well-dressed, with recently styled hair and a hint of eye makeup. She stops a few feet from the necropsy table and looks on while she chats.

She tells me in Spanish that she often walks the beaches of San Carlos, picking up garbage. "The people here," she says, "they think the beach is a trash can."

But the day before she had found more than empty bottles and wastepaper. She had found a dead turtle, or really its skeletal remains, entangled in fishing gear. With her cell phone, she shows me a video of the remains. Her recorded voice provides commentary. As the clip pans over the scene, I catch a few sentences. "No tengo palabras," she had said while standing next to the animal on the beach. She had no words to describe what she had found washed up.

Even now she is distressed by what she had seen, though she seems comfortable to be standing next to and presumably smelling a more recently dead turtle.

The flock of flies has grown. Thirty or forty of them buzz over and occasionally land on the carcass.

The woman leaves and the work continues.

When there are so many people in the world, it is no wonder that at least some of them do good deeds, both great and small. Elsa and her husband and Diana, Eduardo, the volunteers who walk the beaches day after day, the Jains, the millions behind the massive conservation movement that has exploded since I was born, all working to save animals and plants that they and their kind have pushed to the brink. Despite what might seem to be the futile nature of all this frantic effort, it nurtures my optimism.

Among these, people raising monarch butterflies offer an example. Such people exist. They bring egg-laden leaves into their homes and protect them until the eggs become first ravenous striped caterpillars, then quiet hanging pupa properly called chrysalides, and finally orange-and-black flying adults. The task, especially the husbandry of hungry caterpillars, can become a full-time job, hour after hour and day after day spent finding the right fresh leaves for food and sweeping away the inevitable droppings. But monarch raisers are not paid for their trouble. They do not receive medals. As far as I know they cannot even legally deduct expenses from their taxes.

They raise monarchs because they know that monarchs, once very common, are in trouble, their population on the steep downward slope of a decline curve. They raise monarchs because they know that a world without monarchs is a lesser world.

But there is an ugly flip side, a dark lurking shadow. The very people who raise monarchs benefit from those things that humans are doing that kill monarchs. They eat food routinely grown under the protective cloak of pesticides, they live in neighborhoods that were once monarch habitats, they drive cars and wear clothes that could not exist in the absence of the fossil fuels that emit greenhouse gases.

In the complicated calculus of environmental degradation, it is hard to know who among us does more good than harm. Not even Jain monks can claim innocence. We are all guilty. I am, like it or not, a killer and destroyer of the world I love.

This is not a new idea. "As he mounts toward civilization," wrote Nathaniel Shaler in 1905, "man becomes a spoiler."

But still, people raising monarchs show us how we can counteract the inevitable harm caused by being modern humans. People raising monarchs feed my optimism. Likewise, those who protect turtles. Or wolves. Or ordinary looking fish found in tiny isolated ponds.

These people give me hope not because they provide the only way forward for conservation in the long-term, but because they show that humans, despite our faults, have the capacity to care.

Our turtle's liver, the part of it that is visible, is the size of my hand, fingers included. Parts of it are pale. "Not good," remarks Elsa. Blood analyzed while the animal was still alive did not show liver damage, but here it is.

"Very bad," Elsa adds. "Not only scarred but also a little small."

The two women cut and slice, and a moment later Diana has the liver in her hand. Although it may be smaller than normal, it spills over the edges of her palm. Abnormal blood vessels stand out as a network of distinct black lines crisscrossing the flabby organ.

But liver damage can be the result of chronic illness as well as the cause. Elsa, her hands now covered in congealed and congealing turtle blood mixed with bits of cartilage and assorted tissue, asks me to photograph the liver. I am after all a biologist, hardly squeamish about these sorts of things, so I snap closeups while trying not to bloody my notebook and camera.

Diana slices the liver into half-inch strips, looking further at the damage. Elsa pokes around with forceps, looking for visible flukes, for parasitic trematodes, but finds none.

"It is congested with blood," she says. With a quiet splash, pieces of it go into the now open jar of formalin.

Just over one hour has passed since work commenced. Elsa cuts away at a shoulder blade. Somewhat weirdly, but really not surprisingly, the shoulder blade sits inside the ribcage—that is, inside the shell. The turtle is the only vertebrate designed and manufactured in such a manner. The rest of us keep our shoulder blades outside of our ribcages. In any case, out comes the shoulder blade. It will go to a researcher in Sinaloa who is looking at something to do with age in turtles.

A lymph node, swollen to at least twice its normal size, perhaps as big as a pack of playing cards, is cut into two pieces. One goes into the formalin jar and the other goes into a freezer bag.

More cutting, slicing, sawing. Elsa holds up a length of intestine, its loops bound together by a membrane of tissue interlaced with blood vessels. Like the liver, like the lymph node, it is abnormal, speckled with yellow fat. I take more pictures.

"When they are starving," Elsa says, "little by little the intestines are damaged." Thickened nodes punctuate an otherwise shrunken straw of an intestine. Elsa runs her fingers along the intestine, squeezing gently. Most of the nodules are full of liquid, but at least one is unyielding, like thickened clay. Elsa cuts it open, exposing the flat blackness of volcanic sand. But it contains chunks of something other than sand. She describes it as hard and compacted. It is possible that it was the root cause of sickness, or the start that led to cascading effects ending in death.

She searches the entire intestine for plastic, but finds none.

"This turtle was sick for a long time," Elsa says. "Mucho tiempo enferma."

The two women pour more blood from the carapace.

The plastron, now on a white tarp lying on the weeds next to the necropsy table, becomes a depository for discarded parts. A chunk of liver. Unwanted muscles. A length of intestine.

They cut out the heart. It is dark and bloated. They slice it into ribbons and then run the pieces through their gloved fingers, searching for cysts. They find none.

Elsa points out the trachea, now exposed, which looks like a reinforced plastic tube three-quarters of an inch in diameter.

The spleen is unusually small. "Ridiculously small," Elsa says. But there is no apparent infection. A piece of spleen goes into the formalin and another into a freezer bag. Sweat drips into Elsa's eyes now, apparently unnoticed. She remains cheerful.

The esophagus is spiked, like a one-way valve. The stomach is deflated, empty. Poking around, Elsa finds minuscule remains of food, bits of sponge and calcareous remains of the stuff she had fed her patient over the past weeks. She describes the stomach lining as "completely irritated." She slices off samples and then drops the rest of it—that is, the bulk of the stomach—onto the growing pile on the plastron.

Blue-green flies, a larger species than the ones that were out earlier in the morning, land in force on exposed organs and parts of organs.

"Blood analyses showed problems with the pancreas," she says. "And here it is. Tiny." She cuts it in two, half for the formalin and half for the freezer.

I comment that, in her shoes, I would have gone straight for the lungs, to what I thought was the root cause of this turtle's death. But she says no, it is a systematic process. In the case of turtles, from this perspective, looking from the belly downward, the lungs lay hidden behind other organs, lodged against the carapace. "When turtles are upside down," Elsa explains, "the weight of their organs against their lungs can suffocate them." She mentions, too, that the lungs can be damaged by the sun, its rays shining right through the carapace, when sick turtles spend too much time on the surface.

The conversation turns for a moment to poachers and fishermen who grew up eating turtles. I tell her of a man I know, a worker in the boatyard, who told me of eating turtles when he was younger. Like many others, he found green turtles to be tastier than olive ridleys.

At just shy of two hours Elsa lifts the left shoulder, completely exposing a permanently deflated and surprisingly small lung seemingly plastered to the inside of the carapace. "It should be more transparent," she says, "not this white." This is the left lung, which was not, based on what she had heard through her stethoscope before the turtle died, as bad as the right lung.

In many vertebrates, including humans, the ribcage expands as the lungs fill and contracts with exhalation. The turtle's ribcage, the animal's shell, remains rigid, lungs full or lungs empty. The turtle—this particular turtle no longer, but the living turtle—relies on what has been called a "unique abdominal-muscle-based ventilatory apparatus whose evolutionary origins have remained mysterious." In other words, it breathes like we do, but differently, not quite like we do. The presence of the shell has forced development of a new approach to breathing.

Elsa exposes the right lung. Even a biologist and writer can see the difference between this and its left side twin. It is swollen throughout, parts of it a yellowish inflamed mass. "She may have a virus because we see very little puss," Elsa points out. Puss would suggest a bacterial infection. "Maybe she had a bacterial infection too but the antibiotics helped with that and she improved. But the virus was still there."

She removes the lung and with forceps holds it up in the bright sun. "In other turtles I found puss and some tumors," she adds. "But this lung is very infected. This is very bad. This is a terrible lung." She points out clotted blood in air passages. "This is completely horrible." She points at blood trapped in the bronchioles.

We look at the ovaries, lined with immature eggs, hundreds of white spots that could have become turtles had things gone differently.

We look at the kidneys. "At least her kidneys look good," Elsa says. "At least one thing was still working." With a syringe she pulls a sample of urine. "It is a little turbid," she remarks.

And we are done, all of us by now hot and sweaty and tired of flies.

Knowing of the work that goes into saving turtles, knowing that what I see here is the tip of an iceberg, I ask Elsa about the value of a sea turtle. Specifically, I ask how much a sea turtle is worth. I expect to hear one of the answers floating around in the academic literature, appraisals provided by environmental economists. Inevitably estimates show that live turtles attract tourism valued at far more than anyone would pay for the meat or eggs. One of my favorite estimates comes from a study in North Carolina. To avoid the extinction of loggerhead turtles alone, residents were willing to pay two hundred and twenty-five million dollars, and this was in the dollars of 1991.

She politely evades this question. Perhaps she is like other veterinarians I know who are uncomfortable with putting monetary values on life, even if it is those very values that biologists sometimes use in arguments favoring conservation expenditures.

She talks instead about their role in ecosystems, their function in the environment, suggesting they are part of a balance.

"We are part of an advisory board for the government," she says, referring to herself and colleagues scattered along the coast. "And of course the government wants to protect turtles. But there are lots of priorities, and sea turtles may not be the top priority."

Others, both foreigners and Mexican nationals, say that the government does not always hire the most competent people. Instead, someone's sister or cousin is hired, and the pay is far too low to offer incentives in and of itself.

I offer to dig the grave. My offer is immediately accepted.

The ground is too hard for the shovels on hand, so I drive to a nearby hardware store for a pick. In the sun, I chip away at the hard Sonoran Desert. My pick bounces off rocks. I scoop up chipped earth. I swing the pick some more. I sweat.

A hole approximating the shape of a turtle appears. Elsa and Diana drop the carapace into the hole, upside down, so it forms a bowl. They pour the contents of the blood bucket into the bowl. They dump in the pile of body parts stacked on the plastron. They lower the plastron itself into the grave. The turtle is now complete but for the samples that have been saved and what some might call the animal's vital essence, its life.

The samples will go to a laboratory for various tests and analyses. Someone will learn something, but we will never know what killed this turtle, aside from an almost complete systemic failure. She was riddled with infection, with damage, but how it started and why it went unchecked is impossible to know. It is easy to assume but impossible to be certain that humanity played a role, perhaps through one of our oil spills, or one of our sewage outfalls, or even because something like underwater noise from ships and fishing boats caused the kind of stress that weakens the immune response. Or maybe she died from entirely natural causes, if that is still possible in the ocean today, for a life to come and go with no influence at all from humanity. Most likely she died not from one thing, but from many.

Hot and sad, I shovel earth onto the remains. In the weeds nearby I find a half-rotten length of plank, and with the shovel I pound it into the ground, a marker.

Ashes to ashes, dust to dust.

SIX

Rancho San Basilio

With Judith and others, Lisanne and I find more nests. We participate in more releases. But hurricane season ends and our boat maintenance tick list grows smaller and smaller, in part because we defer two of the bigger jobs at hand—the removal of an unwanted diesel generator and the replacement of rigging—to another year, another boatyard. Now it is time for us to do what wandering sailors do. On a favorable forecast we sail away, headed south and west.

The wind, as often happens in the Gulf of California, behaves as if it were entirely unaware of the forecast. We leave the mainland behind to encounter seas that grow until they are breaking, foaming white. We progress, surfing down wave faces, crashing into troughs, climbing back upward, all repeated every few seconds. After a rough and noisy thirty hours of headway we reach the peninsula, the Baja, unscathed. Such is sailing at times.

We cruise the coast looking for turtles, watching whales and dolphins and leaping rays, enjoying nature at sea and ashore, hiding in remote bays and behind uninhabited islands from the strong northers that blow through once or twice each week at this time of year.

Now, in early January, anchored, we walk a coastal trail with the familiar cactuses and scrubby plants of this part of the peninsula—cardón, pitaya agria, and cholla cactuses dominating the landscape, but mixed with stands of jojobas and scattered thorny Adam's trees and white toxic-sapped slipper plants that can be used to make a substance akin to rubber. A handful of car and truck campers on a nearby beach sport license plates from California and Washington and North Dakota. They have arrived over a rough road that runs through an arroyo. The drive requires at least an hour after the last of the pavement is left behind, an hour of bouncing over rocks and washouts, of slipping in soft sand. A few employees of the landowner, of Rancho San Basilio, keep small but well-maintained adobe houses scattered through the bush, living, some would say, rather remotely.

We turn off the trail and onto a beach where we find a cage, a round cylinder three feet across. It is made from fine chicken wire. Here on the beach, its only purpose can be the protection of turtle eggs. Around the base, a perimeter of chain-link fencing has been staked flat on the sand, probably to prevent coyotes, raccoons, and possibly foxes from excavating the nest.

A half mile farther along, around a rocky headland, we find another.

To find nest cages here, in a spot this isolated, this challenging to reach, surprises me. As does finding them in January, when temperatures drop into the forties at night.

We walk on, eventually leaving the beach to climb uphill, where we see one of the ranch's adobe homes. The home could be described as functionally elegant, full of cool shadows cast by wood and stone, but also tasteful in that it complements its surroundings. Its occupant welcomes us. He is a mestizo in his forties with a face etched by dry air and sun. We converse. His eyes light up when he talks of the land and its animals and plants. He tolerates my Spanish, perhaps because my interests match his own.

The man lives here ten days at a time, watching after a handful of cattle and horses and mules—mulas, he calls them. But his real job is to protect the land, to prevent poaching and keep squatters away. He does this from the adobe house, which, it bears mentioning, has what would in more accessible locales be a multimillion-dollar view of the sea.

He grew up in a nearby coastal village. When he was younger, he was a fisherman. He used diving gear—a long hose connected to a gasoline powered compressor on the surface—to collect sea cucumbers and clams and lobsters.

He goes by the name Chavelo. He offers a long and complicated explanation about the nickname. Nicknames in Mexico are commonplace, though most are simple—Flaco for men of a slender build, Memo as the rough equivalent of Bill for those christened Guillermo. But his explanation makes no sense to me or Lisanne, whose Spanish is far better than mine.

The talk turns to turtles—tortugas, of course, but here also known as caguamas. Chavelo explains that it is a word that once meant something like turtle stew or turtle soup, but that is now used to mean a sea turtle of any species, although some say that it should only be applied to loggerheads. It also serves to designate a large bottle of beer of a particular brand in this part of Mexico, while another brand is known as ballena, or whale. Sometimes it is used to indicate gringos of a certain type, generally of the complaining, clumsy, corn-fed variety.

There are many caguamas here, sea turtles of various kinds, and they come to nest all year long, in every month of the year, he says, but most come in the summer months. We ask if he knows what species they might be—¿que tipo? But our Spanish fails us. Lisanne forms the outline of a hawksbill's carapace with her hands, pantomiming the serrated marginal scutes toward the back of the shell, and I use my hands to mimic the animal's overlapping beak.

"Si, si—tortuga carey," he says with a smile, apparently glad to convey this information across the language barrier. But he is only being agreeable. Hawksbills certainly occur here, but far less frequently than greens and olive ridleys.

There are more turtles now than when he was young, he tells us. Every year, there are more and more turtles.

I ask if he ever ate turtle, perhaps as a boy. He answers by saying that he does not like turtle, that he would not eat it, not quite saying that he had never eaten it. I do not press the issue.

He tells us that a man named Martin looks after the nest cages. When needed, Martin comes down from Loreto, a city of twenty thousand people or so that was, until 1777, the capital of Spain's Baja settlements.

Chavelo searches for nests daily and checks known nests every morning, but Martin is in charge of the program. I ask if he can put me in touch with Martin. He cannot, but his friend can. He gives us directions to the home of José Manuel, also known as El Chollo. The house is about a mile away. There, he says, we can also buy vegetables, grown by El Chollo onsite. We are in need of fresh vegetables.

Before leaving, I ask if he thinks people might start hunting turtles again someday. If there are more and more turtles every year, maybe they will become so abundant that people will return to eating them. Or they might go back to harvesting eggs. Not anytime soon. Not next year or the year after, but in twenty or thirty of forty years. For me this is hard to ask in Spanish, not only because it is a question that rivals his nickname in its complexity but because it might come across as rudely superior. And also because I do not want it to be a leading question, a question that has only one right answer. It takes an intervention by my wife and several tries before he registers understanding.

"Of course there will always be poachers," he tells us. "There will always be some people taking turtle eggs and eating turtles. But most people will not go back to eating turtles. Why would we? The turtle is better in the sea. And we can get better food at the grocery store."

I am more surprised by his words than I was by the presence of nest cages on these remote beaches. My translation may not be perfect, but I am dead certain of his meaning. This response, coming not from a biologist or a politician but from a one-time fisherman who grew up on the shores of the Gulf of California, sends a gratifying chill through my being.

Before we leave, he imitates the sound of a turtle surfacing and breathing, surfacing and breathing, surfacing and breathing, a sound that he makes by pursing his lips and exhaling. He spent his youth at sea in a small boat, and on calm days it would have been a fairly common sound, yet it is one that even now delights him.

In 1940, John Steinbeck passed here aboard a diesel-powered fishing boat named *Western Flyer*, ostensibly on a trip intended for the collection of biological samples. The boat was seventy-five feet long. It carried, among other things, seven people, including the author himself and his close friend Ed Ricketts, the biologist Steinbeck fictionalized in *Cannery Row, Sweet Thursday*, and other novels.

The two men coauthored a nonfiction book about their Gulf of California trip, originally published as *Sea of Cortez: A Leisurely Journal of Travel and Research* but later reprinted in a revised form as *The Log from the Sea of Cortez*, with Steinbeck as the sole author.

In his nonfiction, Steinbeck sometimes exaggerated to the point of fabrication. He did not hesitate to leave out key facts if they proved inconvenient, such as the presence of his soon-to-be ex-wife aboard the *Western Flyer*. But he included what appears to be a factual account of a turtle hunt, of one of the crew members harpooning a turtle. He and the crew found the animal hard to kill. Even after they cut off the head, the turtle remained lively, flippers waving uselessly.

In its gut, they found "small bright-red rock-lobsters." The contents of the gut and the description of the gut itself—"lined with hard, sharp-pointed spikes"—suggest that the now-headless and dying animal was a hawksbill, consistent with Steinbeck's description of "a tortoise-shell turtle," one of the many common names sometimes applied to the species.

The heart continued to beat even after the gut had been dissected.

They carved up the turtle's muscles, cutting them into "little cubes of white meat." But their culinary skills were not up to the task. "The cooking was a failure. We boiled the meat, and later threw out the evil-smelling mess."

A wasted useless death at the hands of inept humans, one of them not only a biologist, but in part thanks to Steinbeck and in part thanks to his own writings, a renowned biologist, an icon of the conservation movement. In today's world, it is safe to say that no biologist, and certainly no conservation biologist, would participate in such a killing.

El Chollo's house is similar to Chavelo's in the way that it makes the most of stone and wood to provide protection from wind and heat and cold, but it is different in that the front yard is full of free roaming chickens, a corral with goats, and a few mules. It is the kind of house I would want were I to give up the sea in exchange for the Baja desert.

He shows us around with pride, then sells us tomatoes, carrots, and spinach from his carefully managed raised gardens. He gives us a phone number for Martin. The ranch has neither telephones nor internet, but, El Chollo tells us, we can reach Martin in Loreto.

So the next day we sail twenty miles south to Loreto. Once in range, we call Martin. He agrees to meet for a drink in the restaurant at the head of the town pier.

He shows up wearing a long-sleeved shirt and a green San Basilio ballcap. The word CONSERVACIÓN is printed in black capitals on the side of the ballcap. Martin speaks English but is more comfortable with Spanish. His full name is Luis Martín Castro Romero.

He spent thirteen years working for the Procuraduría Federal de Protección al Ambiente, something like the Federal Attorney for Environmental Protection and typically abbreviated to PROFEPA, which is part of the Secretaría de Medio Ambiente y Recursos Naturales, roughly the Department of Environment and Natural Resources and almost universally abbreviated to SEMARNAT. He did not get the job through a sister or a cousin. He is a trained and dedicated biologist. Before he left government service, he had taken more than thirty classes on turtles and turtle management. He has the names of the classes printed on a page that he shows me with pride. He also became well-known and well-connected within the realm of environmental governance, both in the Baja and on the mainland.

He left SEMARNAT to work for Rancho San Basilio. His creation, the turtle program at Rancho San Basilio, is only two years old.

Even with his background it has not been easy to get a permit, which comes from his previous employer, for handling turtles and eggs. But of course, he explains, the permits are necessary. Without them, handling of turtles and their eggs would be entirely illegal.

Under permit in 2020, he and his colleagues at Rancho San Basilio managed twelve olive ridley nests. The 2020 nests failed. All of them. "Coyotes," Martin tells us. "That is why we now put fencing on the ground around the nest cages. To keep the coyotes from digging up the nests."

This year they managed thirteen olive ridley nests and one black turtle nest, that is, a black green turtle, tortuga negra or prieta. In his report to the government, a required follow-up on the permitting process, Martin wrote of the black turtle nest: "¡Algo maravilloso! Por tratarse de una especie que está aún más en peligro de extinción, en comparición con la tortuga golfina." Roughly, "Something marvelous! Because it is a species that is even more in danger of extinction than the olive ridley turtle." It is the kind of language generally missing from reports of this kind written in English, where training in the sciences strives to restrain passion, to temper enthusiasm, no matter how justifiable that passion and enthusiasm might be.

This year has been far more successful. Eleven of the thirteen nests have hatched out and the hatchlings have been guarded as they made their way to the sea. The fencing kept coyotes out. When some of the nests hatched early in the morning and late in the season, he would keep the tiny turtles warm until late in the afternoon, when they would be released. There are usually eighty to one hundred and twenty eggs in a nest. Of these, maybe 80 percent will hatch. Of those, he says, maybe one in one thousand will grow to adults. It is of course the same one-in-one-thousand number that I heard in San Carlos.

Two nests remain, the two we had seen on the beach, turtles maybe still developing in their eggs, buried in the sand. Or, as seems likely to me this late in the winter, dead in their eggs, too cold to develop into hatchlings.

Martin lists the predators hatchlings face once they are in the water: "dorado, frigate birds, octopus, crabs." He can protect the nests from coyotes, but once the hatchlings are in the water they are on their own.

He talks, too, of the lost years, the años perdidos, when the young turtles are at sea, out of sight, no one knows where. Well, no human knows where. The young turtles themselves may have a fairly good idea of their whereabouts.

I had first come across this phrase, "the lost years," the años perdidos, in a book by Archie Carr, in reference to green turtles in the Caribbean. Hatchlings of all species, when they leave the beach, quickly disappear. It is said somewhat vaguely and often accompanied by a certain amount of hand-waving that some species mature in vast mats of floating sargassum, a brown algae that sometimes forms extensive mats caught in ocean gyres. Christopher Columbus wrote of the Sargasso Sea, claiming he feared he would be caught in the mass of seaweed, but reporting no sign of turtles, large or small.

But scratch the surface of the sargassum explanation of the lost years with care. It is not in fact easy to find young turtles in the Sargasso Sea.

To my knowledge, no one sampling Sargasso Sea algae or invertebrates has reported young sea turtles in abundance. A few tagging studies have followed young turtles in the Atlantic out into the Sargasso Sea, but these animals were several months old with shells four or five inches long.

I ask Martin if he has ever heard of anyone putting satellite tags on hatchlings. He has not. The newly born animals are too small, too fragile. No one knows where they go. And while there is sargassum floating in the Gulf of California, it occurs in intermittent patches. Nothing like the Sargasso Sea exists here.

I ask, too, about egg poaching. There is more poaching on the mainland, he says. "La cultura no exista aquí." The culture of egg poaching does not exist here. He thinks most of the poaching that occurs in the Baja can be attributed to fishermen from the mainland. They see turtles as easy money.

He has, in the past, had the opportunity, the responsibility, to arrest turtle poachers. This was during his time as a government employee. In one case, he says, the poachers were sentenced to ten years in prison—eight years for poaching, and two additional years for poaching in a national park. Ten years in a Mexican prison. Hardly, one might reasonably think, easy money.

I do not like to hear of anyone going to prison. The possibility of long-term loss of liberty terrifies me, all the more so when rendered worse by the conditions of incarceration and the horror of what prisoners do to one another. But there is a small and shameful piece of me, a vindictive fragment of my character, that delights in hearing of jail time for turtle poachers. Until, after a moment of reflection, I remember that relatively few turtles are killed intentionally, and no one goes to jail for accidentally drowning turtles in gillnets or trawls, for running over them with boats, for poisoning them with toxic runoff. Then long sentences for poachers seem especially unjust.

But here is an optimistic point: Martin has a job in the field of turtle conservation. He is not alone. Later, after talking with him, a quick online search for "sea turtle conservation jobs" yields more than twenty hits. Turtle conservation programs need divers, plumbers, biologists, veterinarians, fundraisers, beach walkers, security guards, and regulatory personnel. This is just in the English-speaking job market. Worldwide, thousands of people have jobs in a field that was all but nonexistent fifty years ago.

Rancho San Basilio, despite its name, is not the sort of place where one might find hundreds of cattle or sheep or even goats. The land is far too dry, especially now, after several years of drought. Even after talking to Martin, I am not sure of exactly what sort of ranch it might be. So a few days later I have breakfast with Tom Woodard, an American who is the property's overall manager.

Tom's midsixties exist only in memory, but he talks with the energy of a man at the front end of his career. He leaves little room for asking questions and scant time for notes.

When I ask him to tell me about himself, he talks instead about the people employed by Rancho San Basilio. He describes them collectively as "the best team he has ever worked with, anywhere, period." They are motivated, creative, clever, hard working. "And they know the land. They come from this land and they know it." Unlike Martin, many of them have little or no formal education, yet they have designed and built some of the small buildings on the property. "Americans come down here and make all kinds of wrong assumptions about Mexicans. It is sad to see. The truth is that there are great human resources here. This team of ours, really it is unbelievable."

Then he talks about the land. Rancho San Basilio now covers something like 19,325 acres, or about thirty square miles, including the land surrounding Bahía San Basilio, the Bay of San Basilio, sometimes called

San Juanico. Tom believes this latter designation, widely used in the sailing community, to be incorrect, an artifact of poorly informed modern map makers. There is a village of San Juanico northwest of San Basilio as well as a generally dry river that goes by the same name, both beyond the headland that delineates the northern extent of the bay, but the old maps, the Spanish and Mexican maps, invariably show the bay as San Basilio. This sort of geographical ambiguity is anything but uncommon on maps and navigational charts translated from Spanish to English.

Without pause he goes on to talk about a survey conducted two years earlier, an investigation of the biological resources of San Basilio. The work had been done by a consortium of scientists with diverse affiliations, including organizations based in the United States like the San Diego Natural History Museum, Scripps Institution of Oceanography, and the University of Arizona, but also Mexican organizations like the Instituto Politécnico Nacional and the Centro para la Biodiversidad Marina y la Conservación. Forty-seven professional scientists participated. They were assisted by an additional twenty-seven participantes de la comunidad, community participants. These were people who knew the area, some of them since childhood. These were people who could sweet-talk mules, who recognized the signs of wildlife large and small, who could find cougars and ring-tailed cats, who knew the locations of hidden cave paintings, who were comfortable handling scorpions and rattlesnakes.

The report begins with a subjective yet accurate description, in English and Spanish: "The bay of San Basilio, Baja California Sur, is immediately remarkable to any visitor for its stunning landscape and heterogeneity of landforms and habitats." It also uses the words "incredible biodiversity." Had this report been written in Spanish by Martin, it is a dead certainty that the word "¡maravilloso!" and its various synonyms and near synonyms would have found multiple applications.

The text is backed up by photographs: spiders, insects, fish, plants, birds, lizards, snakes, starfish, sea pens. And, of course, turtles.

The report includes species lists: 15 kinds of bats, 14 of other mammals, 88 birds, 40 reptiles, 60 spiders, 284 plants.

"One of the scientists from Scripps," Tom says, "told me that San Basilio was the most species rich site he had seen in twenty-five years of surveys in the Baja."

It is only now, forty minutes into our conversation, that he begins to talk about himself, about his own role. Many years ago, he had started college as a biology major, then switched to creative writing, then settled on a business degree. His wandering path led him to start an organization called Floresta to reforest denuded lands in the Dominican Republic. It is now called Plant with Purpose, and its work extends far beyond the Dominican Republic.

Life moved on. He went to work for the medical industry and stayed long enough to realize that the job could kill him. In his last two years of that career, he drove 8,500 miles. To escape what he refers to as the "rat race," he founded the Rancho San Basilio project on behalf of a collection of partners and investors. That was years ago. The owners hoped to eventually develop the land with hotels and a golf course. A marina was to have been built in an area that was and still is occupied by a mangrove-shored saline lagoon.

Not long after he started with San Basilio, litigation commenced. It was not intended to stop development, but rather to transfer the land from the hands of one set of owners and would-be developers to those of another. By 2013 and 2014, he explains, there were forty-two legal actions in play. Litigants included relatives of highly placed politicians. At least one relied on forged documents in what amounted to outright fraud. Other cases were more complicated. "We have a great lawyer," he says. "An amazing lawyer."

Some of the litigants were not above the use of extrajudicial threats and intimidation.

"At one point someone sent fishermen to string gillnets across every beach in San Basilio. Strictly harassment. They would not catch many fish where they put the nets. I wanted to tell our guys to pick up the nets and burn them. But I didn't." There is regret in his voice, a tone bemoaning a lost opportunity, a missed shot at an action that might not have been helpful in the long-term but that would have been at least momentarily gratifying.

One litigant, a man who Tom refers to as "a very bad guy," spread poison on the land, killing goats and leaving one of the resident ranchers with neurological damage. Much of this sounds a little unbelievable, but by now I have been in Mexico long enough to have heard and read newspaper accounts of other land disputes that turned deadly, including some that involved systematic mass killings of one set of claimants by another.

"I came here to relax, to spend the last part of my career in a laid-back atmosphere. You know—Mexico! But instead I woke up every morning to what amounted to a new bar fight. This went on for fourteen years. A bar fight punctuated by long periods of waiting and uncertainty."

"I thought about walking away," he tells me. "But I realized that I am both stubborn and resilient."

One by one, the cases against the Rancho San Basilio project were overcome. Along the way, investors sold out and new investors bought in. The project occupied the land with small ranch houses, establishing the physical presence that is a legal requirement in a nation known for problematic and confusing property laws. A master plan for the resort was developed.

Over time, the possibility of multiple hotels and a marina looked less and less promising. To Tom, it looked less and less appealing. He talked to the owners about a new plan, one that would convert Rancho San Basilio into a nature reserve.

A major partner balked. Tom hired a mediator, but mediation was a nonstarter. The partner wanted a resort or nothing.

He got nothing. That is, he dropped out.

Another partner, tired of pouring money into the project, wrote off "a sick amount of money," as Tom put it, simply walked away from it with the proviso that the land must be put into conservation in perpetuity.

How much, I wonder, is a sick amount of money in this context? "Thirty-three million dollars," Tom tells me.

Tom took measures to raise operating funds. Donations trickled in. At this point, the operation was on a shoestring. Then, somewhat miraculously, an extremely wealthy heiress who prefers to remain anonymous stepped forward. The future remains amorphous, the conservation plan existing mainly in Tom's head and in conversations with his partners and his angel funder. In general terms, the hope is for Rancho San Basilio to become conservation land in perpetuity supported by an endowment and perhaps a small very high-end educational ecolodge and research center.

By the way, that same angel funder, the anonymous wealthy heiress, provided a grant to advance Martin's efforts. However Rancho San Basilio's plan may develop, sea turtles will play a role.

We sail back to Bahía San Basilio, and Tom drives out from Loreto. We meet for a glass of wine on the patio of a large house overlooking the bay. The patio and the adjacent building had been built long before Tom arrived on the scene by a marquesa, a Swiss woman who had married into Spanish royalty. But the marquesa had run into property problems of her own. She sold the land to the San Basilio project. By the time the San Basilio project acquired the land, termites had reduced the wooden parts of the structure to sawdust. The new owners renovated. It is possible, even likely, that the marquesa's house, big and airy, will become the centerpiece of the planned or at least dreamt of eco-lodge.

The vista is nothing short of astounding. Rock spires, the cores of long extinct volcanoes, pop up from the bay's clear water. The bay itself is outlined by cliffs of various colors, expressions of andesite and silt stone and limestone, folded bending layer upon folded bending layer. Beaches punctuate cliffs. And behind it all dry hills extend into the distance. There are no paved roads in sight, no cell towers, no power lines.

I ask Tom where this project would be now if he had walked away, if he had not been stubborn and resilient, if he had opted out of the bar fight. His face falls as he considers his answer. "Nowhere," he says. "There would not be a project. The investors would have dropped out. The land ownership would remain in question."

I had come to Tom because of the turtle nest cages I had found on the beach, but it is obvious to me that Tom's interest here goes far beyond turtles. I ask if he has ever heard of the biologist Edward O. Wilson, the aforementioned man who had written *The Future of Life* and discovered more than 400 ant species before recently passing away.

Tom smiles broadly. "I love E. O.," he says. "You know I am a Half-Earther myself?" Here he refers to another book by Wilson, *Half-Earth*. In addition to the book, there is his Half-Earth Project. Both advocate setting aside half of the globe for the preservation of nature.

Some might dismiss Edward O. Wilson as something of a nut. "Devote half the earth to nature conservation?" some would ask. "Crazy. Insane. Impossible."

Others might disagree. "Inspirational and not at all crazy," others would say.

I would say optimistic. But I would also ask, "Which half?" And I, along with many others, might add something along the lines of, "half is probably not enough."

E. O., as he is often referred to in the conservation community, was not a turtle man. In conventional science circles he was known for his ants as well as for work in island ecology and sociobiology. But his interests did not stop with academic articles. He introduced and promoted the term biophilia, for the human desire to seek connections with other species and with life in general. He was instrumental in moving the Encyclopedia of Life forward, a database that now captures information on more than a million species. He founded the E. O. Wilson Biodiversity Foundation, he wrote books for nonspecialists, and he even wrote a novel. Etcetera.

Regarding all those ant species he discovered, a time came in which he was running short of new and unique names. This is why today certain ant species are named after conservationists.

His novel is about ants.

As to his Half-Earth proposal, where are we now? The 2020 Protected Planet Report from the United Nations, in collaboration with others, says that just under 17 percent of the terrestrial world is now protected, not including Antarctica. For the seas, the figure comes in at just shy of 8 percent.

Of course, not all protected areas are created equally. Not all are managed in the same way. Some enjoy far more protection than others. Some enjoy little more than protection in name. But still, 17 percent and 8 percent are not horrible numbers. For perspective, protection is in place for an area of land more than twice the size of the United States. Protected oceans cover an area about three times the size of the United States. The number continues to rise. From a June 2023 United Nations media release: "Today, in New York, the United Nations adopted a historic agreement aiming to ensure the conservation and sustainable use of marine biodiversity of areas beyond national jurisdiction which cover over two-thirds of the ocean."

Yet turtles continue to perish needlessly. As do other species. So, congratulations to all concerned, nice work, but we can do better.

The reality of our ability to do better—this is the key to hope and optimism.

One morning not long after meeting Tom, Lisanne and I head out to dive on one of the rock spires in front of Rancho San Basilio. As sometimes happens in the Gulf of California, even in winter, the water sits flat under brilliant sunlight. We wear thick wetsuits in our dinghy, propelled by an electric outboard and with an electric hookah diving compressor aboard. The electric hookah provides air through hoses, allowing us to dive to depths of around thirty feet for up to an hour at a time. Between uses, we recharge both the outboard and the compressor through solar panels aboard our boat.

Another dinghy approaches us from astern. They are strangers, but fellow boaters. "Some guy named Tom is looking for you," the man in the dinghy says. "He's headed to that beach over there to release some turtles."

Lisanne and I alter course, guided by the stranger's pointing finger, heading to one of the two remaining turtle nests at San Basilio. It is beyond what most people would think of as the hatching season. The air is cold. These thick wetsuits are not mere fashion statements.

Tom is on the beach with Martin and Chavelo. Martin works the sand, scooping it away, bringing up hatchlings and in some cases eggs. The hatchlings and eggs amass on the ground next to the nest.

Martin expresses delight at the survival of the nest. This late in the season, he did not expect hatchlings. But the hatchlings, to my eyes, are not as energetic as other hatchlings I have seen. "Maybe they have been in the nest too long," Martin speculates. I wonder if it is simply too cold for them, but Martin does not see this as a likely explanation.

I kneel and then bend over the nest, smelling it. Tom joins me. To me it smells exactly as one might expect a nest with recently hatched eggs to smell, not terribly pleasant but hardly overwhelming. To Tom it smells something like a chicken coop.

"No wonder the coyotes can find the nests," he says.

Martin checks each hatchling for umbilicals. We talk about the nests, and how air gets into the nests, pumped in and out as the tide rises and falls on the beach. Martin mimics a turtle digging its nest, his hand imitating the rear flipper of an adult female, first digging the chimney down a foot or so into the sand, and then scraping out the egg chamber at the bottom of the chimney.

As we talk, the breeze builds. It is hardly a roaring wind, but it is enough to kick up waves along the beach. And it is growing.

Martin names the turtles. "Martin Uno, Martin Dos, Martin Tres," he says, laughing. Martins One, Two, and Three, his babies. There are forty-five little Martins on the beach now. They are all males, Martin is sure. His certainty does not come from their appearance but from the temperatures of the past month. In sea turtles and many other reptiles, sex is determined by the temperature of the nest. Male sea turtles arise from nests incubated at temperatures below about 81 degrees Fahrenheit. It is remotely possible that these late nests reflect a survival strategy, a way to ensure that a dramatically warming world has enough male sea turtles

Since they are males, today will be their last experience with a beach. They will never return to shore.

Immediately after emerging from their eggs, the turtles are jet black, but they turn gray as they dry. They become more active. It is time to let the little Martins swim.

With agreement from Tom and Martin (Martin Senior, of course), Lisanne and I enter the water before the turtles, tasked with capturing photographs. My wife is the photographer. I am there to help find turtles and to manage the hookah compressor. We will follow the turtles out and dive with them, watching and documenting their sudden transition to the life aquatic. I also want to see what the turtles will see, what sort of bottom they will traverse in their first hour of life, in this first stage of their lost years. And what sort of predators they might encounter.

While Lisanne photographs turtles just beyond the surf in a few feet of water, I swim offshore. I use the hookah to submerge and swim east, toward the mouth of the bay and the open sea. I swim over a bottom interspersed with the trails of olive shells, small snails that crawl just below the surface of the sand. In slightly deeper water, starting at maybe fifteen feet, I come across patches of sea pens, feather-like relatives of coral and jellyfish that extend upward from invisible burrows. I swim through a school of porgies, each perhaps ten inches long, bottom-feeding fish for the most part, eaters of tiny shellfish and worms; as far as I can tell, they offer absolutely no threat at all to turtle hatchlings.

The lost years for the Martins will begin with a view of mostly barren sand. But in fact the sand is alive not only with scattered olive snails and sea pens but with creatures too small for my aging eyes to see. And the water column above the sand is thick with tiny comb jellies and salps, more than big enough even for my vision, gelatinous things, bite-sized and sufficiently soft for young turtles to eat, if they are so inclined. Young turtles will likely eat almost anything they can find, provided it is small enough, and small prey is plentiful here.

I swim back to shore, watching for turtles. I see none until I am near the surf zone, where Lisanne works with her camera.

The wind blows at ten knots now, still growing in strength. Some of the turtles have swum away, but many appear to struggle. They float on the surface, unable or unwilling to dive beneath the waves. They are thrown back onto the beach or caught in a current running north, toward a rocky point.

Tom is gone now, called away to some urgent business. Only Martin and Chavelo remain on the beach. At their urging, I gather up the hatchlings closest to the rocky headland. It is clear that these hatchlings will not survive even the light surf crashing against the hardened shore.

Once the hatchlings have had a short rest, they swim free once more. But again waves hold them back. They drift back toward the rocks. As before I gather them up and take them to Martin and Chavelo.

It is the surf that stops them. Maybe they can survive, or have a better chance of surviving if we can deliver them beyond the surf. Lisanne and I stow our dive gear in the dinghy while the hatchlings rest, then we load them as well next to the dive gear. We are now in charge of twenty-nine hatchlings, twenty-nine Martins, with instructions to release them a few hundred yards offshore, well beyond the surf and the rocks. We shove off and slowly head offshore.

We stop the motor. Our tiny dinghy, overloaded with dive gear and turtles, bobs low in the water. One by one, we gently set each hatchling into the sea. Some fold their flippers backward, pausing for a moment before submerging. Some simply float, bobbing in the waves just like our dinghy until they drift out of sight. Some swim on the surface, then pause, then swim some more before submerging.

We of course have no idea how many of these hatchlings will survive. Possibly none. If it is true that only one-in-one-thousand hatchlings survive to adulthood, or even if three or four in one thousand survive to adulthood by virtue of the assistance offered by Martin and his colleagues and his cages, then almost certainly none of these twenty-nine animals will survive long enough to reproduce. But that unpleasant thought is easy enough to dispel. What we can say with some certainty is that these turtles have at least a chance. Without Martin, they would have been coyote food. Without us, they would have been dashed onto the beach or smashed into the rocks. Realistic or not, that is the thought I hold onto as the last of the hatchlings, the last of the little Martins, disappears in the sea.

SEVEN

The Fishers

Tom drives back to Loreto and we sail into a strengthening norther, clawing away at it, tacking back and forth, making slow, tedious headway upwind. It takes five hours to close the ten miles between Bahía San Basilio and the headland known as Punta Púlpito, named, I think, because the rock face looks something like an octopus, a pulpo, when viewed from the right angle and with imagination. But Lisanne thinks it is more likely named for its resemblance to a pulpit, a púlpito, and of course she is right.

It stands nearly five hundred feet above the water's surface, the remains of a volcanic vent with a distinctive black band of obsidian running through otherwise gray rock. It appears ancient, but in fact it is not so old at all, almost certainly younger than five or ten million years. The direct ancestors of turtles that swim in its shadow have been around far longer than this seemingly permanent rock.

We anchor in its lee, entirely protected from the waves and more or less sheltered from the wind. By morning of the next day the waves and wind have subsided, so we take the opportunity to dive beneath the cliff face of Punta Púlpito, using scuba gear to reach beyond the depth capabilities of our electric hookah rig.

The seascape is nothing less than one would expect; in other words, it is spectacular. The water swarms with fish, including large sea bass and grunts. Sponges and sea fans and tube worms blanket the vertical rock walls. The temperature is a hypothermic sixty-one degrees. For reasons I do not know, the marine community here is less depleted than the many we have seen elsewhere in the Gulf of California.

At a depth of eighty feet, rock gives way to a steeply sloping seabed of sand and gravel. It is there that I am excited to stumble upon what I believe at first to be a sleeping turtle. It is a green, twenty inches across the shell, so probably a teenager. It will be ten or possibly twenty more years before it is old enough to reproduce.

In my collection of scientific papers I have "Winter dormancy in sea turtles: Independent discovery and exploitation in the Gulf of California by two local cultures," published in the prestigious journal *Science* in 1976. It describes dormant green sea turtles, or sea turtles that are, in a very loose sense, hibernating. The paper is a work of anthropology as much or more than a work of biology. The authors offer accounts given by Seri people, the same people whose ancestors lived on the islands and shores of the Gulf of California long before the Spaniards arrived. The Seri told the authors about hunting dormant green turtles in the winter. They called the turtles "mosni ʔant kóit," translated by the authors as "green turtle land touch." The animals, as the Seri hunters described them, were half-buried in the mud, often in groups. They could be harpooned at low tide. In the distant past the Seri took them for food, but as early as 1959 they were hunting dormant turtles for the markets in cities like Guaymas and Hermosillo, near San Carlos on the mainland.

Later, in 1972 or 1973, according to the authors, fishermen from Kino, the city closest to the remaining Seri communities, were diving in the fishing grounds of the Seri. The Kino divers took lobster while breathing from gasoline-powered hookah rigs or from scuba tanks. While decimating the lobster stocks, they, too, discovered or rediscovered dormant green turtles. These divers called them "caguama echada," which the authors translated to "sea-turtle lying-down." A one- or two-hour dive could turn up five or ten caguamas echadas, all destined for the markets. In their paper, the authors included a black-and-white photograph of a young diver escorting an immature green turtle to the surface. The diver's right hand grasps the leading edge of the turtle's carapace. The turtle's eyes are open and seemingly alert, and his or her fore flippers are stretched outward and upward. At first glance, the poor creature appears utterly terrified. But on closer examination, I cannot determine what makes the animal look terrified. A turtle, for all its beauty, is inexpressive. The appearance of terror must come from me, not from the turtle.

I had read the article with skepticism, finding it difficult to believe that an air breather the size of a sea turtle could lay on the bottom for days on end. Unlike some freshwater turtles, there is no convincing evidence that sea turtles can take on meaningful amounts of oxygen directly from the water, through the cloaca or their mouths. I had found no follow-up papers. There was nothing else to confirm the existence of winter dormancy in the literature, not a single word since 1976. But now I may have my own evidence, not from dusty papers but from real life, right in front of me.

While Lisanne photographs our turtle, what I am thinking of as our mosni ʔant kóit, our caguama echada, I look more closely. My excitement diminishes. This turtle may be more than asleep. The eyes are glassed over; the limbs and, more disturbingly, the neck are entirely limp. This animal may be dead.

After taking eight or ten pictures Lisanne backs away and I move in. I do not want to disturb a dormant turtle, but I want to know for sure if this animal is still alive.

Some of the flesh appears to be rotting away. The eyes, which had looked glassed over even from a distance of four or five feet, look very dull close up, certainly lifeless.

Almost convinced that the animal is dead, I look for a cause of death. I suspect a gillnet. Carefully, I lift the carcass. The animal does not react. From the short length of the tail, it seems that the turtle was a her. She shows no signs of wounds, no cuts in her limbs from a gillnet. I turn her over on her back. Her flippers and head flop uselessly downward. I am now certain that she is dead. But still, I see no signs of a cause of death.

Lisanne takes more pictures, documenting our unfortunate discovery. I have seen the remains of dead turtles underwater before, but only their bones and shells or badly rotting carcasses. This is the first time I have seen one intact, and I think it might be of interest to Martin.

We surface, cold and saddened by what we had seen.

A few days later, back in Loreto, we show Martin the photographs. Zooming in on the eyes, he suggests the turtle had died two or three days before our dive. With some certainty, he says she died in a gillnet. Gillnets do not always scar the leathery skin of turtles, he tells us. It depends on how long the turtle struggles before drowning, and mild marks from a gillnet would disappear quickly.

There are environmentalists who disagree with E. O. Wilson, who do not see the wisdom of protecting at least half the Earth for the preservation of biodiversity. There are those who say the battle has already been lost, nature has been crushed, and the real hope lies in accepting the losses and managing what is left of the defeated ecosystems and their inhabitants.

Wilson, in *Half-Earth*, quotes Erle Ellis. "Nature is gone," Ellis wrote in *Wired* in 2009. "It was gone before you were born, before your parents were born, before the pilgrims arrived, before the pyramids were built. You are living on a used planet." All of us today, he goes on, live in the Anthropocene, a time defined by the extraordinary influence of humanity. People have taken control of the air, the water, the soil, the biosphere.

Many others align with Ellis's way of thinking. Rather than promoting the preservation of vast areas of wilderness, some of these people find hope in semiwild areas, carefully managed unkempt gardens. Instead of setting aside half the planet for nature, their argument goes, we should instead manage habitats and species, forming a sort of paternal partnership. In this arrangement, humanity would be, by far, the senior partner. Some species would disappear, but through stewardship, through wise choices, the important ones would persevere.

Backed into a corner, some who side with Ellis might say that the only way to save what is left of nature is to commodify it, to monetize it.

Wilson refers to Ellis and those who agree with him as "Anthropocene ideologists." His unwelcoming view of their approach to conservation can hardly be overstated. From his writings: "A prediction can't yet be made of the damage from procedures suggested by Anthropocene ideologists." He elaborates on his objections, pointing out, among other things, that humans do not understand nature well enough to selectively manage ecosystems. We are not adequately wise to make reasonable choices when it comes to managing nature. Unintended consequences are inevitable.

Wilson has passed away, so I cannot ask him why a two-pronged approach might not make sense, one that preserves and restores wilderness to the greatest extent possible—more than half the planet if I were in charge—but manages the rest as a partnership.

Really, it may not matter what Wilson might have thought, or what Ellis might think. In reality, both approaches have gained ground. Both contribute to the protection of species. It is possible to see that now, in the realm of the sea turtle. Marine preserves, some of them covering vast reaches of ocean wilderness, already exist, unmanaged by humans if for no other reason than an absence of funding. Smaller preserves actively protect turtles in places like Cabo Pulmo in Mexico, Palau in the South Pacific, and the Flower Garden Banks Marine Sanctuary off the coast of Texas. Nesting beaches have been set aside for turtles in places like

Costa Rica's Pacuare Reserve and Oman's Ras al Had. At the same time unprotected oceans and beaches are under new management. Turtles in most of the world cannot be legally hunted, at sea or on land. Measures are in place to limit the risk to turtles from certain kinds of fishing. Unprotected beaches are patrolled by volunteers. Nests are guarded and if necessary moved. Eggs mature in incubation centers. People release hatchlings by hand.

Too little of the ocean is preserved as wilderness. There are too few managed coastal habitats and beaches, not enough management measures in place, and woefully insufficient enforcement capabilities. But the world is changing. My internal optimist sees at least the shallow upward curve of a positive trend, but at the same time this optimism lies under the shadow of what I know about people. People, at least some people, possess a remarkable ability to ignore rules. People, at least some people, including far too many in positions of power, pursue their own short-term best interests regardless of positive trends.

We sail thirty-five miles south and slightly east of Loreto to anchor with several other small yachts in front of the fishing village of Puerto Agua Verde, population about two hundred. Walking on one of the village's packed sand roads, we encounter a woman with a young child. The woman asks us for money. She insists on handing us a letter written in English. The letter explains that she needs cash for medical expenses because she is pregnant. Medical services require a two-hour drive and she has no car.

It is not clear if the woman realizes that the date printed in the letter makes it four years old. The child with her may be the result of the pregnancy described in the letter. But we give her a little money anyway. She tells us about the town. There are two stores, a school, and two restaurants. Most people here fish for a living. Freshwater is piped in from five miles away, carried through a plastic tube coming down from the mountains, where, she says, there is a river.

Later we talk to a fisherman. He is perhaps sixty-five years old. He once enjoyed caguama, turtle stew, he says, but no longer. He says the beaches here are no good for turtles, that turtles seldom nest here. There are too many people. This makes me think of San Carlos, of turtles laying eggs between tire tracks on beaches and well within sight of the lights of restaurants and hotels, on beaches far busier than those of his village.

In any case, he tells us that if we want to see turtles nesting we should go to the next bay to the southeast, behind Punta Marte. There he is sure that turtles nest. Not now, but in the summer.

Even though summer is months away we sail to the bay behind Punta Marte, only to discover the beaches are rock and heavy gravel. They are not laying beaches.

We sail out to Isla Montserat, eight miles to the north, uninhabited, dry, and designated as a protected area. But like the beaches lining the bay behind Punta Marte, the beach near our anchorage is gravel and rock, entirely unsuitable for nesting. On that designated protected beach of gravel and rock we find eleven slaughtered rays. Based on the size of their barbs, which exceed six inches, they are probably diamond rays, a kind of large stingray. And we find the heads of twenty-two hammerhead sharks, all from animals that, were their heads still attached to their bodies, would not have exceeded four feet in length. Sadder still, we find the carcasses of five angel sharks, an unusual looking animal, in appearance a cross between a shark and a ray but whitish or at least light gray even when alive, with deltoid pectoral fins. No part of these angel sharks has been harvested. They have simply been killed and dumped on this protected beach.

What does this have to do with turtles? Why should a turtle hugger care if sharks are going to the slaughterhouse?

Aside from the wanton loss of life and the role of sharks in the ecosystem, these particular sharks, like the turtle we had seen dead on the bottom at Punta Púlpito, were caught in gillnets, which were very likely set in a protected area. The fishermen know that protected areas offer better fishing. And we know that gill nets kill turtles.

That night, bobbing on our anchor in settled weather, my optimism fades. But I fight back with rum as I read about the history of nature protection in general and about regulations protecting the Gulf of California from that most dangerous of predators, a human being in need or want of money.

Words alone, whether written into law or scrawled across signs posted on beaches, provide little protection. Managing wildlife requires management of people.

This sort of management can be traced back to medieval gamekeepers, the King's protectors of deer and wild boar and perhaps rabbits and foxes.

Management of people interested in exploiting protected areas and protected species is not an especially safe line of work. Take one of the earliest wardens in the United States, Guy Bradley. A one-time hunter himself, later in life he was employed to prevent the ongoing illegal slaughter of birds such as egrets and herons, spoonbills and ibises, whose feathers fed one of history's more ridiculous fashion fads.

Poachers—plume hunters, as they were called—shot Guy Bradley and left him to die at Oyster Cay, near what is today Flamingo, Florida, on July 8, 1905.

Hundreds of game wardens have been killed in the United States since then, making the job one of the most dangerous within the nation's realm of law enforcement. The average American game warden is far more likely to be killed on the job than the average police officer.

I cannot find similar statistics for Mexico, perhaps because the Mexicans are too smart to send lone armed officers out to do battle with armed poachers, or perhaps because it is simply not something that is tracked.

Consider for a moment the 17 percent of land area and 8 percent of ocean area currently categorized and inventoried as "protected." Some permit certain kinds of hunting and fishing. Others allow mineral extraction. Still others consent to logging. Many encourage recreational use. Most do not have sufficient funding for enforcement. In the Gulf of California the Mexican navy helps out, as do groups like Sea Shepherd, a nonprofit organization that implements what amounts to officially sanctioned nongovernmental law enforcement, one step removed, some would say, from vigilantism.

On several occasions we have seen navy boats on patrol in the Gulf of California, well-armed and fast. We have never seen a Sea Shepherd boat off the dock, but presumably they are out here too. In contrast, we regularly see fishermen in supposedly protected areas.

I attempt to suppress these thoughts with an additional ration of rum.

A day later, *Rocinante* rides on her anchor just off the southern tip of the seldom visited Isla Santa Catalina. Also known as Isla Catalan, it is yet another protected island.

I walk inland, stepping carefully, hoping to see a rattle-less rattlesnake but avoid its bite. The serpent is yet another species close to extinction. For two hours I pick my way through forests of cardón and giant barrel cactus that stretch across steep windswept sunbaked hills and then, dropping downslope, I wander through arroyos that meander between the hills.

In all the world, this snake occurs in the wild only here. Unlike other rattlesnakes, it is not a shy species. It is known to sprawl across the branches of shrubs, up off the ground.

The International Union for the Conservation of Nature's Red List suggests that an attentive person walking for four or five hours would be likely to see from one to eight of them. But the last official record of their abundance, or at least the last one that I can find, is more than ten years old.

Information offered alongside that aging record suggests that the snakes are or at least seem to be in decline. Thanks to collectors and the small size of their island home, about eight miles long and two-and-a-half miles wide, the rattle-less rattlesnake stares extinction in the face.

I see exactly zero snakes.

Later, I kayak beneath a sheer cliff of what looks like layered andesite and rhyolite. I paddle over clear water, intent on shaking away recent injuries to my optimism. Beneath me I witness an abundance of fish—giant damsels, hogfish, Cortez and king angels, grunts, chubs.

It would be easy, if I knew less about the sea, to be deeply impressed by such plenty. But certain fish stand out because they are missing. I see far too few piscivores fish, the fish that eat other fish rather than plankton or algae or invertebrates, and that in so doing unintentionally render themselves desirable to the human palate. Scallop shells are common, but living scallops are rare. Lobster are seldom seen and almost never full-grown.

Do not take my word alone. Turn to the erudite words of scientific journals. Read a paper published in the journal *Frontiers in Ecology and the Environment*, "Remembering the Gulf: Changes to the marine communities of the Sea of Cortez since the Steinbeck and Ricketts expedition of 1940." The paper describes an expedition that followed in the footsteps of Steinbeck and Ricketts, sampling where and how they once sampled, but sixty-four years later. The new expeditioners found fewer of almost everything. The ranges of many species had contracted. The animals they found were often smaller than those seen in 1940.

Or turn to the writing of educator Aaron Hirsh, who taught field science in the Gulf of California's Vermilion Sea Field Station for many years. He writes of, among other things, the dramatic decrease in the size of typically caught yellowtails, a sought-after food fish, and about the disappearance of a species of sea cucumber, precipitated in part by a legal ban on its harvest, which drove the price up, leading to a boom in illegal gathering. A type of starfish, too, had become uncommon.

Yet the underwater world here remains beautiful and full of life, distractingly so, despite the abuse. The sea, like the land, can be simultaneously tremendously rich and badly depleted. Ecologists often talk about shifting baselines, a common-sense idea adopted from the field of landscape architecture by the fisheries biologist Daniel Pauly in 1995. It works like this: People look at an ecosystem—say the Abaco Sea or the Georges Banks or the Gulf of California—a hundred years ago, and they see biological abundance and diversity beyond belief. Then, as they grow older, they see less life and register decreased abundance and diversity. But along comes a new generation of people, and they see what is to them biological abundance and diversity beyond belief. Then they age and see fewer fish and turtles and shells. But they are followed by yet another generation. And so on.

The baseline shifts. Expectations change.

For those of us who have grown up surrounded by horribly degraded ecosystems, that is, almost all of us alive today, an ecosystem that is merely badly degraded appears to be a wondrous thing.

But here is where my optimism kicks in. Two of the biggest problems faced by the Gulf of California are inadequate enforcement of mostly existing regulations and a lack of opportunities for people aside from fishing. Address these two problems and watch as badly degraded becomes, very quickly, merely degraded. Before long one might be able to apply the term healthy. One day, the finest of adjectives in the ecologist's lexicon might be brought back into play: Pristine. Not entirely pristine, because the species we have driven into extinction will never return, because the footprint of humanity can never be erased. But pristine enough to warrant the word, even if it is not literally correct.

These problems, inadequate enforcement and a lack of opportunities, are easily addressed. Well-spent money is all that is needed. Money well spent changes behaviors. Changes in behaviors give ecosystems the space they need to fix themselves. It shifts baselines back toward where they belong.

It is easy to be optimistic when paddling alone over shallow clear water under the shadow of a towering wall of andesite and rhyolite in the company of fish.

As per our nature and that of our boat, we move again. We anchor in twelve feet of water just south of a lagoon at Bahía Timbabiche, back on the Baja peninsula. The bay stretches in a mile long crescent, all of it good sand, suitable for nesting turtles.

Onshore, we walk toward the scattered buildings of a fishing village, a tiny pueblo. We encounter bony free-ranging cattle and healthier looking goats. We step over the bleached shell of a turtle, probably an olive ridley, long dead. We pass a new but apparently abandoned school building.

The first fisherman we come across tells us that eighteen families live here, but that the children now attend school in Constitución, a city of forty-five thousand people at the heart of one of the Baja's agricultural centers. A crow would fly about forty miles to reach Constitución, but a student riding in the family's truck would zigzag on rough sand and clay tracks beneath that crow's flightpath, doubling and tripling the distance, spending close to four hours to cross that same stretch of dry land. The children, the fisherman says, cannot come home on weekends. It is too far. But they come home for vacations. They like it here. It is better here than in Constitución, he says, but the trip back and forth is expensive. This is why the children are only here for vacations. He goes back to work on a boat that rests on a rusting trailer in front of his brick house.

Walking on, we find another fisherman. He tends a well-fed bull and two well-fed goats in a small pen. He introduces himself as Modesto, smiling broadly, and in so doing exposing a few missing teeth and a friendly openness that is a pleasure to see. He glances at his livestock as he talks.

The beasts chew green branches of the desert shrub palo verde that he has gathered and stacked in their pen. We talk for a few minutes about the village, about the healthy appearance of his bull and his goats, about the drought. A jackrabbit dashes through the scrubby brush behind him.

"Un conejo," I say. A rabbit.

"No, una liebre. El conejo es mas pequeño." No, a hare. The rabbit is much smaller. He says also that the liebre is very good to eat.

I ask if turtles nest on the beach. Yes, many turtles. In the summer. But the coyotes take their eggs.

Lisanne tells him that in other places we have seen people put protective cages around turtle nests. He nods. He knows about this. In some villages, he says, people are paid to look after the turtle nests. He wishes the same were true here. The village, he says, could use the money.

I do not have the heart to ask him if people here eat turtles or eggs. It seems certain that they do, at least at times.

We take a different route back to the anchorage, back to our boat, and along the way we come across three large gillnets, neatly folded and stacked, the bread and butter of this village and of a hundred others spread up and down the coast.

The next day, aboard *Rocinante*, still anchored near the childless village of Timbabiche, I sit in the cockpit. This is another of those rare winter days in the Gulf of California. We may be in the heart of the season of strong north winds and nighttime temperatures dipping into the fifties or lower, but the water rests as flat as a mill pond, generally ranging in color from blue to gray. Its surface reflects the white of scattered clouds and the reddish brown of sea cliffs and the sudden glare of the sun. Now it is early evening. An almost full moon hangs pale in the remains of daylight.

I watch for turtles. In conditions such as these, I am sure that a surfacing turtle will be visible for at least a quarter of a mile. Probably farther. With binoculars, certainly an easy half mile.

I watch a pelican glide low over the water, riding the cushion of air between its wings and the sea, its ridiculous pterodactyl-like bill out front, its broad wings elegantly extended. Ahead of it, I see a flock of eared grebes sitting on the water. There are at least two hundred grebes in this raft of nervous birds. I know they will dive—all of them, synchronously—as the pelican approaches. And dive they do. The pelican flies past, uninterested, no threat at all, and forty seconds later the grebes resurface just as they had dived, not one or two at a time but the lot of them. This is something to love about eared grebes, their ability to stay together underwater, like a school of feathered fish.

I keep looking for turtles, scanning the water through my binoculars with something approaching a systematic search. The smarter ones have likely gone south to warmer water. Or possibly they have just moved away from here, from this village that might harbor predators.

I hear a launch, a panga, the irritating buzz of internal combustion. The noise arrives long before the boat itself rounds the headland in the northeast corner of the bay. When I see it the first thing I notice is the mound of gillnets heaped midships. The boat passes without slowing, on its way to land in front of the pueblo.

The moon brightens as the sky darkens. When the sun slips behind the mountains, the Sierra Gigantea, the air cools quickly.

No turtles. Not a one. But still, time spent looking for turtles has value. Whether or not time spent looking results in time spent seeing, it brings more life to my life.

We move on, this time to San Evaristo, another fishing village, but one that seems more prosperous than most of its neighbors along this coast.

Ashore, walking along the beach, Lisanne and I encounter five fishermen, ranging in age from nineteen to sixty-five. They ask about the binoculars I am wearing. I pass them around. The men take turns scanning the hills for deer and bighorn sheep. They say that these are very good binoculars, much better than the binoculars they have seen before.

I tell them about bighorns I had seen on the steep hillsides just to the north, right at the edge of town. They express surprise bordering on disbelief. They consult among themselves. The oldest of them agrees that it is possible. He has heard of people seeing them there before, once or twice. The younger men, it seems to me, remain doubtful.

I talk at length to one of the men. He is in his thirties, wearing white waterproof boots and lounging spread-eagled across a neatly folded mound of gillnets that stands three feet tall. He looks remarkably comfortable.

He tells us about fishing life. The nets they use from their pangas, their open boats, can be three hundred feet long, but the ones used by the big commercial boats stretch out for over a mile. They hang them at different depths, but always deep enough that we should not worry, that we will not hit them with our boat. They are hanging at depths of fifty feet, a hundred feet, three hundred feet. It depends on what they are fishing for. Lately they have been fishing for sharks, with the nets set at a depth of several hundred feet. I ask about turtles, and he says they do not catch turtles. Their nets are too deep for turtles.

I point out that leatherbacks, laúds, can dive to almost four thousand feet. Even olive ridleys, golfinas, venture beyond nine hundred feet. Both greens and hawksbills, prietas and careyes, dive beyond three hundred feet.

He nods his head but points out that the mesh of his net is too small for turtles. Turtles are only trapped in the larger mesh nets used for larger fish. And I know that this is, for the most part, true.

I ask what has become a standard question. In the past, did people here eat turtles? Not often, he tells me, because the taste is very strong, muy fuerte, and the people here prefer fish. They have always preferred fish. They like fresh yellowtails or stews made from the flesh of sharks and rays.

He talks about the business of fishing. Here in San Evaristo, a man from La Paz buys the catch, a man who he casually refers to as "El Patron." This buyer sometimes provides boats or motors or nets in what I understand to be a sort of a lease-to-own arrangement or possibly a form of contract employment. Some of the motors are paid for in part by government grants or government-backed loans.

As politely as my Spanish allows, I ask about the cost of a net such as the one upon which he sprawls. The question prompts discussion among his colleagues. With their input, he suggests a cost of about 26,000 pesos, about 1,300 dollars. He asks, with equal politeness, about the cost of my binoculars. About the same as your net, I tell him. With a winning smile he immediately offers a trade, binoculars for net. But I have no use for a gillnet, other than to retire it. As wrong as this may seem I value my binoculars more than I value the possibility of putting a gillnet out of commission. What good would come from removing one net of thousands? And I would miss my binoculars, the best pair I have ever owned. Even as I recognize the validity of my choice, my decision to hold onto my binoculars, my own behavior saddens me.

Wandering on, we visit the village's only store. It has no refrigeration and far fewer goods than, say, a poorly stocked convenience store of the kind found on every second corner in any Mexican city. On the hill above the store, we visit a small school where an American couple offers English lessons to children. Today four students attend. They read essays from their notebooks aloud. Their written English is good, far better than my written Spanish. But they need practice with spoken English, and so we practice.

One of the students, who is fifteen years old, hopes to be a biologist one day. His says that his family founded the village. He thinks that was a hundred years ago, but he does not seem sure. The village is now home to twenty or twenty-five interrelated families. The fishermen here use only lines and nets. If they see fishermen with air compressors, diving for fish and lobster and octopus and sea cucumber, they chase them away. Likewise, they chase away smugglers. Now, his family runs a salt evaporation operation on the flats just outside of town. They bag and ship twenty tons of salt per year, a few truckloads. It goes to La Paz, where, he says, it is further processed. His teacher interjects, explaining that from La Paz it is marketed as boutique salt, with special qualities because it comes from the Gulf of California. It is, she claims, the only active salt production operation in all of the Gulf of California, where salt production was once commonplace.

The fifteen-year-old biologist-to-be tells us that he has seen leatherback turtles. He has seen them crawl up onto the beach near his house to try to lay eggs. But the sand there is too hard. Turtles do not lay eggs on these beaches. Even if they did, he explains, the coyotes would take the eggs.

Later, Lisanne and I visit the town's only restaurant. It caters to passing sailors and occasional campers. We eat fish tacos, making ourselves complicit in gillnetting.

On the wall of the restaurant, patrons have painted seashells with the names of their boats, but one has painted a boat name on a turtle rib. The handles on the restaurant's trashcan lids are also made from turtle ribs, and someone has written basura—trash—on them.

On the wall of the restaurant, a poet has hung five lines of verse, in Spanish:

Ojos de gato
Patas de ranas
Que aparezca
En mi mano
Una caguama.

Roughly translated:

Eyes of cat
Feet of frog
It seems that
In my hand
A turtle.

After lunch, we walk to the salt works at the edge of town. It is an artisanal operation, covering no more than an acre or two, entirely unmechanized. It reminds us immediately of pink flamingos.

Why pink flamingos? Because elsewhere, in places like the Bahamas and the Dominican Republic and the Dutch Antilles, we had seen industrial saltworks with evaporation ponds stretching out for miles. The product, the damp drying salt, formed mountains worked by bulldozers and excavators along the edges of the ponds. But the ponds themselves were often dotted by pink flamingos.

From one of those islands, Great Inagua in the Bahamas, comes a conservation story.

The island had been a producer of salt for hundreds of years. In the 1950s, Morton Salt moved in and managed what has become three hundred thousand acres of evaporation ponds and associated facilities. In a simplified description of the process, sea water flows into the ponds, is trapped, and evaporates, leaving behind salt crystals. A million pounds of salt came from the operation each year, bringing jobs to the island's thousand or so people.

As water evaporates from salt ponds, algae grow. Brine shrimp—not actual shrimp at all but branchiopods, a several-times-removed cousin of the kind of shrimp caught in turtle-killing trawls throughout the world—eat the algae. And flamingos eat both the algae and the brine shrimp.

With regard to Great Inagua, we are not talking about one or two flamingos, or two or three hundred flamingos. We are talking about an estimated fifty thousand birds.

These are flamingos that were once subject to the same kind of plume hunting that killed Guy Bradley. Pink flamingos were targeted as part of the slaughter of birds to provide feathers for the strange hats once favored by women of fashion. Hunting pressure drove flamingos to the brink of extinction.

Even after they were protected, locals continued to hunt them. Flamingos, by many accounts, are surprisingly tasty. And there is the problem of pigs. Flamingos are ground nesters, and pigs introduced to the island in Spanish times take both eggs and chicks from nests.

With flamingos seemingly disappearing from the Bahamas and the Caribbean, the Audubon Society's Robert Porter Allen visited Inagua in 1952. He found some guides who knew the island, who knew how to find flamingos. How did they know? Because, of course, they hunted flamingos. A few years after that visit, one of those guides was hired as the island's first game warden.

We learned all this from a man named Casper Burrows, a man who showed us around Great Inagua while *Rocinante* was anchored offshore. This was years before we transited the Panama Canal into the Pacific and sailed up to the Gulf of California.

Casper found flamingos for us, and parrots, and burrowing owls. He spoke highly of Morton Salt. He told us of his late uncle, the poacher-turned-game warden.

Casper's uncle and many others like him followed in the footsteps of Guy Bradley, happily giving up hunting to become stewards. Put another way, they gave up a destructive way of earning a living for a constructive way. Fishermen in the Gulf of California, as Elsa had told me months earlier in San Carlos, can become great protectors of sea turtles too.

We sail thirty miles southwest to spend a week at various anchorages around Isla San José and the neighboring Isla San Francisco, sometimes alone and sometimes in the company of other boats. We walk miles of shoreline. In places, walking along the shoreline is a matter of boulder hopping or strolling across long sheets of sloping bedrock. Elsewhere, there are beaches, but they consist of what I take to be andesite and rhyolite gravel. These shorelines would be no more useful to a nesting sea turtle than, say, a freeway in Los Angeles. But other beaches appear suitable and even ideal for turtle nesting, with thick sand and no more than scattered rocks and pebbles. There are no coyotes on these islands. Neither are there dogs, cats, or raccoons. The only people are visiting fishermen and occasional sailors or kayakers. In the heat of summer, when expectant turtles might be most eager to dig a nest, some fishermen and almost all sailors and kayakers disappear, avoiding the heat. These would be very good beaches for nesting turtles.

John Steinbeck and Ed Ricketts wrote of their 1940 visit to Isla San José. They described a nearby rock known as Cayo Islet. At low tide the island is half a mile long and, at its widest point, not quite two hundred feet across. It is steep-faced and surrounded by boulders. Steinbeck found iron rings and chains set into the rock.

When we paddle our kayaks to the island, we find the rings but not the chains. Eight decades of oxidation have taken their toll.

"In the shallow caves in the cliff there were evidences of many fires having been built," Steinbeck and Ricketts reported, "and piled about the fireplaces, some old and some fresh, were not only thousands of clam-shells but turtle-shells also." We found shallow caves, but the shells were no more present than the iron chains.

Steinbeck and Ricketts did not understand what anyone would have been doing on this waterless rock. "It is a riddle we cannot answer," they wrote, "just as we can think of no reason for the big iron rings."

With all due respect to the esteemed authors, a likely answer occurs to me. Someone harvested guano from this island.

Here is a story of something terrible followed by something magical. It is a story of how gathering bird droppings kills birds, even when the eggs and the birds themselves are not taken. But it is also a story of the resilience of nature.

In the 1850s, guano was gathered from the islands of the Gulf of California and shipped to, among other places, England and Germany. Guano, for the uninitiated, is nothing more than bird or bat droppings. The droppings are full of nitrogen. They smell, but make wonderful fertilizers. Guano was guaranteed, proponents of the product claimed with some justification, to more than pay its own way through increased crop yields.

A guano boom occurred that impacted small islands scattered around the globe. Nations, including the United States and Great Britain, annexed uninhabited islands for the sake of their guano. In places where annexation would have been politically awkward, as was the case in Gulf of California, negotiations provided access.

In dry regions like the Gulf of California, bird droppings accumulate to become several feet thick. Or more. Some rock islands are—or were, before they were mined—more guano than rock.

As to guano mining, we are not talking here about a couple of guys with shovels. We are talking about single contracts calling for five thousand tons per year of guano. We are talking about operations that could remove, from one island alone, well over ten thousand tons of guano.

The miners were not on the islands to gather eggs, or at least they were not there to gather more bird eggs than they could eat. Others gathered eggs for the markets on the mainland, but the miners were interested only in the guano.

But no one stopped mining operations just because a few birds might be interested in nesting or roosting.

Guano was scraped from rocks and carted away. Plant communities were destroyed. And along the way rats found their way from ships to island shores.

For ground-nesting birds, rats are about as welcome as pigs. Sea bird populations, even of those species that as adults are unpalatable and with feathers not necessarily sought after by the fashion world, declined precipitously.

Then the bottom fell out of the guano market. First, potassium nitrate, or salt peter, found its way into the fertilizer market. Not much later, in 1913, the invention of what became known as the Haber–Bosch process allowed large-scale relatively inexpensive synthesis of nitrogen fertilizers. Guano miners had to seek other forms of employment, which, given the terrible conditions under which they worked and the low wages which they earned, may not have seemed like such a bad thing.

Decades passed during which the remaining birds nested in the company of rats. Then, in the 1990s, rat eradication efforts came to previously mined islands in the Gulf of California.

The birds bounced back. Nature prevailed. The baseline shifted in a positive direction.

I have not found any records of guano mining on Cayo Islet. I am not even sure where one might look to find records of guano mining on Cayo Islet. But guano mining would explain the rings and chains. Hungry guano miners would explain Steinbeck's shells, both those of clams and those of turtles.

We sail on toward the city of La Paz, stopping along the way to walk more beaches at Isla Espírito Santo, and finding once more a mix of rock and gravel and sand, some good for nesting and some not, but all free of the four-legged predators that make egg survival so tenuous on the Baja peninsula.

EIGHT
Grupo Tortuguero

A north wind carries us past tankers and freighters and a fast ferry into the long curving narrow channel that leads to La Paz, a Baja city of a quarter of a million people. We pass by one packed marina after another, eventually finding a spot to anchor in the lee of El Mogote, a low-lying sand and mangrove peninsula. We come to rest in front of the navy base, among a hundred other small yachts, where a strong current, especially near the full and new moons, turns us and the other boats to point alternately to the northeast and the southwest, changing directions with the tide.

Steinbeck and Ricketts stopped nearby more than seventy years ago. They wrote of complaining fishermen, of a crewmember who refused to wash dishes, of drinking beer. They waxed philosophical about the nature of time and its perception. They collected specimens.

While here, we will have shoes repaired, eat out, and see a doctor for annual physicals. We will wash dishes without complaint and drink beer, also without complaint. We will see more traffic lights in an hour than we have seen collectively in several months. But it is really Grupo Tortuguero that draws us. They are headquartered here, and from here they coordinate, to one degree or another, turtle conservation throughout the Gulf of California and down the west coast of Mexico.

In 2014, a man named Wallace J. Nichols published a book called *Blue Mind*. The book explores the virtues of oceans and lakes and their impact on the human brain. He is widely credited with founding the field known in some circles as neuroconservation to discuss and promote nature's calming effect on humans, its ability to make us smarter and more content. He is also active with the International Union for the Conservation of Nature's Turtle Specialist Group, he is a research associate with the California Academy of Sciences, and he coaches graduate students in both Mexico and the United States. He has been called a "Keeper of the Sea" by *GQ*. And he has appeared in a full-face shot on the cover of *Outside*, under a banner saying "breakthrough science."

In his book, he talks about three possible ways to relate to nature. One can have an egocentric relationship, seeing nature through the lens of more or less direct exploitation, of what it can do for me, nature as a provider of a fish or two and perhaps a place to swim or walk in the woods. One can adopt an anthropocentric relationship, putting nature at the service not of the self but of humanity as a whole, a place from which oil can be extracted or fish can be harvested on a massive scale, in some ways a scaled-up egocentric view. Or one can cultivate a biocentric perspective, with humanity as part of nature, as one of many dancers at a complicated multispecies ball, a setting shared with our millions of cousins no matter how distantly removed.

"Nature needs us," he wrote, "and we need nature."

Why do I bring up Wallace J. Nichols? Not just because he talks about the need for a move toward biocentric thinking, but because he was one of the founding forces behind Grupo Tortuguero. When asked, he often suggests that it grew from a turtle tagging effort, one in which a turtle that he and his colleagues tagged in Mexico famously swam across the Pacific, showing up in Japan 478 days after they set it free. From there,

Nichols and his friends started intentionally nonconfrontational discussions about turtles with Mexican fishermen. The fishermen, at least some
of them, grew more reluctant to eat turtles. Some stopped eating turtles
altogether and made the switch to the conservation arena, the conversion
from egocentric to biocentric, from hunter to if not quite a game warden
at least an advocate for turtles.

In his book, Nichols also described a study in which volunteers were put
into two groups. Each group was tasked with seeking donations by telephone. They were given an instruction sheet identical in all ways but one.
The first group's instructions included a photograph of a runner winning a
race, while the second group's instructions did not. The group working with
the photograph in front of them raised more money than the group without,
even though many of those in the first group, during exit interviews, did
not recall seeing the photograph. The experiment, Nichols claims, was
repeated, yielding the same results. And it was repeated again, once more
with the same results.

Optimism, one could argue, really matters.

Go to the Grupo Tortuguero de las Californias website and the first thing
up is an aerial photograph of a group of people standing on the beach to
form the outline of a sea turtle in the sand. Next are these words: "Somos
una red de individuos y comunidades que trabajamos para la conservación
de las tortugas marinas." The site does not offer an English option, but
this simple sentence translates into something like, "We are a network of
individuals and communities working for the conservation of sea turtles."

They work with people spread across not only the Baja peninsula but
most of the west coast of Mexico. They also work outside of Mexico, with
collaborations in the United States, Japan, Cuba, Nicaragua, Costa Rica,
El Salvador, and Ecuador. Lest one is left thinking that this is a network

of well-established conservation organizations staffed by professional environmentalists closely tied to government agencies, read on: "El trabajo y la convicción de pescadores, estudiantes, maestros, amas de casa, científicos, organizaciones de la sociedad civil e instituciones de gobierno hacen que esta red se mantenga activa." Translated: "The work and the conviction of fishermen, students, teachers, housewives, scientists, civil society organizations, and government agencies maintain the activity of this network." Whether intentional or not, in this list fishermen come first, housewives come before scientists, and everyone comes before government agencies.

This is not some gringo outfit trying to tell Mexicans what to do, as often happens. Even though the organization traces its roots to Wallace J. Nichols and another American, it was conceived in 1999 by a group of forty-five people, mostly Mexican, who met together in Loreto, midway along the Gulf of California coast of the Baja peninsula, where I had talked to Tom and Martin of Rancho San Basilio, both of whom know Nichols.

Eight years later, Grupo Tortuguero became an Asociación Civil, a nongovernmental organization. In the United States, such a group might be called a nonprofit, or even a 501(c)(3), in reference to the part of the United States tax code that exempts certain nonprofit organizations from federal income tax. But again, this is a distinctly Mexican operation. It is Mexicans helping Mexicans. It is an organization that does some work of its own but that also provides an umbrella for other groups working to protect and save sea turtles.

There is, incidentally, a prominently placed "To donate" button on the website. It says "Donar," and clicking on it takes would-be donors to additional information in Spanish and a drop-down of suggested donation levels in pesos only. It is not that a non-Spanish speaking donor could not navigate the process, but it is clear that neither the site nor the organization are hungry for American handouts. It is, again, a distinctly Mexican operation that works from the bottom up. It might be described as organic activism, a conservation movement growing and nourishing itself.

Lisanne and I take our dinghy ashore, leaving *Rocinante* to swing in the tidal currents on her own. We walk for forty minutes on sometimes cracked and weed-choked sidewalks past homes, restaurants, hardware stores, and hotels toward the address I have scrawled in my notebook, ending up at what looks like an ordinary middle-class house in a modest residential neighborhood. But behind a white iron fence in front of the house stands a sign saying "Grupo Tortuguero de las Californias" in white letters against a blue background. Above the words are the white outlines of the leatherback, the hawksbill, the green, the loggerhead, and the olive ridley, along with a human, and the righthand edge of the sign has been cut into the shape of a turtle.

By rattling the locked gate we attract the attention of someone inside. We explain that we are here to meet with the director, Karen Oceguera, and the gate is unlocked. We are led inside. We wait for a few minutes in the entryway, next to the stairs, sharing space with a stack of sea turtle dolls, life-sized with anatomically correct shells—a leatherback, a hawksbill, three greens, and an olive ridley, ready to be deployed to classrooms.

Karen appears, offers us coffee, and leads us upstairs. She wears a fashionable gray sweater accentuating long black hair, but within her sense of style there is room for a necklace from which hangs a metal turtle pendant. On the floor of her small office there is a turtle doorstop.

"When I started," she tells us, "my parents thought I was crazy, out walking beaches alone at night, looking for nests." This is all in Spanish. Her parents thought she was loco.

Although she is to my eyes young, she has been at this for some time. Her parents no longer think she is crazy. When she started no one foresaw a real career in protecting turtles. And yet here she is, the director, with a core staff of four or five people overseeing a network of more than a dozen member organizations. Through this network, she has affected the lives of fishermen, university students, mothers, teachers, children, retirees, biologists, and, of course, turtles. And in turn they have affected her.

In addition to supporting member organizations that work directly with turtles, she and her staff provide advice to the government. She no longer has time for much hands-on biology. She is for the most part a coordinator, a raiser of funds, an organizer of people.

But now, when she can get out into the field, when she can eke out the time to walk beaches at night, her mother sometimes joins her.

The biggest challenge faced by Grupo Tortuguero?

"Dinero, por supuesto. Siempre dinero." Money, of course. Always money.

She tells me this past year was extraordinary for nesting in the Gulf of California. She does not yet have final counts, but everyone up and down the coast is reporting very high numbers. It is the year of the turtle.

I ask if she has any idea how many turtles there might be in the Gulf of California, the total number of turtles, a population estimate. She does not. But she is certain that the numbers, at least for the greens and olive ridleys, must be increasing, because the number of nests found each year is steadily increasing. This is not just a matter of having more beaches covered by more turtlers. On individual beaches where volunteers have worked for years, the numbers steadily climb.

She thinks it is important for us to talk to her staff, not to her. Her staff keeps things running. Or perhaps the unbearable sound of my Spanish urges her to push us off on someone else. In any case, she directs me to talk to Dr. Agnese Mancini, a resident scientist, and she is adamant about a man named Chuy Lucero. We must, she insists, talk to Chuy.

Agnese Mancini is an Italian scientist who earned her PhD here in Mexico and who currently works with Karen's organization. Her work, among other things, assesses the effectiveness of the ban on turtle hunting. In other words, she is doing what so many other environmental scientists do: She is documenting the obvious.

"Olive ridleys," she tells me, "are recovering. And the green turtles in Michoacán are now at numbers as high as they were in the 1970s and 1980s. They are recolonizing abandoned beaches. Why? Because of the protection of nesting beaches in the 1970s and the later ban on the turtle fishery."

We talk for a time about enforcement of regulations. She is not, she says, entirely comfortable with the topic. There are, she intimates, bad feelings in some of the communities. There are those with family members who have been jailed, and there are many others who take turtles but who, so far, have never been punished.

These are not necessarily bad people, she explains. They are fisherman from families who have always eaten turtle. They see turtles frequently and do not understand why such a common beast should be protected. They see fishermen from other communities, coming from faraway places in boats, taking turtles—taking, that is, their turtles. They know that politicians eat turtles, that public officials publicly consume turtles.

Just how many turtles are eaten in Baja villages up and down the coast? I have been told, straight-faced and with direct eye contact from local people, that turtles are seldom eaten, that most people here do not like the meat, that it is too strong for their taste, that there has never been much of a tradition of turtle-eating here. But on the other hand, surveys administered in a handful of communities some years ago, the most recent source of information I could find, suggest that at least one turtle was, at that time, consumed each week in each village. In bigger communities, more were consumed.

There are at least 150 permanent communities on the Baja coast. If the surveys are to be believed, yearly consumption would amount to 7,800 turtles.

I press Agnese for more information on the matter of poaching, because, more than ten years earlier, she had published a paper entitled, "To poach or not to poach an endangered species: Elucidating the economic and social drivers behind illegal sea turtle hunting in Baja California Sur, Mexico."

In that paper, she and her coauthors reported that as many as 35,000 sea turtles were illegally killed in the state of Baja California Sur every year well after turtles had been legally protected. Turtle meat was consumed in households, locally traded, even "sold via a network of well-organized black market circuits to local, regional, and even international markets." Turtle trafficking in at least some cases is tied to drug cartels.

For people who live in Mexico, for people with even a basic understanding of Mexico, none of this is especially surprising. But it is also not the sort of thing that one typically puts in writing for public dissemination. It is more the sort of thing that falls squarely in the large category of "topics to be avoided by foreigners who do not want to run afoul of the authorities." Or worse.

For the "To poach or not to poach" paper, the authors asked twelve known poachers if they would be willing to talk. Ten agreed, although two changed their minds once they understood the questions. All were males, aged twenty-eight to sixty. On average, they each took 1,328 turtles per year. Also on average, each turtle sold for 1,200 pesos, or about $58.

When not poaching turtles, they all worked as ordinary fishermen.

It is worth pausing here to consider this: Independent fishermen working out of the lower half of the Baja peninsula, fishermen legitimately working from the many registered small boats known as pangas, the kind of fishermen likely to have the opportunity to poach turtles, may earn as little as eighty or a hundred US dollars per week. Do the math. On average, a turtle poacher could earn $77,024 per year, a small fortune in Mexico, well over ten times more than the typical earnings of a legitimate fisherman—a handsome payoff, even if adjusted downward to account for the fact that fishermen have a well-known tendency to exaggerate, and even if adjusted further downward because fishermen, poaching or not, have to pay expenses out of their earnings.

Almost always, an argument can be made that crime does not pay. The paper, like most good scientific papers, applies calculations. In this case mathematics is used to determine if the crime of turtle poaching pays.

The mathematics look at the profits versus the costs of catching and selling turtles, of being caught, fined, and jailed, of paying bribes. Since almost all of the study participants had indeed been caught, and most had been caught more than once, the researchers had data on which to base the cost side of their analyses. Sometimes the cost of an encounter with law enforcement was a few dollars' worth of gasoline; the culprits simply escaped, being in possession of faster boats than those used by the authorities. Sometimes the cost involved bribes, which averaged $1,472, but which, as is always the case with bribes, were open to negotiation. Sometimes it involved fines. Although the law allows for fines of more than $11,000, they more typically came in at around $2,500. Very occasionally the cost involved jail time, during which lost income was considered a cost. Although the law allows for a penalty of up to nine years in prison, the few poachers interviewed who were actually sentenced served less than two years.

To quote from one of the men interviewed in the turtle poaching paper: "Of course there's some law enforcement, but most of the time you can easily escape. The inspectors have small boats so they can't catch us, on the other hand the marines are more efficient but most of the time they don't care about turtles. They look for guns and drugs. And sometimes when you get caught you just need to give them some money and there's no problem."

As an aside, I have in my life known a handful of criminals, ranging from drug dealers and burglars to an acquaintance convicted of accounting fraud cumulatively valued at many millions of dollars. To my knowledge, none of these people have run cost-benefit analyses. I suspect they would laugh at the very idea of it. They simply assumed they would not be caught.

But if a turtle poacher in Mexico ran a cost-benefit analysis, the poacher might be pleased by the results. It turns out that, in most cases, the crime of turtle poaching pays.

So if enforcement does not work very well, and if crime pays, what is the way forward? Wallace J. Nichols—the man behind *Blue Mind*—advocates a "conservation mosaic." Sure, keep laws in place to protect species and habitat, and enforce those laws, but attack the problem from other directions, find alternatives to "hard enforcement." Apply what some have called "soft power." Involve communities in turtle monitoring. Back environmental education and communication. Sponsor things like turtle statues and turtle murals and turtle paintings. Wear turtle T-shirts and necklaces. Convince everyone turtles are cool. Make people love turtles.

In other words, do the things Grupo Tortuguero does.

When I think of the work done by Grupo Tortuguero, it occurs to me that, in the course of writing this book, seldom a day goes by in which I do not hear good news about the fight against human-caused extinctions. It is not just Grupo Tortuguero that has found ways to protect biodiversity and to promote conservation.

Example one: A story of the slow recovery of the kākāpō, a chubby flightless parrot from New Zealand that manages to look both somewhat dim and undeniably cute. These birds, typically two feet long and weighing three or four pounds but sometimes reaching nine pounds, were easy targets for Māori hunters. The kiore, a Polynesian rat that the Māori brought with them when they settled New Zealand seven centuries ago, also took a toll, preying on eggs and chicks. By the time Europeans showed up, the Māori and their rats had eaten most of the kākāpō, and, in the case of the Māori but not their rats, turned them into feathery cloaks. European settlers worked on the remaining pockets of kākāpō, eating them but also catching them for zoos and private collectors. The poor birds were further harassed and killed by the black rats, cats, stouts, weasels, and ferrets set free by the settlers. Meanwhile, land clearing for crop fields, by both the Māori and the later arrivals, destroyed kākāpō's habitat.

Despite conservation efforts, including several attempts to relocate kākāpōs to offshore islands believed to be predator free, the birds were feared to be extinct by the early 1970s. But they were not. In 1977, on the island that the Māori called Rakiura, south of New Zealand's South Island, more than a hundred kākāpōs survived, but barely. Feral cats were killing them off with quiet efficiency.

The survivors were removed to four islands that were, more or less, predator free. Their wild diet was supplemented at feeding stations. Nests were monitored and protected from any predators that had slipped past control efforts. Some eggs and young were hand-reared by humans. Some birds were flown by helicopter to veterinarians who treated them for fungal infections. A handful of females were artificially inseminated.

The latest news puts the population at 252 birds. Perhaps this does not seem like a very big number, but it is more than nothing. It is also 25 percent greater than it had been only a year earlier and 100 percent greater than it had been only six years ago.

Example two: Australian scientists announce the discovery and naming of 139 new species. Among them are two blind weevils, a millipede with more than a thousand legs, an ant that raises caterpillars in exchange for their sugary secretions, four species of fish, and a brown frog with a call described as a bopping croak. Experts tell the media that maybe three-quarters of Australia's species remain undescribed. There are more species being discovered than being lost.

Example three: In an academic article, researchers evaluate green turtle populations that had been reintroduced in the Cayman Islands. The animals in question were the children and grandchildren of individuals released as long as fifty years ago by what was once a turtle farming company but that had, over time, reinvented itself as a conservation organization. Some of these released turtles had been raised in captivity for more than a year to give them a better chance of long-term survival, "head-started," as the practice is called, while others were released as hatchlings. Today's introduced populations appear to be healthy, genetically diverse, and loyal to the beaches where their parents and grandparents had been released. The authors saw their findings as not only good news for the turtles, but also for other reintroduction programs. It was possible, it seemed, for human interference to have positive outcomes on conservation.

But on second thought, are any of these good news stories? It is good news that we humans are saving or at least somewhat desperately trying to save the world's only flightless parrot. But it is bad news that we almost drove it to extinction, and especially bad news that this reality, this deadly relationship history between man and beast, is so commonplace as to be unremarkable. It is good news that there are more species being discovered, but what bearing do humanity's inventories, its score sheets of total species in existence, have on extinction rates? In terms of the extinction crisis, the discovery of new species is nothing more than interesting news, a broadening of our knowledge about the species with which we share a place and time. It is information with the capacity to confuse the issue, to convince the dullards among us, the pudden-heads, that human-caused extinctions may not be such a big deal after all. Regarding the success of turtle reintroductions, sure, that is good news of the same ilk as the news of the kākāpō, humans working hard to save what they had almost wiped out. But the same paper on turtle reintroductions underscores the costs involved. The authors choose to highlight economic drivers, writing, "Sea turtle reintroduction programs can, therefore, establish new populations but require scientific evaluation of costs and benefits." If sea turtles and other endangered species have to compete as commodities, if they have to be evaluated against various widgets, balanced against competing consumer interests, their future prospects dim considerably.

And, by the way, at least some of those just discovered species in Australia are hanging on by a thread, already in danger of extinction, and not at all likely to attract the kind of attention that has come to sea turtles, with no chance at all of coming out ahead in anything resembling a cost-benefit analysis.

When I consider that I hear good news about the fight against the extinction crisis on a daily basis, I realize that I hear bad news at least as frequently.

From *Yale Environment 360*, take this little tidbit: "The number of species facing extinction may be much higher than previously thought." Higher? That is indeed bad news.

Researchers came up with a model, a computer simulation using machine learning techniques. They associated extinction risks for more than twenty-eight thousand well-known species described in the Red List with the effects of climate change, invasive species, habitat loss, and hundreds of other threats. Their computer spit out the probability of extinction for each species, the PE. Then the researchers went to the Red List and found more than seven thousand "data deficient" species. These are species known to science, that have been named and described, but for which little additional information is available. For example, little may be known of their breeding habits, their population levels, of where they live, of how they do or do not migrate. Among these species were killer whales, hundreds of kinds of bats, many amphibians, and the pink fairy armadillo. PEs were calculated for the data deficient species, and what came out was the suggestion that they faced a risk of extinction greater than twice that of their better-understood cousins. The effort did not even consider newly discovered species and undiscovered species.

In the extinction game, there is a difference between good news and bad. The good news can be interpreted as either good or bad, or at least as news with both positive and negative aspects, while the bad news is just plain bad. The bad news comes with nothing even resembling an upside.

Come on world, give the would-be optimist a break.

Chuy Lucero has a small office near the front door of Grupo Tortuguero's headquarters. He is older than his colleagues. When we meet, he is sitting behind a computer wearing a brown jacket, a black COVID mask, and the white hard straw hat favored by the region's ranchers. On a shelf next to him are two turtle skulls, one from a green and one from a hawksbill, a prieta and a carey. On his wall is a clock shaped like a turtle. A small stuffed turtle toy sits on his desk, next to the computer.

At first I think he is a biologist, but I am wrong. He tells us that he is a pescador, a fisherman. He has been a pescador since he was six or seven years old. He learned the trade during school holidays. By his own accounting, he was seasoned in the use of nets, traps, and lines before he noticed girls for the first time.

As a boy and a young man, he tells us, he had no reason to think there was anything wrong with killing turtles. He and his friends and coworkers killed them for food and to sell. There was a season for lobster, for tuna, for shrimp, for octopus, for rock fish. And for sea turtles.

They ate the meat, mainly of the green turtle, but in his community they did not eat the eggs.

He jokes in the easy way of this part of Mexico about changing from a poor fisherman to a man who now knows how to use a computer. The joke grows to a comparison of biologists and fisherman. I point out that it is possible, in fact not even very challenging, to train a fisherman to work as a biologist, but training a biologist to work as a fisherman would present real difficulties.

Regarding Grupo Tortuguero's efforts to stop fishermen from killing turtles, the most important thing, he says, is to work with communities. By communities he means in general the small pueblos scattered up and down the coast, many difficult or impossible to access by road. And he has this to say: "What better way to influence communities than for fishermen to talk to fishermen?"

Although he spends a great deal of time talking to other fishermen, part of his job involves monitoring turtles. In this sense, he continues his career as a pescador, but what he catches he releases. And he manages, on behalf of Grupo Tortuguero and its member organizations, a database with information on thousands of turtles.

He assures me that the numbers of olive ridleys and blacks, the golfinas and the prietas, is up. But the numbers of leatherbacks, of laúds, is down.

The threats turtles face depend on the area. In some places tourist development destroys nesting beaches. In others the turtles drown in gillnets or on longline hooks, and as fish in the Gulf of California grow scarcer and smaller, fishing effort increases. Gillnet mesh, properly sized, can limit the risk to turtles, but in reality mesh size reflects prey size. Gillnets snare fish and other animals small enough to push a head or fin or beak through the mesh, so smaller mesh means smaller prey. And mesh size small enough to protect turtles may only catch the smallest of fish.

"Nosotros somos la mayor amenaza," he says. "We are the biggest threat." His "we" is all of us, the collective humanity.

I mention the man Lisanne and I had talked to in Timbabiche, the man who wished someone in his community could be paid to protect turtle nests. Chuy explains that someone in Timbabiche, or someone working on behalf of Timbabiche, would have to write a proposal to raise funds. It is not as though there is a treasure chest from which funds for turtle conservation can simply be scooped out and served around. There is a process. It is competitive.

I ask if he is optimistic about the future of turtles. "Poco poco," a little. But then he leans back in his chair and pauses to think. When he was young, he tells us, the job he has now did not exist—"no existió." Of course he knows some people are still eating turtles. He knows too that people are occasionally arrested and sent to prison for trafficking in turtles.

"But in this life you never know how things will turn out," he adds. "I killed and ate turtles once, but now I have probably saved more turtles than I have killed. Turtles have something for people. For me, they have changed my life."

If we constitute the biggest threat to turtles, as I have been told more than once, in fact repeatedly, it is worth considering exactly what constitutes "we."

Collectively, we are eight billion people.

For perspective, there are almost two people alive today for every year in the history of the Earth.

For another perspective, the planet supports about ten pounds of human for every pound of wild mammal still alive. If ten to one does not sound so bad, add in the weight of our livestock and the ratio more than doubles, with about twenty-three pounds of humans and their cows, pigs, and sheep to every pound of wild mammal.

Our chickens, for anyone who might wonder about such things, outweigh wild birds by almost three to one.

None of these numbers, incidentally, include our stuff. They do not consider our bicycles, cars, furniture, clothes, houses, driveways, bridges, office towers, airplanes, or boats. Taken as a whole, as us and our livestock and our stuff, we outweigh all other life on Earth combined.

This does not even consider our crops, our cornfields, our orchards, our pine plantations.

As to humans and sea turtles, we alone, without even considering our livestock or our stuff or our crops, outweigh them by something like five thousand to one.

NINE
Bahía de los Ángeles

We sail north again, to some degree retracing past steps, making our way toward Bahía de los Ángeles, a mere 330 straight-line miles more or less north. Nautical miles; in statute miles, in miles of the land, it would be 380 miles. But land prevents us from sailing in anything resembling a straight line. And worse, at this time of year, the prevailing winds come from the north, often with significant strength. It has been said more than once and frequently with a seasoning of expletives that one is better off sailing a thousand miles downwind than a hundred miles upwind. Sailboats cannot sail directly into the wind. They must zig and zag, zag and zig, always at an angle to the moving air, stalling completely if they venture within thirty or thirty-five degrees of the wind, sails emptying and then slapping, backwinded. Building seas create bumps over which the boat must climb and pound, forcing a steeper angle to the wind as the hull slips down wave faces. Such a voyage tends to be hard on vessel and crew alike.

But nevertheless we sail for Bahía de los Ángeles, where old friends, he a biologist and she a musician, keep a permanent camp on the beach. And of course there is something of turtles to be learned there.

Along the way, along those three hundred and thirty straight line miles, we stop fourteen times. We anchor at places with names like Bahía Falsa and Punta Mangles and Punta Chivato, as often as not hiding from the strongest of the north winds, dashing ahead when the winds abate. But at each stop we walk the beaches, always wondering, "Do turtles nest here?" When opportunities arise we ask strangers if they know of turtles nesting.

Many of the beaches are far too rocky for turtles. One is covered in a thick layer of seashells, hardly suitable for the digging of nests. On the mainland, all sandy beaches show signs of raccoons in the form of tracks. Most also reveal the presence of coyotes through tracks and scat and often in the howling of the animals themselves and even in the arrogant daylight presence of individuals and groups trotting up and down the beach, sniffing the sand, sitting to rest and peer out to sea. They appear entirely unconcerned by the presence of humans.

But when we stop on islands, we sometimes see sandy beaches with signs of neither raccoons nor coyotes.

I should mention too that at every stop, without exception, we find the remains of turtles. Once or twice we find entire or nearly entire shells, but more often we find pieces of bone or shell, unmistakable in their porosity and their shape.

We sail past a whale shark, twenty feet long, making its slow way northward, scooping up plankton, its long tail swinging gently back and forth. No one knows how many whale sharks remain in the world, but it is safe to bet that they are fewer in number than sea turtles. In 2016, the International Union for the Conservation of Nature ranked them as endangered. To quote from one of the organization's media releases: "Numbers of whale sharks, the world's largest living fish, have more than halved over the last 75 years as these slow-moving sharks continue to be fished and killed by ship propellers."

Within a few miles of Bahía de los Ángeles, we take shelter from a raging norther in the well-protected and uninhabited bay known as Puerto Don Juan. While listening to the wind I write for a while, catching up on notes, fleshing out ideas. But a turtle interrupts me.

I can see her short tail, making her a her rather than a him. She is a solid four feet long across her shell. She swims on the surface so close to our starboard bow that we could, if we were so inclined, touch her with a boat hook. We can plainly see the four costal scutes along each side of her carapace, and the three vertebral scutes, both marking her as a green turtle. She is the black variety of green turtle, a prieta or tortuga negra. She is the same kind of turtle that we had found dead, lying on the seabed in seventy-five feet of water near Punta Púlpito two months before. That one had also been a female.

For a moment, her presence fills me with joy. But only for a moment, because that is all it takes to see that this animal is far from healthy. Her presence so close to our boat serves as a warning. Turtles in the Gulf of California tend to be cautious around boats, perhaps remembering past encounters with humanity. But more importantly she floats high in the water. She tries to dive, headfirst as turtles do, but her hind flippers thrash around on the surface. With what appears to be a monumental effort, she pulls her body downward, disappearing into the darkness of the plankton filled water, but within two or three seconds she pops back up, tail first.

She is so close to our boat that when she lifts her head to breathe I hear her sudden exhalation over the noise of the wind and I can see milky whiteness clouding what should be marvelously black eyes.

The sight drains me. Here is a turtle that as an egg escaped coyotes and raccoons, that as a hatchling evaded sea birds and predatory fish, that as a growing animal dodged gillnets and seines and that refused the bait of longlines. Here is a turtle that is at least thirty years old, based on her size, and that could be, maybe, as old as I am. Now she appears very sick. And if she is too sick to dive, she cannot eat. Her chances of survival seem slim.

I watch her until she swims well away from the boat. She struggles to submerge, then rests, then struggles again, then rests.

Elsa, the turtle veterinarian, is on the other side of the Gulf of California. There is nothing I can do but watch. In fact, the law does not allow me to help. There is no Good Samaritan clause in Mexico when it comes to sea turtles, which is just as well, because while many people might be overwhelmed with concern, few would have the skills needed to assist a sick turtle.

There is before me the tragedy of a single life, an individual turtle that, in all likelihood, will soon be dead. But I take solace from the possibility that at her age she may have nested six or seven times by now. She may have laid upward of two thousand eggs in her lifetime.

Then it occurs to me that this is a poor form of solace. If only one of every thousand eggs survives into adulthood, the two thousand eggs that she laid have resulted in a total of two adults. Perhaps she has replaced herself and one of her mates, and now she is dying. It is this kind of math that underscores the need for turtle stewardship, for efforts to help the young, to increase their odds of survival.

The next day we see the turtle again, still marooned on the surface.

We row ashore and walk for an hour through dry scrubby desert interrupted by hills of crumbled igneous rock and steep arroyos to reach the beach surrounding the next bay south. And there on the beach we find another turtle, the same species and sex and size as the turtle swimming near our boat, but this one has been dead for at least several days. Its head is gone, but three of its flippers and its tail remain intact. It has not been slaughtered. Perhaps it drowned in a gillnet. Maybe it died of natural causes, possibly of the same ailment afflicting the still living animal in Puerto Don Juan.

I do not know why coyotes have not more thoroughly scavenged the carcass.

Another day passes and we see our sick turtle again, still unable to submerge.

We row to a different shoreline and climb high above the bay, walking through large stands of coach whip and cactus. The still vicious north wind lashes plants and walkers alike.

Scattered across the slopes we find outcrops of limestone, some rich with marine fossils, with the ancient remains of sand dollars and snails and bivalves. The hills here, like so many in this area, were uplifted from the sea. We also find what archaeologists sometimes call a chert mine, signs of people chipping away at an outcrop of hardened silica dioxide, used in the not-so-ancient past to make spear tips and knives and scrapers.

Returning downhill, but still at an elevation of several hundred feet, we find the partial and broken remains of a turtle shell, bleached by the sun. It is impossible to know how long ago it might have died. Two years? Ten? Surely not a hundred? Likewise, it is impossible to know how it got here, so high above the beach, so far from the sea and across rough, rocky country.

Finding the remains here reminds me of a seal found more than a mile inland in northern Alaska, apparently lost and in need of help. But the seal had obviously walked or rather shuffled on its flippers and belly across the tundra, whereas this Baja mountainside would be impossible terrain for a sea turtle.

The remains make me think, too, of Ernest Hemingway's "The Snows of Kilimanjaro," of his description of the frozen leopard carcass near Kilimanjaro's western summit, well above the cat's normal habitat. Hemingway's words, which I read decades ago, remain imprinted in my memory: "No one has explained what the leopard was seeking at that altitude."

I could say the same of this turtle, but I suspect it was dragged here, hauled up the hill by humans and for unknown reasons abandoned on the tough terrain.

The wind subsides overnight and in the morning we sail to the village of Bahía de los Ángeles, anchoring in front of our friends' camp, just south of the village itself.

Steinbeck described the village as it was in 1940: "There were new buildings, screened and modern, and on a tiny airfield a plane sat." He harbored suspicions that guns were being smuggled into the bay, weapons that would be used in an upcoming election, but that may have just been a product of Steinbeck's imagination, dramatic seasoning for his writing. Although there were new buildings, the community had been around for some time, supporting miners who extracted gold and silver from the surrounding hills since at least the nineteenth century. There were also ranches on which families ran cattle and sheep. Before that, there were missions in the area. And before the missions, several thousand Cochimi called this place home.

Fewer than a thousand people live here now, year-round, extracting a living from visiting tourists interested in what remains an end-of-the-road kind of place, isolated despite the paved highway built well after Steinbeck's time.

Our friend the biologist tells us that when he first started coming here, decades ago, he would sometimes see turtle meat for sale in local shops. On at least one occasion, he saw an entire turtle carcass, its shell sawed open to provide ready access to its flesh, hanging in a store.

But no more. That has changed. To find turtle meat now, one would have to know someone. One would have to buy the meat from an unsavory character willing to ignore both the law and the changing ethos.

A veterinarian lives nearby. She was born here, the daughter of the community's much loved but now retired physician, who happens to be with her when we meet. Both speak perfect English. They tell me about their whale shark study, which the doctor had started decades ago out of personal interest and that the daughter continues today. Whale sharks visit the bay every summer.

I ask them how the whale sharks are doing.

"Not good," the doctor tells me. "The numbers are very low. Something is happening. Something is not right." We talk about how they tag the whale sharks and he shows me one of their tags. To deploy them, a swimmer approaches a whale shark and when within a few feet of the animal launches a sharp-tipped tiny harpoon using a Hawaiian sling, a type of hand spear. The tip is attached by stainless steel wire to a numbered label that identifies the animal. The whale sharks here are small, which is to say up to twenty or twenty-five feet long. The work is not for the faint of heart.

His daughter, the veterinarian, grew up swimming with whale sharks. She has tagged more whale sharks than the vast majority of humans will ever see.

I show her a video of our sick turtle. The animal, she says, suffers from what is broadly known as buoyancy disorder. In the parlance of turtle conservation, the animal is "corking," that is, submerging or almost submerging before floating back up. The cause is trapped gas somewhere in her body cavity. If the animal were to be taken to a well-equipped clinic, a CT scan or an MRI could determine exactly where the gas is trapped. It might be possible to remove the gas.

Possible sources of the gas? Lung tears, infections, tumors, trauma.

I ask if she would be interested in trying to help, if she would come with us back to the bay of Puerto Don Juan. She confirms what I already suspect. She cannot. It would be illegal. She does not have the appropriate permits. Even with whale sharks, the research permits held by her and her father do not allow her to help distressed individuals.

Changing topics, I ask them if anyone here still eats turtle. The answer is a variation of one I have heard up and down the coast. In effect, fishermen who pull dead turtles up in their nets may occasionally eat them, rather than throwing the carcasses away, but they no longer sell them. There is no longer a market for turtles.

I ask the doctor when he last knew of turtle meat being sold here. When did it stop?

"It was not immediate," he says. "When it became illegal, the trade slowed down. But I think I last saw a truckload of turtle meat five or six years ago." Confirming what I have heard from others, he shares his belief that turtle meat has gone up in value sufficiently to attract the attention of organized crime. It is widely known that the cartels are engaged in the harvest and sale of the dried bladders from totoaba, the same large fish I had heard about months earlier from Elsa in San Carlos, the drum endemic to the Gulf of California whose swim bladder is worth more by weight than most drugs to Chinese buyers who, for reasons that are hard to understand, attribute medicinal qualities to the organ. They believe the swim bladders, properly prepared and ingested, can cure arthritis and perhaps other ailments.

If the totoaba's dried swim bladder is seen as medicinal, what about turtle meat and eggs? It turns out that that some who live in desperate need of an artificial sexual motivator see turtle meat and eggs as aphrodisiacs. The male turtle, after all, has a disproportionately long penis. But aside from this, many are attracted to novel foods, to something that adds variety to their diets. Turtle meat may not be very tasty, but at least it is something different. And the border between Mexico and California remains laughably porous. Illegally harvested Gulf of California turtles find their way into the United States and further afield, wall or no wall.

We return to the topic of the sick turtle. It is a shame to see a female that seems to be of reproductive age dying. Is there nothing we can do? But no. There is no one here, as far as the veterinarian and her father know, with the skills or the permits required to help a sick turtle. But they put me in touch with Erika, a woman in town who has, for well over a decade, worked with turtles in Bahía de los Ángeles.

A strengthening breeze whips up dust devils in the desert. Conditions force us back to the protection of Puerto Don Juan. Before we reach the safety of the anchorage, winds exceed thirty knots.

While it blows, I search for the sick turtle. Scanning the waves and the shoreline through binoculars, I see nothing. The next day, when the wind abates, I paddle around the bay in my kayak, once, twice, three times. For a moment I think I have found her, but the hump in the water several hundred feet away turns out to be a resting sea lion. No turtles to be seen.

A healthy adult sea turtle manages thirty knot winds with equanimity. It has to. Thirty knot winds are not at all uncommon.

In fact, a healthy adult sea turtle can manage hurricane-strength winds. Loggerheads and hawksbills, instrumented with tags that recorded their whereabouts and their diving behavior, have been followed through hurricanes and tropical storms. The animals simply adjusted to the storm conditions, perhaps spending less time on the surface and diving deeper to avoid turbulence, but survived well enough and returned to their normal behaviors when the weather settled. In one case, a loggerhead that had been in nesting mode when the storm arrived drifted northward and offshore with storm driven currents; when the wind died, she was well over a hundred miles from her nesting beach and at least forty miles from shore. She swam toward shore, turned to the south and swam some more, returning in short order right back to her nesting beach.

But a corking turtle in strong winds might not fare so well. Our turtle might, for example, have been blown onto a beach and pounded in the surf. Or she might have been blown onto rocks. Or she might, in her slow decline toward death by starvation, have become exhausted in the waves. Too weak to continue, she might have drowned.

We do not find our sick turtle in the bay, and we do not find her carcass stranded on the beaches or in the rocks of the shoreline. It is possible, I tell myself, that she survived. It is possible she eventually expelled the intracoelomic gases that made her bob like a cork. It is possible that before the winds came she regained her ability to swim, that she is out there somewhere now, living her turtle life. And that, in the spring, she will find a nesting beach and lay hundreds of eggs.

Optimism is, if nothing else, free.

The wind dies and we anchor once again in front of the village of Bahía de los Ángeles, this time closer to the center of town. I watch smoke rise against the backdrop of towering coastal mountains. The gray plume—someone is burning garbage—extends vertically a hundred feet, two hundred feet, and then spreads slowly, evenly. Not a breath of wind carries it east or west or north or south. The sea around us stands millpond-flat.

A turtle raises its head between me and the smoke, four or five boat lengths away, then submerges, leaving a halo of ripples that propagate outward, intercepting two Pacific loons diving nearby, a raft of eared grebes, a flock of elegant terns, and half a dozen pelicans. By the time the ripples pass the birds, the turtle is gone.

Sometimes turtles surface after no more than a minute or two, close to where they dive. Other times, as now, their tolerance for apnea exceeds my tolerance for patient vigilance. Instead I turn toward the broad beach and its even broader fringing mudflat. A snowy egret and a reddish egret forage there, along with two whimbrels and a long-billed curlew. Overhead, an osprey glides, sharing the sky with a few dozen yellow-footed gulls.

Later, ashore, I visit the café at Camp Archelon. Archelon is not an ordinary name for a camp. It is the name of a genus of sea turtle that lived in the company of dinosaurs, known only from the area around what is now the Dakotas. In *Archelon*'s time, the present-day Dakotas were part of a long arm of saltwater stretching north and south through North America, joining the Gulf of Mexico with the Arctic Ocean.

The head of *Archelon* was as large as the entire carapace of an olive ridley. Its own carapace could be fifteen feet across. Sadly, it was lost sixty-six million years ago, long before the first humans breathed.

I ask Antonio Resendiz, the young man at the counter, "Why *Archelon*?" He explains his parents were marine biologists, that they had set up this camp as a marine field station. His father—also named Antonio Resendiz—has passed away, and now he runs the place as an eco-resort for campers, with places for tents and trailers as well as a few bungalows and the café. But he is too busy to talk more about their camp just now. This is Semana Santa, the holy week, the days leading to Easter. In Mexico it is roughly equivalent in terms of frenetic celebratory activity to Christmas week in the United States. I will have to come back another day.

Among other things, the café offers the fastest internet connection in a town without cell towers, without cables connecting it to the outside world. I send a note, some photographs, and a short video of the corking turtle to Judith and Elsa back in San Carlos. My signal moves through repeaters to cross the mountains, and despite the realities of Semana Santa Judith responds right away: "That would be tough to experience—heartbreaking for me." Elsa, too, responds very quickly, saying that she thinks she can get a permit for the veterinarian here in Bahía de los Ángeles. I have to tell her it is too late. The turtle is gone.

Elsa sends a photograph of a turtle in a holding pool, a black green, a prieta. She too had been found corking. Now, after a week under treatment, she is eating. A second turtle is in treatment, an adult olive ridley. Elsa does not say why the olive ridley was captured, but she does share that the animal is "doing better."

Back aboard, I sit in the cockpit once again watching birds and searching for turtles. I share the evening with two species of egrets, pelicans, long-billed curlews, whimbrels, ospreys, American oystercatchers, eared grebes, and a few species of gulls and sandpipers.

Despite the murder of the first real Florida game warden Guy Bradley in 1905, plume hunting ended. Bird populations bounced back. But fifty years later a government biologist warned about the dangers of a pesticide that worked miracles in the world of mosquito control. The pesticide was every bit as deadly to birds as the plume hunters had been. The government biologist was Rachel Carson, the pesticide was dichlorodiphenyltrichloro-ethane, widely known as DDT, and the warning came in the form of her iconic 1962 book, *Silent Spring.*

What Carson warned of was not entirely straightforward. DDT targeted bugs, and a small quantity killed them. Fish ate bugs, both alive and dead. The DDT in their insect meals did not easily kill fish, but with each bug a fish ate the DDT load in that fish's body increased. Certain birds—many birds—ate fish. Each time a bird ate a DDT-laden fish, its own load of DDT increased. In the jargon of the field, DDT loads were biomagnified, concentrated along the food web.

Some birds died from DDT poisoning. Other birds carrying high loads of DDT laid thin-shelled eggs. When those birds sat on their own eggs, the shells broke open. A thin-shelled, breakable egg does not produce chicks. And so the brown pelican, the osprey, the golden eagle, the bald eagle, and the peregrine falcon all wandered closer and closer to the brink of extinction.

My morning bird sightings passed almost unnoticed, unconsidered. But in retrospect, with the day behind me, with time to think, they were remarkable. Stopping hunting and controlling the release of poisons works. Taking action to fight extinction has consequences. It is not just a matter of a few species, of egrets and pelicans and ospreys and maybe turtles, but of hundreds of species. Certain whales and dolphins, manatee, various fish, a number of the great apes, alligators—all saved, at least for now.

Lisanne interrupts my thoughts. She tells me she has just read an article about the worldwide decline in insects. There are, for example, nine hundred million fewer monarch butterflies than there were twenty years ago. And 87 percent of the world's supply of rusty-patched bumblebees has disappeared.

A complete list would be tedious. Here I do not refer to a list of extinctions, which admittedly would also be tedious. No, here I refer to a list of diminished numbers, of crashed populations. Suffice it to say that headlines proclaiming an insect Armageddon are not hyperbolic. As the author of this particular article explained, the windshield phenomenon is real. A short drive that would once have left a car windshield coated with dead bugs can now be undertaken with impunity, without the need for windshield wipers or washers.

My wife is a wonderful woman and a well-trained marine biologist, but no one would accuse her of being held captive by her emotions. At times she can be frustratingly logical and unreasonably reasonable. Overreaction is not among her skillsets. She is not one to be fooled by either good news or bad.

But in this case, she says matter-of-factly that the article makes her want to cry.

No one as yet knows why insects are on the decline. Insecticides are a good bet. As well as habitat loss, including that caused by climate change. Possibly exotic species introductions play a role. Almost certainly, humanity lurks somewhere close to the root cause.

I meet Erika Santacruz Lopez in a restaurant overlooking the harbor. She is Spanish, from Madrid, although she now lives here, brought to this out-of-the-way village originally by a scholarship, but then held here by a combination of marriage, a love of the place, and of course sea turtles. She talks in the animated style of many Europeans, and especially southern Europeans, with eye movements and subtle posture changes that energize her words, that express delight in communication.

She is behind Grupo Tortuguero de Bahía de los Ángeles. Today, on our first meeting, she wears her organization's T-shirt. The organization is one of the many grassroots groups operating under the umbrella of Grupo Tortuguero de las Californias in La Paz.

"Yes," she assures me with a smile, "I know Karen Oceguera and Chuy Lucero and Agnese Mancini. In fact Agnese will be here near the end of the month to monitor turtles. Do you want to go with us? If you are here you can join us."

All of this is said within the first five minutes of our meeting, and all of it is accompanied by a wonderful smile in unfaltering brisk English despite her claim that she does not really speak English.

At times, she admits, it has been frustrating to work with turtles. No, not so much the turtles, but with people. She is like me here, she tells me, a foreigner.

She shares the story of two local women who happened upon a nest as it was hatching, a nest out near the lighthouse. She points to the lighthouse across the bay, a structure badly in need of fresh paint, apparently abandoned at the end of a sandy point. The women reported the nest, she explains, and the local government authorities came with unusual promptness. They immediately chased off onlookers.

"No," Erika says. "This was a big mistake. This was an opportunity to talk to people about turtles, about why it is so important to protect them, and instead they sent everyone away!"

She felt that education was important, that it should be a priority, but the government officials were not interested in educating the public. She talked to fishermen—it is important, she exclaims, to work directly with fishermen—but they were not comfortable in the role of educators. They wanted to catch and tag turtles, but they did not want to talk to the public or to visit classrooms. Knowing the community, she knew that mothers were the educators. She applied for government funds to expand the already existing monitoring program to something bigger, something that would support education through local women. "In truth," she says, "the turtle is a chance to do something beautiful for the community."

More funds came from other agencies. Monitoring continued through the capture and tagging of turtles but also through counting nests and hatchlings and through the documentation of strandings—that is, of dead turtles found on beaches. Nests were of course protected and sometimes relocated. But education became a cornerstone of her program.

Here, this is about more than mere classroom appearances. It involves activities such as having the wives of fishermen accompany their husbands at sea, giving the women a chance to see how the men earn the family's living. She encouraged fishermen to walk the beaches with their wives, who were now at least sometimes being paid to look for turtle nests. It also involved what she calls Campo Tortuguero, in which children—and here she means children of all ages, including octogenarians—have the opportunity to see adult turtles up close during monitoring exercises.

Of course classrooms are part of it too. "It is common for one of the children, for a child of seven or eight years old," she says, "to talk about a turtle that his grandfather has tied up behind the house." This creates an awkward situation. She certainly cannot criticize a grandfather, an abuelo. She cannot, for example, say, "I know your grandfather and he is a son of a bitch and a poacher." She is forced to settle for something more tactful, something along the lines of, "Things are changing." Or, "Things are different now than when your grandfather was young." Along with, "Maybe for your grandfather it is okay, but you are young and the world is changing, and it is not okay any longer." But really, what is most important is putting the children with turtles, with adult turtles or with hatchlings. It is an issue of giving them the chance to think about turtles in a new way, as something other than food. What is important is showing young people a different way of seeing their world and then giving them a chance to make up their own minds.

During the nesting season, she and her colleagues walk four beach zones covering a total of about nine miles of shoreline. On foot. This means that among them they walk a cumulative eighteen miles each day, across a zone and back. I have walked on the beaches here. The sand is generally soft. In summer, during the nesting season, the heat can be appalling. In the twilight hours, rattlesnakes are not uncommon. This would not be easy walking.

Their permits allow them to use all-terrain vehicles, but they do not because they do not want the tourists to think that driving on the beach is okay. "It is not okay," she says.

When they find a nest they sometimes move it, but only if necessary. They do not have an incubation facility, so moving a nest usually means only moving it to slightly higher ground. They protect the nests with fencing. As hatching time approaches, someone camps next to the nest, waiting for the youngsters to emerge. This sort of camping is hot. Buggy. Uncomfortable.

Last year, their nests produced 885 young turtles. But several nests did not survive. She thinks they may have been too dry, that perhaps sprinkling the nests with water would increase survival rates.

She and her colleagues learn from other Grupo Tortuguero organizations, but the fact is, and she is adamant about this, every place is different. "There is a general protocol but every area has to be adaptable. What works in La Paz or San Carlos or San Basilio may or may not work here." That is why a network like Grupo Tortuguero de las Californias is so important. It allows independence and self-reliance. It allows improvisation. It facilitates community pride. All while allowing the free flow of experience and ideas.

"Many times researchers come here to work with our turtles," she says. "Bahía de los Ángeles is famous for its turtles. Especially in the 1990s, there was so much research here with black turtles. But the researchers would come, collect their data, and then leave. Maybe they published papers, but no one here ever saw those papers. The researchers never came back to tell the community what they found."

Years ago, I had heard similar complaints—visiting researchers harvesting data but never to be seen again—in remote villages of arctic Alaska.

She tells me that the blacks—the black green turtles—usually lay their eggs far to the south and on the mainland side, on the beaches of Michoacán. Most of the nesting turtles here are olive ridleys. The nesting range of the olive ridley seems to be expanding along with the number of nesters. They are finding new nesting beaches—beaches not previously known to be used by turtles—close to Bahía de los Ángeles.

It is more than just fishermen and their wives who are involved. The entire community knows about the turtles and that they are in trouble. But even so, poaching continues. During the height of the pandemic, it was very bad. In 2020, 74 dead turtles were found in the area. People needed to eat.

"Sometimes someone will say that a dead turtle was killed by a coyote" she says. "And coyotes do eat eggs. But we talk about coyotes de dos patas. Coyotes with two legs. Poachers."

As I have done with others, I ask her about enforcement. "In Mexico," she says, "it is complicated."

I ask if she is optimistic about the future of turtles.

She started seeing populations recover about ten years ago. "The olive ridleys and the blacks are increasing," she says. "The older fishermen here say they have never seen so many." Regarding the leatherback, the loggerhead, and the hawksbill—the laúd, the caguama, and the carey—she is not as sure. But, and she says this with a smile, "Mexico is a tortuguero country."

And, after a pause, "Yes, we can be optimists."

On another occasion, I run into Erika in a café. A young man sits next to her. He makes his living fishing. I will not name him.

He tells me that, although he protects turtles now, as a child he ate turtles.

"It was awful," he says in perfect English, "a horrible taste. And after eating it, I could smell it in my skin." He swipes his right hand across the skin of his left arm, as if to sweep away the recollected odor.

"Prieto?" I ask. The black green turtle?

"Yes, of course. That is all anyone eats here. In other places they eat any turtle they can find, but the people here will only eat prietos."

Erika chimes in, saying many of her acquaintances occasionally admit to eating turtle. Especially around Easter time, around now, Semana Santa. Some people here might try to impress relatives from out of town, from, say, San Diego, with meals that include turtle.

I tell them of the man in San Basilio who told me that people there would never go back to eating turtles, no matter how abundant they become. The taste, he had said, was too strong, disagreeable for people raised on fish and beef and chicken. The talk turns to gradual change, to generational change, to the need for perseverance.

"Even if it takes three generations," I say, "that is not so long. That is not so terribly long for a patient philosophical fellow."

Semana Santa passes, and I visit Camp Archelon once again. I ask Antonio if he knows Erika. This is a stupid question. They are both long-term residents of Bahía de los Ángeles, and it would be all but impossible for them not to know one another.

"Erika met my father in 2012, so there was some continuity between what she is doing now and what my father was doing," he explains. But more importantly he tells me that, in his father's time, for example in the 1980s, a typical season of monitoring might yield forty turtles. "For him this was really special. Turtles were going extinct, but he and his colleagues could find forty in a season." He pauses before moving back to the connection with Erika. "Now Erika sometimes finds forty turtles in a single day of monitoring," he says. "Forty in one day!"

He shows me a binder full of copies of his father's papers. Among these are budgets for long-ago projects, a notice about a turtle education program in Turkey, a scientific paper about genetic markers used to track the movements of Mexican turtles, a report to a treaty organization, a number of newspaper and magazine articles about his work, and scientific papers he had authored or coauthored. There is also a photograph showing scientists at a folding table on the beach at night. They appear to be conducting the serious business of research with the aid of half a dozen empty beer cans and a well-sampled bottle of tequila. Another photograph shows a turtle in a net hanging from a spring scale in front of a white cylindrical tank. All of the photographs are in black and white.

From the binder, one example of Antonio Senior's own work: "First confirmed east–west transpacific movement of a loggerhead sea turtle, *Caretta caretta*, released in Baja California, Mexico," from *Pacific Science* in 1998. It begins, "The occurrence of loggerhead turtles, *Caretta caretta*, in the Gulf of California and along the Pacific coast of the Baja California peninsula, Mexico, has been puzzling." Why? Because there were plenty of loggerhead adults in the waters surrounding the Baja, but no nesting beaches, no known sources of hatchlings. He—Antonio Senior—released an adult female that had been captured by a local fisherman and raised in captivity for eight years. Four hundred and seventy-eight days later a different fisherman, near Kyushu, Japan, caught the turtle.

This story, of course, sounds familiar. It should. Wallace J. Nichols coauthored the paper with Antonio Senior and later wrote about it in his book, *Blue Mind*.

The binder of papers includes a letter from Japan, written by a turtle conservation organization there in somewhat stilted English. The letter contains a few polite words, the number of the tag found on the turtle that the fisherman caught, and a few notes. Under the heading "Condition," meant to be the space in which the health of the tagged animal could be described, the letter simply says "dead in the set net." There are different kinds of set nets, but in this case it would probably have been a gillnet tied to stakes in shallow water.

When we are done looking through the binder, Antonio tells me about growing up with the turtle conservation movement, as the son of his father. "When I was a child," he says, "I was sometimes not invited to parties. I could not be invited because turtle was being served. People knew my father." Antonio is now thirty-one years old, so when he talks about his childhood, he is talking about the late nineties and the turn of the century.

And this: "My father was sometimes approached by important people from town or from nearby. A police chief, a teacher, even a mayor. They approached him because they wanted a turtle. He kept turtles in tanks down the beach, and people knew he had turtles there, and they wanted to eat his turtles. Sometimes they threatened him. When he refused to share a turtle, to provide a turtle for a fiesta, someone might say something like, 'It would be terrible if something bad happened to you.' And sometimes a turtle in a tank would disappear, stolen to become someone's dinner."

From a few minutes later in the same conversation: "My dad was an educated man, a scientist, and he worked very hard, but there is no money in conservation. We always got by, we always had enough, but he earned something like four hundred dollars a month." In part because of this, Antonio says that he did not pursue a career in conservation science.

But in fact he did pursue a career in conservation, if not in conservation science. Here at Camp Archelon the environmental theme prevails. The café does not use plastic. Signs educate guests. Locals, seeing the guests, are themselves inspired. He may not be a scientist, but he is a conservationist.

"When locals do conservation," he says, "that is best for the town. Foreigners telling us how to do things does not work so well. But when locals come to the café and hear foreigners talking about turtles or see them paying to look at whale sharks in the bay, they get it. It is education."

Before parting, he tells me that his concern for his home is that it could very quickly change. If someone builds a bar here, a real bar, things could change overnight. Because the road all the way to San Diego is paved now, a different kind of tourist could come in. This sort of thing happens fast, he says. With bars comes crime.

He shares his view of consumerism. "The problem," he says, "is that we have too much." He says this specifically in reference to plastics and to waste, but it takes on a broader meaning. He lives simply at the research station that has become an eco-resort, taking his joy not from things but from day-to-day life on a sun-bitten stretch of sand and rock between the mountains and the sea. This is, on the one hand, the kind of conversation that has become stereotypical among environmentalists. It is, on the other hand, nothing short of moving.

Later, walking along the beach toward our anchorage, I notice abandoned tanks in the dunes. Exploring, I find broken glass and old signs scattered around circular concrete pools, recognizable but beyond any reasonable state of repair, with sand heaped against their upwind edges. These are the tanks that once held sea turtles, built by the late Antonio Resendiz and his colleagues, maybe with the help of his then very young son. One of these may once have held the loggerhead turtle that swam across the Pacific only to die in a Japanese net.

For perspective, we have looked at two timelines, each compressing millions of years into a single day, the first capturing the entirety of Earth's history and the second the whole of turtle evolution. For yet another perspective, we can do the same for humans. But where should midnight be set? Is it best to start the clock with the appearance of the first hominids, the first human-like ancestors, such as *Pierolapithecus catalaunicus*, that may have staggered around in a knuckle-dragging manner just shy of twelve million years ago? Or do we start with the first appearance of the genus *Homo*, the genus that includes us, that begins perhaps with *Homo habilis*, in which case midnight would coincide with a bit more than two million years ago? Or do we set midnight at the appearance of our own species, with *Homo sapiens*, which some would place as early as half a million years ago, while others would put at only about 195,000 years ago, the confusion stemming in part from what was a slow transition away from more ancient forms. The exact timing of the birth of the first of our species, clearly and permanently differentiated from *Homo erectus* and *Homo heidelbergensis*, remains and could always remain a matter of debate and opinion.

For simplicity, midnight is set at three hundred thousand years ago, as reasonable a time as many others to claim the birth of this new beast, this first modern human. On such a clock, stone tools have already been around for more than a week, and fires cooked yesterday's dinner and maybe yesterday's lunch. This supposedly smarter version of human, *Home sapiens*, inherits both tools and the use of fire from his predecessors.

For most of the day, nothing much happens. The total human population hovers in the hundreds of thousands, ranging up and down, reaching heights of as many as ten million and depths of as little as perhaps a few hundred thousand. Around dinner time, massive volcanic eruptions and related climate change sucker punch the planet, putting humans in the position of holding on by the thinnest of threads. There may have been fewer than ten thousand human survivors, leaving behind the characteristic signature of a genetic bottleneck.

But we carry on, along the way killing off various ground sloths, saber-tooth cats, a true American horse, a few terrestrial crocodiles, Stellar's sea cows, dodos, and a host of others.

Around eleven at night, fairly late in the game, agriculture emerges. Human numbers grow slowly but steadily.

In the last few minutes, humans invent vaccines and antibiotics. We use both on ourselves and our livestock. In these same busy minutes, we also invent chemical fertilizers. Agriculture takes us from a few million to almost two billion in ten thousand years, but the inventions of the last two centuries—the last few minutes—take us to eight billion.

As to conservation laws? The first show up, not coincidentally, in these very same last few minutes.

As to the concerted effort to save turtles and other creatures, this changing of our ways on a noticeable scale, the passing of the Endangered Species Act in the United States and the widespread adoption of the Convention on International Trade in Endangered Species of Wild Fauna and Flora, this seemingly late in the day Hail Mary pass attempt to dampen the extinction crisis: They started just fifteen seconds ago.

All of which is to say that humanity, for most of our existence, was a bit player on planet Earth. It was about an hour ago that we started causing big problems, less than a couple of minutes ago that the extinction crisis gained a firm toehold, and maybe thirty seconds ago that we began to start thinking seriously about cleaning up the mess we created.

When it comes to human endeavors, one cannot expect miracles to occur in the passing of a handful of seconds.

TEN

Puerto Peñasco

We sail from Bahía de los Ángeles across the Canal de Ballenas, the Channel of Whales, to Isla Ángel de la Guarda. The distance is a mere seventeen miles. Despite the promise of the channel's name we see no whales.

I have been eager for some time to visit the island, the second largest in the Gulf of California, some forty-one miles long and eight or ten miles across, covering 361 square miles. Despite those many miles, reports dating back hundreds of years claim that the island has no permanent freshwater sources, and therefore the island supports no large mammals. The island does not harbor a single pueblo, ranch, mine, or settlement of any kind. Its terrain, in places, is rugged, and one can fairly say that parts of the island probably have not been explored by humans.

Isla Ángel de la Guarda was not long ago part of the Baja peninsula, noting that not long ago, in this context, indicates one to three million years. The two localities share the same geology, the same rocks that flowed freely in the Miocene, between five and twenty-five million years ago, well before the rifting that would create the Gulf of California occurred. The island is a reminder of the youthful nature of the Gulf of California, the youngest sea on Earth. The turtles that witnessed the birth of the Gulf of California had been among the living for millions of years, swimming around out in the Pacific, when the ground split open and was flooded, first from connections to the west, and over time from what is today the opening to the south.

Despite the short distance from the peninsula and the short time that has passed since the island's birth, the Canal de Ballenas is several thousand feet deep, its water sitting on top of the tear in the Earth's crust, the rift that separated the mainland and the island. The place is as emblematic of plate tectonics as one might hope to see even within the broader Gulf of California, where plate tectonics is evident everywhere.

Among the things I hope to find here are turtle nesting beaches, long reaches of them, free of actual coyotes and mostly free of coyotes de dos patas.

But I am, at least at first, disappointed. The island is steep-sided and rocky. Surveying several miles, I see mostly cliffs and beaches of mixed cobble and heavy gravel, entirely unsuited to nesting turtles. I visit one of them by kayak, coming upon nests of yellow-footed gulls just above the tideline. They are ground nesters, users of hollowed out divots in the gravel and cobble. They sometimes line their nests with sargassum and bits of driftwood. The nests hold eggs roughly the size of those produced by chickens but with dark irregular spots on a creamy background. A few of the eggs have hatched, liberating downy chicks that share the colors of the eggs.

Two nests hold pipping chicks, their tiny beaks poking from within cracked shells.

Angry guardians swoop upon me from the sky, shrieking, screaming. I beat a hasty retreat, leaving them to themselves.

A beach that is no good for turtles is, at least, good for gulls. And I have only seen one short stretch of the shoreline. There is every reason to hope for long stretches of sand elsewhere.

Paddling away, a sea lion accompanies me before losing interest, and I see three turtles, probably prietas, in less than thirty minutes.

We stop for a few nights in the bay of Esta Ton, a well-known tiny anchorage almost surrounded by a narrow strip of sand. But two fishermen are camped here. The debris field of cans and plastic wrappers that surrounds their camp indicates frequent and long-term use.

On our first evening, I go ashore to talk to the fishermen. They are divers, working, they say, five hours each day, breathing compressed air from a long yellow hose attached to a gasoline-driven compressor mounted in the middle of their panga, scouring the bottom for anything they can sell. It is the same kind of compressor and hose that Chavelo, at San Basilio, used as a younger man. It is, for that matter, very similar to the kind of compressor and hose that I used as a teenager working in the scallop fishery in Maine, and a predecessor to the electric compressor that Lisanne and I often use in shallow water.

The men tell me that they come to the island for three or four days at a time, weather allowing, and sleep in the open on the beach, ignoring the flies and the evening chill. They will return home to Bahía de los Ángeles tomorrow.

They show me their catch. Today it is sea cucumbers, the slug-like edible relatives of sea stars, sand dollars, and urchins. They call them pepinos, simply cucumbers, and they have boiled the catch over a campfire. In town, in Bahía de los Ángeles, they will sell the boiled cucumbers for fifty dollars a kilo. I would guess that their day's work, in water of fifty-seven degrees Fahrenheit, netted maybe two kilos. From the hundred dollars, they will have to pay for food, gasoline, and boat maintenance before paying themselves.

Yes, they see turtles sometimes, they tell me, but they do not know what kind. And sharks, although not very many, and never very big.

One of them tells me that he hopes his young daughter will grow up to be a diver like him.

The next afternoon, after the divers have left, a new boat with four fishermen appears. I talk to them, too, in my broken Spanish. They use traps to catch octopus, "trampas para atrapar el pulpo." They offer me boiled murex snails as a snack, but fortunately I have just eaten. Despite my decline of their generous gift, perhaps in honor of my questioning, my curiosity, they invite me to join them in the morning. They want to put me to work pulling traps for an hour or so.

And so I find myself directly involved in the exploitation of the Gulf of California, and in particular the exploitation of sentient creatures, octopuses, something I would neither condone or do on my own. But I justify my actions—and I know this is a stretch—with the knowledge that these men would catch octopuses with me or without me. Also, I know that I will learn from working with them, and that engaging with those who make a living from the sea is a necessary part of the conservation movement.

At six in the morning I watch the men retrieve a small gillnet from the anchorage, no more than a hundred feet from our boat. Once the net is up, they come alongside and I join them aboard their boat. They are still emptying the gillnet of its contents. It bears hundreds of porgies and green jacks, dozens of venomous spined stonefish, two venomous spined ocean catfish, a six-inch wide electric ray, and a variety of other species, all small. No turtles, possibly because the mesh is too small to foul even a young turtle.

Some of the fish go over the side, still alive. The rest go into a pile in front of a bait cutting board. They put me to work cutting, and as I cut the captain takes us to the next bay along the coast and to our first string of fifty traps.

I cannot follow all of their Spanish, and they seem to find mine more amusing than communicative. With hand signals, they urge me to move from the bait table to the bow. One of the crew catches the trap line with a boat hook and hands it to me. Following gestured instructions I pull, and traps begin to emerge from the sea. Each is made of chicken wire, about the size of a shoebox and with a small and somewhat funneled entrance, similar in principle to a New England lobster trap.

The traps are spaced at ten-foot intervals along the line. Pulling up one trap from ten or twenty feet of water is not difficult. Nor is pulling up two traps. But pulling fifty traps is a workout.

The first five traps come up with sea stars, murexes, and untouched bait. They throw the sea stars over the side and the murexes into a bucket. The sixth trap holds a moray eel, an anguila, which follows the sea stars back to the depths. But our luck turns for the better, and the luck of our prey turns for the worse. The seventh trap holds two octopuses and the eighth trap a singleton. One of the fishermen dumps the octopuses from the traps into an open plastic barrel while another stacks the retrieved traps astern. By the time we have all fifty traps aboard, we have nineteen octopuses in the barrel, squirming, inking, trying to climb the walls of their plastic prison. Each animal has an arm span of perhaps eighteen inches, although this is only a rough estimate as they do not fully extend their arms but rather work them in a bizarre dance, smooth but without rhythm. The octopus harbors a distributed central nervous system, a brain, in a sense, for each arm, and that strange reality shows itself here.

Without comment, the captain circles around to where we had started and the crew lowers the trap line back to the bottom, rebaiting each trap as it goes over the side, working with the efficiency that comes from repetition. For my benefit the captain uses dumbed-down, repeated sentences, supplemented by gestures, to explain the operation. With a total of thirteen trap lines, they fish an area for two or three weeks, after which the catch rate declines and they move on. But they will return after a few more weeks pass, and the slaughter will continue. Where do the octopuses come from? He does not know. Maybe, he thinks, from deeper water. He only knows that he never runs out of octopuses to catch.

He and his crew earn their money from octopuses five months of each year, after which they switch to other prey, but the octopuses pay well compared to other quarry.

We move to the next trapline, not far away, and repeat the process. My hour turns into an hour and a half, three traplines, close to sixty octopuses, and noticeable fatigue in my biceps and forearms. My curiosity is satisfied, and although I am not at all fond of what I have seen, of my participation, I again take shallow solace in the knowledge that my presence did not change the catch rate. For octopus lovers, and at heart we all love octopus, it is perhaps easy to condemn these men. But in reality they are no more guilty than the clients who buy their prey. They seem to be decent men, cheerful, hardworking, respectful of each other and of themselves and even of their prey.

The Gulf of California generates just shy of half of Mexico's fisheries' catches and supports fifty thousand jobs. In the northern Gulf, which includes Isla Ángel de la Guarda and Bahía de los Ángeles, almost 80 percent of the people are directly or indirectly involved in fishing, mostly from small boats, from pangas. By scientific authorities, the Gulf of California has been classified as a "Class I highly productive ecosystem" and one of the five most productive marine ecosystems in the world, and it is possible that the fisheries or some form of them can continue, adjusted, of course, to protect species that are or have been at risk. But those adjustments are already in place for sea turtles, totoaba, and the diminutive vaquita, the tiny porpoise with a remaining population too small to reasonably estimate. And the adjustments seem to have mixed results. There can be no doubt that this is a badly diminished sea.

All of us eight billion people want stuff. I want stuff, the fishermen diving for sea cucumbers and trapping octopuses want stuff, the fishermen's children want stuff, the readers of this book want stuff. In the struggle for resources that pits us against other species we tend to get what we want. With our oversized *Homo sapiens* brains and opposable thumbs, we out-think and out-build the competition. Which is why today we and our stuff outweigh the rest of the living world.

In polite mainstream company, discussion of consumerism has become awkward at best. People—especially people in the developed world—have been trained since birth by advertising and social interactions to define themselves by what they own and what they hope to own. They perceive any criticisms of consumerism and capitalism as a threat, as something unpatriotic, as hypocritical, or at best as naive. Regardless of the past and present existence of individuals and cultures that entirely eschewed excessive ownership, they often claim that the habit of acquiring things is simply an expression of genetic destiny, an undeniable and inalterable aspect of human nature. They often assume that any discussion of consumerism is a criticism, a call for austerity rather than, as in this particular case, merely a call for rational consideration, possibly for moderation.

I include myself as one of the "they."

But in my better moments I pry open my mind to the words of others.

Take those of the late Quaker sociologist, Elise Boulding: "The consumption society has made us feel that happiness lies in having things, and has failed to teach us the happiness of not having things."

From Fulton Sheen, the late celebrity bishop who hosted long-running radio and television shows: "Advertising tries to stimulate our sensuous desires, converting luxuries into necessities, but it only intensifies man's inner misery. The business world is bent on creating hungers which its wares never satisfy, and thus it adds to the frustrations and broken minds of our times."

From actress Jennifer Stone: "Consumerism is our national religion."

And my favorite, perhaps because I am hardly known as a snappy dresser, from the *Analects* of Confucius, written well before the birth of Christ: "A fellow who is ashamed merely of shabby clothing or modest meals is not even worth conversing with."

Despite these pithy words, to criticize consumerism is to swim upstream. But even against that strong current, the movement known as minimalism has managed to find its way. It is a movement that questions unfettered buying and accumulation. It does not require a vow of poverty. Instead, it asks adherents to make conscious choices about what to own and what not to own. It espouses the belief that happiness comes to those who own only those things that are important to them rather than those things that others claim should be important to them.

I have ascended a soapbox, summiting to a dizzying height. What, one might ask, does consumerism and minimalism have to do with saving turtles and other species faced with extinction? Quite a lot, it turns out. To state the obvious, as is regularly done by those perched atop soapboxes, our often irrational desire for things that we neither need nor truly want leads to overexploitation of resources. In the end, the pursuit of stuff deprives our fellow living beings of life. Our desire for fish promotes the use of gillnets, which kill turtles. Our desire for inexpensive crops leads to the overuse of fertilizers and pesticides, which run off into the sea and kill turtles. Our desire for cheap and easy transportation encourages production of gasoline, diesel, and jet fuel, all of which warm the climate and spill into oceans, both of which kill turtles. And so on.

We sail south to another uninhabited island, Isla Partida, not to be mistaken for another island of the same name that sits farther south. The Seri people who once lived in the area, the same people who hunted sleeping turtles, called the island Hast Simle, or Barrel Cactus Mountain. Barrel cactus do not occur here, but it has been suggested that perhaps the island looks something like a barrel cactus, even though I cannot see any resemblance at all, no matter how hard I try.

We anchor in an open-mouthed bay on the island's north side and paddle ashore. We find the rubbish of modern man in modest quantities, and with some searching we find signs of long-ago visitors. There are collapsing stone shelters of unknown age, but also talus pits where someone had moved rocks, possibly to hunt whatever might have been living among them—lizards, of course, but also the Mexican fishing bat.

We walk across the island. Looking southeast, a half mile across the water, we see swarms of birds hovering over Isla Cardonosa Este. When I refer to swarms, I do not mean hundreds. There are many thousands of elegant terns and Heermann's gulls.

Isla Rasa sits farther away and more toward the south, four miles out and barely visible from here. Isla Rasa is known as the nesting home of 95 percent of the world's elegant terns and Heermann's gulls. The multitudes we see on Isla Cardonosa Este are nothing more than overspill from Isla Rasa.

Here is another tale of optimism, or really another case of something terrible followed by something magical, something akin to the story of guano harvesting.

Less than a hundred years ago people came to Isla Rasa to harvest bird eggs. One trouble with harvesting wild bird eggs, they found, is that the eggs may be of various ages and in various states of development, some newly laid and others ready to hatch. It is not possible to tell the young from the old, but the egg harvesters knew their customers did not want to feel the crunch of tiny bones in their eggs, in their huevos rancheros.

The harvesters came up with a simple solution. On day one, smash every egg in every nest. On day two, and every day after that, harvest newly laid replacement eggs, young and boneless. Problem solved.

Reports from the 1920s indicate that people took eggs from the entire island, everything they could find, twice each day. One egg gatherer, one of many who had been working on Isla Rasa in 1947, reported selling 27,000 eggs in the Baja mining town of Santa Rosalía.

In 1964, in response to noticeable declines in sea birds throughout the Gulf of California, Mexico declared Isla Rasa a Natural Reserve Zone and Seabird Refuge. The birds bounced back. In 1999 biologists reported finding 260,000 Heermann's gulls and 200,000 elegant terns on the island.

Eggs may still be taken by occasional poachers, but the days of gatherers sweeping across the island and a single entrepreneur selling 27,000 eggs in just one season are over.

I walk the beach overlooking Isla Cardonosa Este and the more distant Isla Rasa, watching the birds near and far. Occasionally I look down at my feet, at the beach on which I walk, and I see scattered turtle remains, bits of carapace and very occasional scattered bones. I think about the culinary history confronting me. Eating wild bird eggs and slurping turtle soup were once signs of wealth and sophistication. Now, for most of us, they are nothing less than obscene, repugnant, indecent.

What will be considered obscene a century from now? Eating meat? Private jets and bus-sized gasoline-powered recreational vehicles? Private offices? Personal ownership of cars? Houses of three thousand square feet heated and air conditioned for a family of three? Golf courses in deserts? Privately owned sailing yachts, no matter how old? Hunting of octopuses, certainly.

We are no more capable of imagining our hundred-year future than my own great grandparents were, and none of them saw all this coming, this accelerated world busy with video calls and transatlantic flights, farms full of genetically modified crops, people manically focused on material wealth, the oddities of social media and virtual friends. Nor would they have foreseen the environmental regulations searching for ways to reel in abuses of the air, the water, the soil, and the biosphere.

In the hundred-year future, it seems to me that almost anything is possible. And by anything, I include things that would be considered very good, that would be very welcome, by someone like me, by a lover of nature. It is not outside the realm of possibility that global norms and values will tip toward those currently held by, say, the Jains. But also I include things that could be very bad. It is not outside the realm of possibility that global norms and values will continue along a trajectory of thoughtless consumption for its own sake, other species and our own future be damned in the endless Sisyphean pursuit of fantasies engendered by advertisements. What will it take to tip things one way and not the other? Perhaps the world's seven sea turtle species hold the key, along with polar bears and various whales and tigers, along with all of the charismatic endangered species that are out there, focusing our attention, making us say and think, "Hey, wait a minute." It is these species, the ones that draw our attention, that might help us change our ways.

Thick fog pins us down for several days at Isla Partida. At times *Rocinante*'s stern cannot be seen from her bow, a mere forty-four feet away. We can wipe droplets of freshwater from the deck even at midday and throughout the afternoon.

At times, light breezes momentarily open the view, offering a stray glimpse of the island, but then the fog descends again. The effect is both pleasantly surreal and disquieting. I turn on our foghorn, signaling to anyone or more likely no one that we are here and that we would rather not take part in a collision.

When the miasmic shroud lifts we sail on, making our way back up the Canal de Ballenas, still free of whales, past Esta Ton and onward to an anchorage near Isla Ángel de la Guarda's northern tip. There we spend a week alone, catching no more than glimpses of other boats, listening to sea lions barking night and day from a nearby beach. Beneath our boat, we dive with guitar fish. We have seen guitar fish before on rare occasions but for reasons beyond my grasp they are surprisingly common here and now.

There are also, of course, turtles.

I think about ways that one might influence consumer behavior. What would it take to get me to buy less stuff that I neither need nor sincerely want? What would it take to make me and others think about the consequences of purchases?

In January 1, 1970, Richard Nixon signed into law the National Environmental Policy Act. The Act required federal agencies to consider the environmental effects of projects. Want to build a highway, a dam, a military base? Need to dredge a channel? Hoping to grant an oil lease on federal land? Or approve a pipeline right of way? Stop and think, the act declared. The courts, hearing arguments that continue to be restated and refought, formalized the process. For many projects, the documentation required and the process needed to produce that documentation can cost millions of dollars and take years to complete. Whether a project goes forward or not, at least the consequences have been considered.

Not so with the environmental consequences of consumer products.

Unrelated to the National Environmental Policy Act and Richard Nixon, by 1966 the government required ingredients labeling of packaged foods. If you were about to eat corn syrup when you thought you were going to eat actual sugar from sugar cane, the government wanted you to know. If a beverage contained chemicals that seemed more at home in a laboratory than in a person, the government wanted you to know. In 1990, labeling rules expanded. Both ingredients and nutritional values were required. Some people—lots of them—paid attention. Labels impacted buying habits. In some cases producers worked toward a more palatable list of ingredients and acceptable nutritional values, changing their ways not because of an inherent sense of right and wrong but from a desire to satisfy consumer demands.

Would it change the way we buy things if all products included standardized environmental labels? If the new golf clubs that you neither need nor truly want come with a label describing the product's environmental footprint, would your credit card slip quietly back into your wallet? Like-wise with that laminate flooring? That new suit? That steak and lobster dinner?

Sometimes, yes, it would. Or at least it might move you toward considering competing products and brands, at least considering their environmental footprint as part of a purchasing decision. If this were not true, companies with environmentally benign or at least less problematic products would not voluntarily use environmental labels and there would be no marketing push behind natural, environmentally friendly products.

Goldilocks winds propel us toward Puerto Peñasco. Our route skirts the edge of known vaquita habitat. During the crossing, we see slightly fewer of the very rare porpoises than have been seen cumulatively by every other person on Earth in the past two years. No more than seven confirmed sightings have been reported in two years, and even those are questionable. As to us, we see zero animals.

This is also totoaba country, but we see neither the huge fish nor the fishermen who might be supplying the illegal trade in totoaba swim bladders.

We do see shrimp boats. On and off through the night and into the morning we change course, trying to give them a wide berth. As often as not they change course with us, and we change course again. Occasionally, two or three of them, seemingly working together, box us in.

Around two in the morning, we radio a shrimper to ask his intent, his navigational plans, and to confirm that he sees us. Someone responds politely enough, but it is hard to believe that he and the other shrimpers are not playing with us. Shrimping involves long slow runs dragging a trawl across the bottom, and who can blame the fishermen for occasionally entertaining themselves by harassing passing sailboats? Even more so since most of the sailboats fly American flags, flaunting symbols of the same country that banned Mexican shrimp, claiming these fishermen are killing too many turtles, citing endangered species protection as a rationale for, as many of them see it, restricting trade and inflating the value of shrimp caught north of the border while slowly but surely driving their own fishery mercilessly toward bankruptcy.

About four decades ago, fisheries biologists in the United States developed what came to be known as Turtle Exclusion Devices, frequently abbreviated to TEDs. The first ones were nothing more than mesh strung across the opening of shrimp trawls, the idea being to let shrimp pass through while keeping turtles, at least the big ones, out. But the mesh clogged with debris, perhaps saving a few turtles but definitely sparing millions of shrimp. From the viewpoint of the fishing industry, these early TEDs were way off the mark.

The biologists began working with the fishermen to adopt an approach using an existing device intended to keep nets from filling with jellyfish. The improved TEDs sat inside the throat of the trawl nets, sweeping turtles out through an opening to one side while letting shrimp pass through. They worked reasonably well, but biologists, realizing that panicked turtles tend to head for the surface, moved the opening to the top of the nets. The number of turtles killed while using the top-pointing TEDs dropped by 97 percent.

Fishermen loved it, as long as there were jellyfish around. If there were no jellyfish around, the TED was in their view more trouble than it was worth.

The biologists made further improvements, including shrinking the TED, making it easier to manage. The fishermen complained that it was still too big, too heavy, too unwieldy.

Fishermen and regulators met. They yelled at one another. Aggravated faces took on the color of cooked shrimp. Turtles continued to die. More modifications were made to TEDs.

June 29, 1987, was or at least should have been a good day for sea turtles in the jurisdictional waters of the United States. On that day final regulations requiring the use of TEDs were published. Four and later five TED designs were approved.

Lawyers on both sides made hay. State laws were passed in reaction to federal laws, suits were filed, enforcement actions were suspended, temporary rules were promulgated, modified, and replaced. Confusion and anger reigned while fear and loathing matured on both sides. More turtles died.

In 1989, better federal regulations went into effect. TEDs were more widely used. Turtles, at least more of them, survived encounters with trawls.

That same year, George H. W. Bush required the Department of State to start talking with other nations about protecting turtles from shrimpers. No one, including George H. W. Bush, likes to suffer alone, so the United States banned import of shrimp from nations failing to impose requirements that limit the killing of turtles in trawls.

Gear improvements continued. Fear and loathing held onto their own, with shrimpers hating environmentalists and environmentalists hating shrimpers.

In April 2021, the United States decided that Mexican shrimpers were killing too many turtles. Mexican shrimp could no longer be legally sold in the United States. The value of Mexican shrimp plummeted, while the cost of shrimp fishing in Mexico did what it always does. That is to say, it increased.

Hundreds of shrimp boats rested in port. Mexican shrimpers sat on sofas watching television novellas or on barstools drinking watery beer.

Mexico's Secretary of Agriculture and Rural Development, Víctor Manuel Villalobos Arámbula, had his staff work with representatives from across the border. An agreement was reached. Mexican shrimpers would face the same requirements faced by shrimpers in the United States and Mexican shrimp would once again be certified for import in the United States. "This certification," Arámbula told the media half a year after the ban had been put in place, "clearly demonstrates that there is openness, respect and a strong commitment between the governments of Mexico and the United States to strengthen dialogue and relations in international fisheries matters."

Shrimpers got off their sofas and barstools and went back to harassing gringo sailboats and catching shrimp, while at least presumably not catching nearly as many turtles as they had in the recent past.

We arrive in Puerto Peñasco in midmorning, turning into a rock-lined harbor to escape the long low swell that had built up over the past thirty hours. In this harbor, it is all but impossible to have and hold a reservation for dock space. The norm is to show up and claim the first available spot. We motor around the harbor, sharing space with a few tourist boats, one or two dozen yachts in various states of disrepair, and uncountable shrimp boats. We pick a spot and secure *Rocinante* to a dock.

With our eyes biased by weeks in remote anchorages surrounded by nature, we walk down streets in need of repair past seedy strip clubs and low-end restaurants. We stroll next to vacant weedy lots and piles of garbage. On a nearby beach we see thousands of tourists, many of them Mexicans and Californians of Mexican descent, here for a few days of inexpensive seaside life. The beach is backed by tall condominiums and a long stretch of recreational vehicles. A couple of dozen small stands sell drinks, snacks, and trinkets on the sand. I stop at one to quench my thirst and am pleased when the young woman running the stand slops a very heavy measure of rum into a sixteen-ounce ice-filled cup, contaminating it with no more than a couple of splashes of coke, consumerism at its finest.

Over the next few days, I discover that there is more to the town than the rundown area around the harbor. Housing blocks stretch inland and along the coast, enough for a population of sixty thousand. There is a woman who voluntarily operates a small but well-done seashell museum. Cartels occasionally fight, usually quietly, over turf here and in the nearby communities. The Center for the Study of Deserts and Oceans, a nonprofit organization, promotes regional sustainability. There are many hardware stores, ferreterías, one of which has shallow tubs lining one wall, each holding a freshwater turtle, all of which, the owner tells me with obvious pride, are his pets. Some of the turtles have lived in his tubs for more than twenty years.

There is no coordinated turtle conservation activity in Puerto Peñasco, no one to talk to about patrolling beaches and protecting nests. There is nothing here resembling a Grupo Tortuguero organization. But a building a few miles from the harbor on an out-of-the-way street houses a few big tanks holding sea turtles, the primary purpose of which, as far as I can tell, is to amuse and perhaps incidentally educate visitors. The sea turtles, including a large green that has been in the tank for years, swim in circles, brushing their shells against the edges of the tanks as they migrate in meaningless, hopeless circles. But it could be worse. The tanks are clean and the animals seem well-fed.

On the malecón, the street lined with bars and restaurants along the shoreline east of the harbor, kids on skateboards and BMX bikes circle around an iconic bronze statue, El Camaronero, a grand monument to shrimpers. What it depicts is like no shrimper I have ever seen. Instead it is a sombrero-wearing bearded man with a shirtless physique that could shame a Greek god. He holds a long oar, lance-like, in his left hand as he rides upon a giant shrimp. His gaze is one of a sailor staring at a horizon, but, strangely, his back is to the sea, and if his eyes were of flesh rather than metal they would see nothing but a developed strip clearly made to bring in tourists.

A living Heermann's gull—not a bronze Heermann's gull—sits on top of the Camaronero's head.

After all our time away, entirely alone in remote anchorages or in tiny seaside communities, it is impossible to feel comfortable with the people here. It is not the individuals I refer to, but the collective, the population.

The crowds make me think of that horrible number, eight billion, the human population on Earth today. And the even more horrible number, ten billion, which we seem destined to reach in the next few decades.

Talk of population control makes some people even more uncomfortable than talk of consumerism. It conjures thoughts of heavy-handed government controls, of China's one-child policy, of eugenics, and even of Hitler. This is easy to understand. After all, the prophets of old called for what amounts to rampant and uncontrolled reproduction of humans. According to one well-known but some would claim perhaps not entirely reliable source, God is said to have said, "Be fruitful and multiply and fill the earth and subdue it and have dominion over the fish of the sea and over the birds of the heavens and over every living thing that moves on the earth." But God was at the time talking only to Adam and Eve. God was talking to a human population of two. Was the edict meant to be eternally applied? Or did God think to herself that her creations would eventually realize when enough was enough? Did She say to herself, "Surely I don't have to tell these idiots that they can't multiply uncontrollably forever? Should I say something about that now, or just stay on message? It will be fine. By the time it becomes an issue, it will be so obvious that even humans will be able to figure it out."

We have to recall that the same source calling for fruitful multiplication has God reminding anyone who will listen about the importance of biodiversity: "Let the waters teem with living creatures, and let birds fly above the earth in the open expanse of the sky."

Population is, like it or not, at the core of the world's environmental problems. An extinction crisis might exist in a world of a billion people, but clearly it would be more manageable. An extinction crisis in a world of ten billion people will be even harder to manage than it is today.

The good news is this: No one has to try to actively manage human reproduction on a massive scale. It turns out it can and is being managed through individual choices. Educated women tend to have fewer babies, where fewer can often mean none. The next generation is choosing to have smaller families, if any at all, in countries and cultures around the world where both sexes have the freedom to decide such issues. The United Nations projects that humans will no longer produce enough babies to replace themselves by 2050. This will have many consequences, some of which could be inconvenient and even disruptive in the extreme to existing economic systems, but the decline will be slow and manageable. People like Elon Musk can and will continue to say and tweet things like, "Population collapse due to low birth rates is a much bigger risk to civilization than global warming." These people will complain about the reduced number of consumers and workers in future economies, fretting over the possible impacts to markets, to their personal positions of wealth and power, worrying about the end of what is at one level a worldwide Ponzi scheme. Ignore them, because a smaller human population will be better for both humans and our fellow creatures. Despite the problems that might come from declining human populations, the number of people competing for resources with turtles will slowly decline. That applies not only to turtles, but to all other species.

These are the sorts of thoughts I seldom share in public. It has been my experience that utterings like these, random interpretations of the Bible and hand-waving discourses on the economics of population decline, tend to generate a response of stunned silence.

Walking back toward the harbor, we pass an elaborate work of graffiti on the wall of what looks like a neglected building, a wall of a business that once supported the shrimp industry. The painting shows a larger-than-life red-headed mermaid, her body bent slightly backward, her right hand reaching out to touch a vaquita. But the mermaid's face would be at home in a Día de los Muertos festival. It is a Day of the Dead face, the kind seen when Mexicans celebrate their dead, remembering them fondly, possibly drunkenly, always respectfully. This Día de los Muertos mermaid, it seems to me, touches the vaquita with death, with extinction.

Later, I ask around, trying to find out something about the artist, about what he or she intended. No one seems to know. But I walk past the painting almost daily during the rest of my stay, and each time I am moved. I know I will never see a living vaquita, and I am grateful to have seen so many sea turtles. I remind myself that the conservation of nature as we think of it today is a relatively new endeavor and that the decimation of nature has been around for far longer than the conservation movement. Against this backdrop, room for hope emerges.

ELEVEN
Endings

While in Puerto Peñasco, with the aid of a crane, we pull down *Rocinante*'s two masts, sand them, and paint them. While they are on the ground, we remove the complicated mass of stainless steel cables known as standing rigging that hold the masts erect against winds strong as well as weak, and, one by one, we replace them. We cut open the cockpit deck to extricate a diesel generator rendered obsolete in a world of efficient solar panels, then rebuild the opening. Where there once had been a generator, there will now be folding bicycles, tools, and spare cordage. We lift the masts back into place and tune the new rigging, tightening it just enough, but not too much, first here and then there so as not to bend the masts too far forward or aft or to port or to starboard. We sand and paint the bottom of the hull. We sand and paint the decks. We replace an aging propellor shaft seal that keeps seawater at bay. We rebuild a mechanical locking mechanism intended to prevent that same shaft from spinning when we are under sail. These and a hundred other small jobs conspire to keep us occupied. The materials needed immerse us in the world of consumerism, and in that world we make careful choices, limiting our negative impact as much as possible, trying to buy only those things that we want and not those things that others think we should want.

Months pass. During those months, we finally succumb to the COVID virus, suffering through what are classified as mild cases even though they leave us sick for ten days and weak for a month.

After testing negative but while still recovering, I walk along the dock in front of *Rocinante*. A man and a woman approach me, gray-haired, somewhat stiff in their movements. They have come down from Santa Cruz in California. I warn them that I am recovering from COVID, that they should keep their distance, but they seem entirely unfazed. I step back and maneuver to stand downwind from them.

They are retired biologists, employed for years by a research center north of the border. But they are not here on vacation. They hope to find a boat that will take them in search of vaquitas.

I ask if they have seen the mural in town, the painting of the Día de los Muertos mermaid touching the snout of a vaquita. They have not. They express no interest in its whereabouts.

They believe—they are in fact certain, they assure me—that a handful of vaquitas survive in the wild. They claim that there was a reliable sighting within the last year, and that hydrophones—underwater microphones—have detected their high-pitched calls. It seems, they suggest, that a small group of vaquitas has figured out how to avoid gillnets.

I admire their optimism with regard to the vaquita, but I do not share it. Maybe a few still exist, but not enough. Too little has been done too late. The likelihood that a small group of the porpoises could have figured out how to consistently avoid gillnets seems infinitesimally small. I have searched for and even cultivated optimism during these past many months in the Gulf of California, but still that optimism knows certain bounds. I hope I am wrong—I would love to be wrong—but it seems to me that the vaquita is done for, as are many other species. If they still exist at all, the vaquita may be part of what is sometimes called the extinction debt—species still extant but on the way out. More likely they are already gone.

Any optimism I have found in my wanderings carries with it a heavy shadow of doubt, a dark veneer of cynicism that leaves me more than a little ashamed of myself as I talk to these aging biologists. Our conversation quickly turns polite, stilted, distanced. Either they sense my skepticism or they realize that our boat, *Rocinante*, is neither big enough nor fast enough to serve as a research platform.

They turn away and walk down the dock.

I, too, turn away, coughing into my elbow. Facing now to the south, I look out across the harbor. The docks remain crowded with shrimp boats, leaving little room for the occasional longliner or tour boat or sailing yacht. But south is the direction of the channel to the harbor mouth. South a few hundred yards, then west a few hundred yards, and then south again, out into the Gulf of California. Out into turtle habitat.

Finally, a day comes when we feel strong enough to manage ourselves and our boat. The effects of COVID are not yet in the past tense, we are not operating at one hundred percent, but we can no longer bear the restraint of dock lines. We sail away.

Before the horizon swallows the land behind us, a pod of several hundred common dolphins surrounds *Rocinante*. They leap and splash noisily, frolicking, displaying their black backs, their tan and gray flanks, and their white undersides, showing off with what can be fairly described as joyous leaps into the air. Thirty minutes later, a fin whale surfaces a quarter-mile off our port bow, its size—easily longer than *Rocinante*—obvious even at a distance. The fin whale is second only to the blue whale in length, making it the second longest animal on Earth, but it is streamlined and slender, weighing in as only the fourth heaviest of the planet's animals, averaging something like fifty-seven tons. Put another way, this slender whale carries more than four times the weight of *Rocinante*.

Early the next morning dawn light turns up a small pod of orcas, no more than six or seven of the animals sometimes called killer whales, and only one with the straight tall dorsal fin of a mature male. But still, these are the first orcas we have seen during our travels in the Gulf of California.

No vaquitas, of course. But also no turtles. For three hundred miles, we see not a single turtle's head popping up above the waves, not a single shell shimmering at the surface. This I attribute in part to the time of year. We sail in late winter over moderately cold seas. But I also blame our luck. There are turtles here, even now, and it is only luck that hides them from our eyes.

We stop once more in San Basilio, hoping to find Martin and to hear more of his turtles, but he is nowhere to be seen. Likewise, Tom Woodard is not around. On the beach, campers tell us that they have heard rumors of a change in ownership. The land has been bought, they say, by a Walton family heiress, by Walmart money. With dollars accumulated ironically enough through the mechanisms of mass consumerism, she intends to protect the land. No one is even thinking about development.

If this is true, I guess but do not know that it was this same heiress who swooped in with funding to save Tom's financially strapped consortium, the same woman who funded Martin's turtle work. The philanthropic work of one of the Walton family members, Christy Walton, is well-known, both in the arts and in nature conservation. Her generosity can be measured in the billions. I have heard that she also supports efforts to breed the totoaba. If the cartels bent on capturing the fish and selling their bladders cannot be stopped, a breeding program might be the solution to their conservation.

One of the campers worries that the new ownership may put an end to camping on the beach. "Maybe not," I suggest. "Walmart encourages people in vans to use their parking lots. Maybe it's a family thing."

If what people are saying is true, kudos to Christy Walton. She has voluntarily protected a beautiful piece of land and sea not only for herself and her friends but for everything that lives here.

Most of us will never have sufficient wealth to make much of a difference through philanthropy. On the other hand, many Americans are hardly at a loss for funds. What if each person in the United States with a net worth of more than say five million dollars buys one hundred thousand dollars' worth of conservation land? There are, according to those who track such things, three and a half million households in the United States worth more than five million dollars, so those purchases would amount to 350 billion dollars' worth of land. In zip codes where land goes for well over $100,000 per acre, that may not seem like much. But there are places where land can be bought up for less than $10,000 an acre, and in many cases considerably less. Abandoned farms, parcels of marsh, remote and especially roadless tracts, steep slopes, bits of jungle, pieces of swamp, logged forests—all can be had for a fraction of the cost of property in sought-after neighborhoods, and all of them provide habitats. At $10,000 per acres, 350 billion dollars would tie up just shy of 55,000 square miles of land, an area comparable in size to, say, Florida, and larger than, say, Maryland, Rhode Island, Vermont, Delaware, New Jersey, Massachusetts, and New Hampshire combined.

Buying conservation land by individuals may not be ideal. A better approach might be to provide funds to professional organizations set up to acquire and manage important habitat. The Nature Conservancy comes to mind, as well as any number of conservation land trusts, but there are others. While a donation to nonprofit organizations like these might make sense to some, others, having been raised in a system that values ownership for the sake of ownership, might be more comfortable holding the land themselves, even if they know they can never build on it. They may never use the land in the exploitative sense, and perhaps they will seldom even see the land, but at the same time it is theirs, and they have set it aside.

If something like this were to become fashionable among the moderately wealthy, say as fashionable as owning a newer model luxury car, the world would, to those of us who love biodiversity, be a better place.

But still, most of us do not have anything like five million dollars. What can the less well-heeled person do? What can any of us do on our own?

We could volunteer to walk beaches in search of turtle nests. We could raise monarch butterflies. We could in any number of ways become direct participants in the front lines of the extinction wars.

But we could also make lifestyle changes. We could, for example, eat less meat, or even no meat, knowing that many kinds of ranching and modern animal husbandry not only destroy habitats and generate greenhouse gases but also can only function by turning a blind eye to remarkably cruel practices.

We could eat less seafood, or no seafood, or at least none of the seafood harvested in ways that destroy habitats or result in wasteful bycatch. In other words, skip the shrimp and the scallops, unless you know for sure that they come from artisanal fisheries, and even then think twice.

We could drive less. Or not at all.

We could fly less frequently. Or not at all.

We could buy less junk. Or none at all.

The goal of "not at all" or "none at all" is lofty beyond belief. Almost no one will be willing or able to give up driving, flying, and buying unnecessary junk altogether. But almost all of us, with a little encouragement, might be willing to sign on for less consumption, for less damage in a world where eight billion people have to somehow come together to end the extinction crisis.

Or how about this? Drop a note to your local radio station admiring a well-covered environmental story. Or email your local radio station asking why they so seldom run environmental stories.

Track what your congressional representatives do and say about the environment. Send them the same sorts of notes you send your radio station. Let them know that the environment is high on your list of priorities.

Or try on this idea: Wear a T-shirt promoting nature. Do not buy this T-shirt in addition to all your other shirts, but instead when it is time to replace a wornout shirt.

A T-shirt? Is that a joke?

No. A T-shirt campaign, just like letters to editors and notes to elected officials, can raise awareness. Recall Tom Harrison, whose 1964 article "Must the Turtle Die" was picked up by the *Sunday Times of London* and the German magazine *Die Umschau*, leading a German turtle soup producer to worry about the inevitable change in public perceptions. The soup company's worries, it turns out, were well-founded. The way people think about the world, the manner in which we live, can be influenced. Once, just about everyone ate turtle soup. Now, almost no one eats turtle soup.

So instead of apparel advertising some faceless name brand that happens to be trending, wear a shirt that champions for the protection of nature. Use that shirt to strike up conversations. Use those conversations to change minds.

Be infectious. Adopt the contagious passion of people like Elsa Galindo and Tom Woodard and Erika Santacruz Lopez and Chuy Lucero and Karen Oceguera. Speak up whenever possible. Politely but firmly, share thoughts on the extinction crisis, and more importantly on the need for change. Let people know that the status quo is not only unacceptable, it is abhorrent.

Remember that in doing this, in passing on a conservation ethic, in trying to stop the devastation of nature that has become an accepted part of human life, you are only being reasonable and rational. You are only doing something so obviously right that it is all but impossible to understand how humanity has wandered so far off the track.

At remote anchorages, we—my wife and I, my cocaptain and I—like to swim for an hour or so each day, wearing a dive mask and snorkel, looking around while exercising, whether in recovery from COVID or not. It is on such a day, a week or so out from Puerto Peñasco, that our luck changes. But in the saddest of ways.

While swimming, we come across a turtle, the first we have seen since leaving Puerto Peñasco. But the creature is missing a leg. Where the left fore flipper should be there is nothing but a scarred stump. The animal is fifteen inches long, short-tailed so probably a female. Almost certainly, the flipper was lost to a gillnet, an entanglement in monofilament line that lasted long enough to kill the limb but not so long as to immediately kill the turtle herself. Maybe a fisherman, lifting his gillnet, found her still alive, disentangled her, and set her free. Or maybe she escaped on her own. Now she swims with a heartbreaking lopsided stroke that swings her body to the left. She uses her hind flippers as rudders, correcting her course.

Three-legged turtles have been known to survive to adulthood. But in this case, her compressed plastron can only be interpreted as a sign of starvation. She will never live to reproduce.

A week passes and now we swim along the northwestern edge of Isla San Marcos, an island known for a gypsum mine that is run by the several hundred inhabitants of a small dusty company town on the island's southwest shore, making it one of a few permanently inhabited islands in the Gulf of California. It lies within sight of the aluminum mining community of Santa Rosalía on the Baja peninsula.

Offshore, a purse seiner works the water. It is perhaps two miles away, but we can hear its engine both above and below the surface.

On a nearby beach, two fishermen nap close to their panga in the shadow of what had once been a substantial fish camp, with the remains of two buildings still standing. Two other pangas work the shoreline, the steady hum of their outboards producing a higher pitch than the diesel engine of the purse seiner.

Not far from the one-time fish camp, in water ten feet deep, we come across the ruins of a turtle, a mature olive ridley. Now all that is left is flesh-less shell and bones. The skull and jaw lie next to one another in the sand.

We see no large fish. There are scattered damsels, closely packed schools of what we take to be scad, some puffers, and a few other species, no more than the usual suspects. In other words, we see what we have become accustomed to seeing almost every place in the Gulf of California.

I am not sure, but I do not think it is the mining that explains the paucity of fish living among the rocks. That reality probably can be attributed to fishermen, both professionals and sportsmen.

Later, paddling my kayak along the shoreline, I see two species of lizards, a pair of ospreys sitting on their nest, a yellow-footed gull feeding three small chicks, several blue-footed boobies, and the inevitable pelicans and cormorants. I chat with two fishermen on the beach. One has a day job issuing fishing licenses for the government, but he has to fish to supplement his income. He shows me his catch: a bag of the edible abductor muscles from a kind of scallop, a few whole clams, half a dozen octopus, and twenty fish, none of which are big enough to be adults. Everything lies packed in a chest of crushed ice.

The fisherman cheerfully cleans the too-small fish while we talk, throwing their entrails into the shallows next to his boat. A ray the size of a dinner plate swims by to investigate, followed by a fat five-foot-long green moray. The man eats neither rays nor morays, he tells me. They feed unmolested within his reach.

After dark, back aboard *Rocinante*, I look at Venus and Mars in the sky over the Baja peninsula. Hundreds of fish—maybe salemas or grunts of some kind or even small jacks—swim under the boat, unidentifiable in the shadows, taking advantage of the light cast by our anchor lights. Farther away, something exhales in the darkness. Maybe a sea lion or a dolphin, but if so with an unusually strong and prolonged exhalation. Possibly it is a small whale of some sort. I never see the animal, and I will never know with certainty exactly what kind of creature is behind the snorting sigh that I hear, but the sound reassures me. The sight of the fish, too, is reassuring. They are the sound and sight of life prevailing even in this diminished ecosystem. They are the sound and sight of hope.

Here it is, in one place, that all too common experience in the Gulf of California, and for that matter almost anywhere in nature today: the yin and yang of hope and despair, abundant life juxtaposed with devastation, reasons for optimism and pessimism side by side.

My rational mind tends to side with pessimism. Humanity has done so much damage so fast, so much of it entirely irreversible, and still turtles are dying and the ocean is being fished out, each generation shaving off another layer. So many of the people I talk with have no sense of what is happening, no appetite for accepting even partial responsibility, and no desire to change.

Hope is a necessary ingredient for success. How can a thinking person land on an optimistic outlook? I pull out a collection of quotes I have compiled over many years, thumbing through the pages for relevant words. From none other than the Dalai Lama: "Even some political parties have been set up based on the ideology and policy of environmental protection. I think this is a very healthy development. So there is hope."

A few days later I meet a man named Billy at a camp on the shore. His frame carries the softness of age, which is also reflected in a wrinkled face and gray whiskers. He invites me to sit next to the trailer he parked here years ago. He explains that he has driven down from California with his wife and friends. The last three hours of the drive covered no more than forty miles of unpaved tooth-rattling road.

Billy tells me that he has been coming here once or twice each year for more than three decades. When I ask questions, he cannot hear me unless I almost shout. But he smiles as he talks and looks out toward the water. He is too old to fish seriously now, but his friends are slaying them. He uses those exact words: "slaying them."

I ask if there are as many fish as there used to be. No. And, he volunteers, there are fewer birds than there once were. Far fewer. Without the fish, he suggests, the birds suffer.

I ask if the fish are smaller than they used to be. Yes.

Are there fewer different kinds caught? Yes.

I wait for him to conclude that maybe his friends should refrain from slaying them, but he does not.

Then I share with him, politely and with the friendliest tone I can muster, my own opinion on the matter.

I turn again to my compiled quotes, searching for encouraging words. But instead of encouragement I find something more akin to realism.

Wendell Berry, iconic writer and farmer, longed as I do for a stronger conservation ethic. "The great obstacle is simply this: the conviction that we cannot change because we are dependent on what is wrong," he wrote. "But that is the addict's excuse, and we know that it will not do."

Also this: "My faith is that it can't ever get so bad that a person can't do something to make things a little better."

And an offering from Leo Tolstoy, not in the context of protecting biodiversity but still relevant: "Everyone thinks of changing the world, but no one thinks of changing himself."

Finally, from Elizabeth Kolbert, toward the end of her wonderful and influential but distressing *The Sixth Extinction*: "It doesn't much matter whether people care or don't care. What matters is that people change the world."

Nobody—well, few people—think that human-caused extinctions are acceptable. But changing attitudes and beliefs into actions requires alchemy. Or at least the alchemy of time and persistence. So to maintain optimism, patience is a prerequisite. Change is seldom if ever immediate. But if patience is necessary, so is persistence. Without an obstinate, tenacious, dogged pursuit of change, patience would be indistinguishable from giving up. Without accepting the dual necessities of patience and persistence, every excuse for optimism dissolves.

And if optimism dissolves, change will not occur.

During an interlude within reach of a cell tower, I scan the internet for news that I might have missed. I read "The Largest Habitat on Earth is Finally Getting Protection" in *Vox*, describing the Treaty of the High Seas. Then "The Listing of more Australian Bird Species as 'Threatened' is Alarming—but Also Cause for Hope" in the *Guardian*, celebrating the protective measures that would come with new listings. Followed by "Scientists and Fishers Team Up to Protect Bolivian River Dolphin" in *Mongabay*, the nonprofit conservation news platform that publishes original content in at least six languages, including Brazilian Portuguese and Hindi. Next comes "Avian Superhighway: UK's 'Pitstop' for Migrating Birds Seeks UNESCO Status," also from the *Guardian*.

Apparently because of my interest in this sort of thing, an algorithm somewhere directs an advertisement my way. "Join our team of resident biologists," I am told by the Four Seasons Hotel in Tamarindo, Mexico, a luxury establishment with rates far out of my reach.

This is beautiful stuff. None of these stories nor this advertisement would have been found just a few short decades ago. Not because there was no internet, but because such stories and advertisements did not exist.

All of these stories are part of the undeniable trajectory of environmentalism, punctuated with milestones. There were the turtle laws of Bermuda in 1619, game warden Guy Bradley in the early part of the twentieth century, the birth of the International Union for the Conservation of Nature in 1948, the first Earth Day in 1970. In the United States, there was the National Environmental Policy Act and the Clean Air Act Extension, both of 1970, the Marine Mammal Protection Act of 1972, the Endangered Species Act of 1973, the Safe Drinking Water Act of 1974, the Resource Conservation and Recovery Act controlling hazardous chemicals from cradle to grave of 1976, the Clean Water Act of 1977, the Comprehensive Environmental Response, Compensation, and Liability Act of 1980. In a single decade, these laws imposed a level of adult supervision on those who distributed poisons of various kinds and who wantonly killed any creature foolish enough to stand in the way. At the same time, the new legislation created tens of thousands of jobs for people who cared about the world around them. Real opportunities appeared for ordinary people to become professional environmentalists.

The United States was not alone. The United States was not even the first to more aggressively protect nature. Through much of the world, it was as if a floodgate had opened. It was as if *Homo sapiens* everywhere woke up, looked around, and said, "it's time for a course correction."

Society is changing. The pace at which attitudes about our fellow beings transforms seems painfully slow. It is sluggish indeed relative to changes wrought by, say, the internet revolution. But nevertheless, change is upon us.

Will the next generation rely on single-use plastics? Will the manufacture of short-lived consumer goods dependent on water- and land-intensive mining continue? Will people persist in reproducing with the abandon of rabbits? Will they carry on raising their offspring as insatiable consumers, as fodder for advertisers and marketers? How much longer will people own pets that gobble down wild birds and that are, in fact, the largest single risk to song birds in the United States? A decade from now, will visitors to Mexico still slay fish for sport or even for food?

All of these questions place me on dangerous ground. They are the sort of questions that will lead to my name being scratched off invitation lists. As a one-time boss told me long ago, only wet babies like change.

But in this case I am only the messenger. Change is upon us. Too slow, but almost certainly unstoppable.

Two more news items pop up that are worthy of note. First, there is a story on yet another widely reported recent study suggesting that the human population will peak around the middle of the century at, according to this article, something under nine billion people. The era of a human population growing exponentially is coming to a close. Second, a minor news item, but important, from *The Conversation*: "My art uses plastic recovered from beaches around the world to understand how our consumer society is transforming the ocean." Worthy of note, because it is a sign, one of many, of a growing movement that will lead people toward thinking about their consumption habits. The two things together, a reduced population and individuals who consume less stuff, will be good for all of us.

When I talk to people about my optimism regarding the extinction crisis, I am more often than not rebuffed and even at times ridiculed. I am occasionally assaulted, so far only verbally. To be optimistic, some seem to think, is to be a fool, unaware of the facts, perhaps intentionally ignorant of the realities. But I defend myself. I point to the trajectory of change while advising patience and perseverance. Yes, people resist change. They are slow to adjust. It is too late for many thousands of species. Generations have and will continue to witness the diminishment of Earth's biodiversity. Many species, by virtue of tiny population numbers or grossly limited habitat, are already fated to oblivion, part of the extinction debt. But a time will come when we will no longer accept the unnatural disappearance of species, when we will become true stewards to all that swims and crawls and walks, to all that puts down roots or sends up branches, to all that grows upon the Earth. We are fighting a holding action, slowing down the devastation as best we can until real change emerges. But just here there are no people, aside from my Lisanne, and she neither rebuffs nor ridicules.

Anchored precariously next to an island I will not name, an island removed from pueblos and easy anchorages, we dive and see clouds of juvenile fish. There are billions in this bay alone. Later, darkness falls and a school of small silvery fish surrounds *Rocinante*. The individuals dart rapidly and unpredictably, fooling the eye, and I cannot see them clearly enough to say what they are. But they are so densely packed that in a flashlight's beam it looks as if one might be able to stand on their backs. Bumping into *Rocinante*'s hull they make a noise throughout the night that sounds like a strong current running past.

Ashore the next morning, we find well over a thousand pelican nests, recently abandoned for the season. Young pelicans—too many to count—crowd the cliffs and the skies, sharing space with blue-footed boobies. A pair of what look and sound like laughing falcons screech and play in the air above the sharp peaks that reach upward just north of our small bay. To the east we watch ospreys—two adults and their year-old offspring—sitting, sharing the outstretched arms of a cactus in a dry volcanic plain.

Later in the morning, next to *Rocinante*, elegant terns dive suddenly and resurface, almost always with prey. Sea lions swim past. Beneath the waves, we see the same juvenile fish we had seen so many times and in so many places, but also full-sized leopard groupers and schools of mature trigger fish. They swim in the open above the rocks, suggesting the rarity of fishing here.

And there are turtles in the water, turtles popping their heads up every thirty of forty seconds within sight of our boat. This is nothing like what

Columbus and his thugs saw when they came to the New World, nothing like their claim that it might be possible to walk to shore from turtle to turtle, but nevertheless this could be fairly described as a sea full of turtles.

As the sun sets, I watch birds roosting in the rock walls that make up three sides of the anchorage, and in so doing my eyes settle on a lone cardón cactus extending upward from a windswept outcrop at the top of one of the cliffs. The cactus grows directly from stone, or so it seems. Somehow it arrived there as a seed, germinated, rooted, matured. It not only survived, it shot upward, extending its trunk and branches from a piece of terrain that seems entirely hostile, with no regular water supply but subject to frequent severe winds and pizza-oven heat. Now it stands more than thirty feet tall, making it—and this is a conservative guess—at least fifty years old. Maybe older. Authorities believe the species can live longer than two hundred years. This plant could have been here before I was born.

If this were not the sort of thing that occurs so often as to be common-place and therefore all but invisible along the shores of the Gulf of California, I would stare in wonder. But even knowing that what I see above me is by no means unusual, I cannot help but ask myself: How is this possible?

The detailed answer eludes me. I am a biologist, but I have no expertise in the adaptive strategies of cardón cactus. On the other hand, in general terms there is no mystery at all. Given half a chance, life triumphs. It is that simple. And it is this tendency toward survival that gives me my greatest hope. The tenacity of life, it seems, is our greatest ally in this fight to stop human-caused extinctions.

All we have to do, one could argue, is stand out of its way. But that is not possible. We are in fact here and in the way. And so it lies firmly upon our shoulders to right the wrongs we and our forebears have done, to take personal and cultural responsibility, and to convert that responsibility into actions that will give life, all life, both the respect it deserves and a fair chance at surviving on a shared Earth. If we can do that, there is room for optimism.

Acknowledgments

The idea for this book came to me not long after my wife and I sailed into Mexico during the early stages of the COVID pandemic. For wandering sailors such as us, it was a confusing time. In a matter of weeks, concerns about the virus grew from back page news coverage to headlines to border closures. We had the good fortune to sail away from Nicaragua just before that nation closed its ports and the even greater fortune of arriving unimpeded in Chiapas, Mexico. Amid global confusion and tragedy, cautious mask-wearing and gloved authorities processed our paperwork and welcomed us to their country. Six months later, officials graciously granted a humanitarian extension to our visas, and when vaccines became available they were shared with nationals and foreigners alike. Throughout the pandemic and its aftermath, despite widespread and justified concerns regarding both health and the pandemic economy, we never once felt unwelcome or unsafe. For that I thank both the people and the government of Mexico.

Many Mexicans and foreigners living in Mexico, most of whom are named in the text, generously tolerated my basic and mispronounced Spanish while offering their time and wisdom during interviews, site visits, and other interactions. Among the most notable of these were Elsa Coria

Galindo, Eduardo Pérez, Diana Barreto Luna, and Judith Moore (all of El Centro de Rescate, Rehabilitación, e Investigación de Fauna Silvestre, or The Center for the Rescue, Rehabilitation, and Investigation of Wild Fauna, in San Carolos Nuevo Guaymas); Luis Martín Castro Romero and Tom Woodard (both of the San Basilio project near Loreto); Karen Oceguera, Agnese Mancini, and Chuy Lucero (all of the Grupo Tortuguero de las Californias, or the Group of People working with Turtles in the Californias, based in La Paz); Erika Santacruz Lopez (of Grupo Tortuguero de Bahía de los Ángeles, or the Group of People working with Turtles in Bahía de los Ángeles); and Antonio Resendiz (of Camp Archelon in Bahía de los Ángeles).

A number of readers provided helpful comments on early drafts of my manuscript. These included Kathryn Temple, Kristy Sneddon, Jason Hale, Lisanne Aerts, Judith Moore, and Tom Woodard. Fellow nature writers Jonathan Balcombe (author of *Super Fly* and *What a Fish Knows*), Juli Berwald (author of *Spineless* and *Life on the Rocks*), and Andromeda Romano-Lax (author of *Searching for Steinbeck's Sea of Cortez: A Makeshift Expedition Along Baja's Desert Coast* and many other works) offered not only helpful comments but also prepublication blurbs assuring potential publishers of the merit of my work.

My agent, Jill Marr (of the Sandra Dijkstra Literary Agency), brought this book to the attention of worthy potential publishers and placed it with Pegasus Books.

Victoria Rose offered copy edits and spotted far too many embarrassing errors in a nearly final version of the manuscript. Her eye for detail is commendable.

Jessica Case, Deputy Publisher at Pegasus Books, provided insightful suggestions that improved the manuscript while also managing the innumerable moving parts and people working behind the scenes that take books from a collection of words and ideas into print. I am indebted to her for her faith in this book and for her long-standing dedication to the production and promotion of literary works.

Lastly, my wife and fellow biologist Lisanne Aerts was my constant companion and a source of unwavering support as this book progressed, and her contribution to its completion cannot be overstated.

My sincerest thanks to all of you!

NOTES

Preface

Lieutenant William Bligh's words about the value of avoiding "despair" even in a very desperate situation (or especially in a very desperate situation) come from his own *A Narrative of the Mutiny, on Board His Majesty's Ship Bounty; and the Subsequent Voyage of Part of the Crew, in the Ship's Boat, from Tofoa, one of the Friendly Islands, to Timor, a Dutch Settlement in the East Indies*, published in London in 1790. Bligh and the eighteen men who accompanied him slowly starved on very short rations during the forty-eight-day passage. No reasonable person would have had confidence in the success of the voyage, and yet the sailors, according to Bligh, never lost hope. Two side notes may be of interest. First, Bligh, in his quote, mentions the deadliness of despair before reaching New Holland, or Australia, when in fact the open boat voyage did not end until they landed in Coupang, a Dutch settlement in Timor; the northern part of Australia, at that time, had not been settled by Europeans, but it did offer a source of food (mainly oysters and berries) and water, without which the men would never have reached Timor. Second, one man—Thomas Hayward, who accompanied Bligh on the *Bounty* and in the open boat—would later sail on the *Pandora*, tasked with searching for the mutineers. The *Pandora* was shipwrecked, and Hayward faced a second long passage (1,100 miles) in an open boat. Whether or not he maintained his optimism throughout that second voyage I do not know, but I like to think so. If so, it is exactly the kind of optimism and confidence needed as we face today's extinction crisis. In any case, a tremendous amount has been written about the mutiny of the *Bounty*, but the source that brought the Bligh quote to my attention was Caroline Alexander's wonderful *The Bounty: The True Story of the Mutiny on the Bounty* (2003, Penguin, New York).

At least one politician, who represented the Mexican National Regeneration Movement, has promoted the possibility of changing the name of the Gulf of California to the Sea of Yaqui, recognizing one of the groups of people who lived in the region prior to European conquest. In the September 14, 2001, parliamentary gazette, supporters urged "the authorities to change the geographical nomenclature from the Sea of Cortez to the Sea of the Yaqui."

1: The Sexual Turtle

I am well aware that my writing style, in all of my books but especially here, draws often on digressions. I am not ashamed of applying this technique. It reflects how I think. Also, it worked well for Herman Melville in *Moby Dick*; while I am not the writer that Melville was, I stand in good company as a literary digresser.

Many sources, in both academic journals and in more accessible outlets, discuss the Last Universal Common Ancestor. Among others, see https://www.science.org/news/2016/07/our-last-common-ancestor-inhaled-hydrogen-underwater-volcanoes. The example sentence used in the text came from a paper entitled, "When LUCA met gnomAD: Genetic constraints on universal genes in humans," by Alexandre Fabre and Julien Mancini, published in 2022 in the journal *Intractable Rare Disease Research* (11(3), pages 149–152). My use of their sentence in my text should be seen in no way as disrespectful. Similarly specialized and jargon rich sentences can be found in scientific papers everywhere, including many I myself have written.

Elizabeth Kolbert's amazing *The Sixth Extinction* offers (among many other things) a more detailed but very readable history of what might be thought of as "the discovery of extinction."

The *Bioscience* article mentioned in the text is "Where have all the turtles gone, and why does it matter?" by Jeffrey Lovich, Joshua Ennen, Mickey Agha, and J. Whitfield Gibbons, published in October 2018 (Volume 68, Number 10, pages 771–781). It is available in full at https://parcplace.org/wp-content/uploads/2020/03/Lovich-et-al-2018.pdf).

Thomas Molyneux, the author of the paper discussing the large horns found in Ireland, was a medical doctor. In the seventeenth and eighteenth centuries, it was not at all unusual for medical doctors and others to engage in discussions of natural history that today would be considered outside of their realm of expertise. The full paper is available online at https://royalsocietypublishing.org/doi/pdf/10.1098/rstl.1695.0083. This paper is often cited in discussions of the history of extinction.

Thomas Jefferson's words come from "A memoir on the discovery of certain bones of a quadruped of the clawed kind in the western parts of Virginia." The sixteen-page paper was published by the *American Philosophical Society Transactions* in 1797 and is available online at https://founders.archives.gov/documents/Jefferson/01-29-02-0232. This is another paper often cited in the history of extinction.

I have seen early editions of Cuvier's *Essay on the Theory of the Earth* advertised for a mere $600. Fortunately, electronic versions are readily available online in English for as little as $0.00, thanks to Project Gutenberg, at https://www.gutenberg.org/ebooks/62918. Cuvier, if he were alive today, would be amazed by both the high price of the book and the very existence of the electronic version.

Fred Pearce's *Yale Environment 360* article from 2015, "Global extinction rates: Why do estimates vary so wildly," offers an excellent and accessible discussion of the variability in extinction rate estimates. It is available online at https://e360.yale.edu/features /global_extinction_rates_why_do_estimates_vary_so_wildly. Pearce does not point out that some estimates may be exaggerated simply because scientists are humans, and as such a passion for their subject may lead to the exaggeration of seemingly dispassionate estimates. He also refrains from pointing out that anyone seeking research funds may be more successful in the midst of a crisis. Despite these possibilities, the higher end estimates are truly distressing. As are, for that matter, the lower end estimates. It saddens me to think that debate about the validity of estimates, low and high, may detract from efforts to address the situation.

It is sometimes difficult to reconcile published estimates of extinction rates with certain on-the-ground realities. For example, take the estimated background extinction rate of one species lost every 700 years. At any time in the past, species with limited ranges (such as many of the species found in today's Amazon forests or on various islands) would have been lost due to, for example, volcanic eruptions or tsunamis, and this would have happened more often than once every 700 years. Not too surprisingly, different researchers use different methods, with some possibly considering only easily identified and fossilized species and others possibly considering every species found through extensive sampling of contemporary habitats. Despite major discrepancies between researchers and methods, if any single method is consistently applied it is clear that species are disappearing at an alarming rate.

Regarding the use of *darwinii* in species names, as in *Rhinoderma darwinii* (the southern Darwin's frog): There are thirty-seven or more species (including some from the fossil record) that use *darwinii* as a species epithet (the second element in the genus/species binomial name per the system developed by Swedish biologist Carl Linnaeus in the eighteenth century and still in use today, despite its many shortcomings). These *darwinii* include two protists, a mushroom, at least sixteen plants, eight invertebrates, two fish, three reptiles, three birds, a mammal, and of course one very strange frog. I do not know if Darwin himself ever commented on the use of his name, or what he would have thought about, for example, seeing his name applied to a species known only from the fossil record, or to a protist, but I think most biologists would accept the compliment with a smile and keep photographs of their namesakes at hand, perhaps intermingled with those of their children.

For more on Darwin's frogs, skip the mostly superficial accounts available online and go straight to "The population decline and extinction of Darwin's frogs," published by PlosOne on June 12, 2013, by Claudio Soto-Azat, Andrés Valenzuela-Sánchez, Ben Collen, J. Marcus Rowcliffe, Alberto Veloso, and Andrew A. Cunningham, available online. The article was written before researchers realized that the fungi *Batrachochytrium dendrobatidis* and *Batrachochytrium salamandrivorans* could be behind today's tragically remarkable decline in amphibians.

Regarding my father's motivational poster with its adage about turtles making progress only when they stick their necks out: As I recall, at my mother's request or demand the poster was tacked to a wall in the basement. It was only when I decided to use those words that I wondered where they might have come from. According to Quote Investigator, the adage probably originated within the Manhattan Project during World War II, and they cite a *Collier's Weekly* article from October 13, 1945, as a source. They also point out that the saying was further popularized by, among others, chemist James B. Conant, who served as Harvard University President from 1933 to 1953.

Taxonomists place all of the more than 350 extant turtle species into one of two suborders, the Pleurodira or Cryptodira. Pleurodires (side-necked turtles), restricted in nature (that is, in the wild) to southern hemisphere freshwater habitats, withdraw into their shells by folding their necks to the side. The Cryptodira, which includes the freshwater and terrestrial turtles and tortoises familiar to most people who live in the northern hemisphere, can generally retract their heads and necks more or less straight back into their shells. Sea turtles, although members of the Cryptodira, have lost the ability to withdraw their heads into their shells.

Rebecca Tuhus-Dubrow suggested that eco-optimists may be considered morons in her engaging winter 2015 article "The Eco-optimists," which appeared in the online magazine *Dissent*. She did not say that she saw eco-optimists as morons, but rather that they may sound like morons. She is not alone in having made the play on words between oxymoron and moron. Her article is available on www.dissentmagazine.org/author /rebeccatuhusdubrow.

The study of promiscuity in sea turtles, "Reconstructing paternal genotypes to infer patterns of sperm storage and sexual selection in the hawksbill turtle," by Karl P. Phillips,

Tove H. Jorgensen, Kevin G. Jolliffe, San-Marie Jolliffe, Jock Henwood, and David S. Richardson, was published in *Molecular Ecology*, Volume 22, Issue 8, April 2013, pages 2301–2312. The abstract ends with the memorable words, "the primary value of storing sperm in marine turtles may be to uncouple mating and fertilization in time and avoid costly re-mating."

2: Walking Beaches

Although legal harvesting of eggs is, to say the least, controversial, see https://costa-rica -guide.com/nature/wildlife/turtle-egg-harvest/#conservation for arguments supporting the practice at Ostional, Costa Rica.

The description of ways in which sea turtle eggs are eaten in Costa Rica came from the most part from *Saving Sea Turtles* (John Hopkins University Press, 2011), by the eminent turtle researcher James Spotila, who cited both personal experience and one of the fathers of turtle research, Archie Carr, as sources of information. I myself have not knowingly eaten turtle eggs, and I have no plans to do so.

I have heard many people complain about confusing environmental regulations in Mexico, including regulations protecting turtles. But if there were a confusion contest between the United States and Mexico, the United States would probably take the trophy. As an example: According to a long-standing 1977 interagency memorandum of understanding (available at https://media.fisheries.noaa.gov/dam-migration/fws-nmfs_mou_2015.pdf), the United States Fish and Wildlife Service has jurisdiction over sea turtles once they are on a beach, but that jurisdiction is relinquished to the United States National Marine Fisheries Service once that turtle crawls back into the water, unless of course the beach or the water is under the protection of one or the other of the agencies (for example, as a wildlife refuge or a national park). Many of the states also claim some level of jurisdiction under certain circumstances.

The paper about the identity and naming of black green turtles, "Evolutionary significant units versus geopolitical taxonomy: Molecular systematics of an endangered sea turtle (genus *Chelonia*)," authored by Stephen Karl and Brian Bowen, was published in Volume 13, Issue 5, of *Conservation Biology*, pages 990–999, in 2001. The authors seemed genuinely concerned that the name change would impact conservation measures, possibly because some might argue that protecting green turtles in one region would sufficiently protect them in all regions, so, for example, recovery of the Caribbean green turtle populations would result in insufficient protections for the Mexican green turtle (that is, the black green turtle). This can be a legitimate concern, and would have been an even more important concern in 2001, but today species (especially charismatic species like sea turtles) are often managed at the population or "stock" level.

The words of Priest Andrés Bernáldez and Ferdinand Columbus first came to me via the fascinating 2007 book *The Unnatural History of the Sea,* by Callum Roberts (a Shearwater Book published by Island Press, Washington, DC), but I have seen them repeated many times since that first encounter. It is likely that similar accounts exist in the innumerable ships logs kept in various languages at that time. However, I have not encountered any accounts describing sea turtle abundance in the Pacific during the early days of European conquest.

3: The Veterinarian

Many authors have written extensively about past encounters between sea turtles and humans. Of the many papers on the topic, Jack Frazier's 2003 "Prehistoric and ancient historic interactions between humans and marine turtles" (in *Biology of Sea Turtles,* Volume 2, pages 1–38, CRC Press, Boca Raton) offers a good overview. The same author, who writes prolifically about the historical and prehistorical interactions between sea turtles and humans, referred to sea turtles as "the ultimate tool kit" in his engaging 2005 paper, "Marine turtles—the ultimate tool kit: A review of worked bones of marine turtles" (pages 359–382 in *From Hooves to Horns, from Mollusc to Mammoth: Manufacture and Use of Bone Artefacts from Prehistoric Times to the Present* (*Proceedings of the Fourth Meeting of the ICAZ Worked Bone Research Group at Tallinn,* 26th–31st August 2003; edited by J. Luik, A.M. Choyke, C.E. Batey, and L. Lougas), available at http://seaturtle.org /library/FrazierJ_2005_InFromHoovestoHornsfromMollusctoMammo_p359-382.pdf (and elsewhere).

Archeologists often look at changes in fishing and hunting patterns across time. One apparently common scenario on islands involves the gradual shift from shallow water nearshore fisheries to deeper water fisheries, probably indicating a combination of over demand and over exploitation in the nearshore along with development of new fishing techniques and perhaps better boats that allow fishing in deeper water. (I say "perhaps better boats" because I have seen fishermen paddling dugout canoes several miles offshore in Honduras and elsewhere, sometimes in very rough seas, so better boats may not be a necessity at all). With sea turtles, a decrease in turtle remains (bones and shell fragments) over time in the archaeological profile suggests over exploitation or overkill. See, for example, "Long-term trends in prehistoric fishing and hunting on Tobago, West Indies," published in 2006 in *Latin American Antiquity* (Volume 17.3, pages 316–334) by David Steadman and Sharyn Jones. In reading papers like this, it is fun to imagine both the original inhabitants who left behind the signs of their times and the researchers who carefully excavated the past from under a hot tropical sun in a place that most people today would see as a vacation destination.

The survivor of the shipwreck who wrote of Bermuda's turtles was Slyvester Jordain. His *A Discovery of the Barmudas, otherwise called the Ile of Divels* offers an account of the wreck of the sailing vessel *Sea Venture*, a ship bound for Virginia. Badly damaged in a storm, the ship was purposely driven onto the reefs of Bermuda to save the passengers and crew (and one dog). William Shakespeare's *The Tempest* was inspired by the wreck.

Although many accounts of the settlement of Bermuda and even stories of its early rules regarding the hunting of sea turtles can be found in libraries, both online and off, I think Archie Carr's 1967 book *So Excellent a Fishe: A Natural History of Sea Turtles* (University of Florida Press, Gainesville, Florida) should be credited with bringing the legislation to the attention of the modern turtle conservation movement. For the exact wording of the 1620 law protecting Bermuda's sea turtles, see, among other sources, https://www.islc .net/~fripplog/Docs/Bermuda%20Assmbly%20of%201620.htm.

There have been and continue to be many efforts to estimate sea turtle population levels, and many sources exist providing details of individual efforts or summarizing information from numerous efforts. It is easy to imagine the difficulties involved with counting any animal species widely dispersed at sea, but it is even easier to imagine the challenges associated with estimating past sea turtle populations. I am aware of several significant efforts to estimate past populations. The one mentioned in the text is "Roles of sea turtles in marine ecosystems: Reconstructing the past," by Karen Bjorndal and Jeremy Jackson (in *Biology of Sea Turtles*, Volume 2, pages 259–274, CRC Press, Boca Raton). The authors (as I understood it) relied on estimates of carrying capacity based on food availability and back computed prehistorical estimates from there. In others, authors used historical documents to estimate populations that might have existed in pre-Columbian times. For example, J. B. C. Jackson, in his 1997 "Reefs since Columbus" (*Coral Reefs*, volume 16, pages S23–S32), made speculative estimates of pre-Columbian sea turtle populations in the Caribbean using a series of assumptions about native hunting pressure, concluding that there were between thirty-three and thirty-nine million adult turtles in the region; this put the biomass well above that of, for example, the biomass of ungulates wandering in the Serengeti at the time of his writing. It may be worth noting that the estimate from Bjorndal and Jackson assumed there was no hunting pressure from humans while that of Jackson was based on assumed hunting pressure, although that in itself does not explain the difference between the two estimates. Although Jackson's estimate was considerably smaller than that of Bjorndal and Jackson, it still drives home the simple point that there were, at one time, far more sea turtles than there are today.

Most of the information regarding the legal hunting of sea turtles comes from the 2014 paper "So excellent a fishe: A global overview of legal marine turtle fisheries," published in *Biodiversity Research* (Volume 20, Issue 5, pages 579–590) and authored by Francis Humber, Brendan Godley, and Annette Broderick.

To my knowledge, the earliest reports of attempts to relocate sea turtle nests came from Tom Harrison in 1947, when he was the curator of the Sarawak Museum in Borneo. He knew of earlier requirements to "plant" eggs from females that were slaughtered in the turtle hunt in Australia, but his reports seem to be the first to describe actual transplanting of nests. However, transplanting turtle eggs is so straightforward, so simple, that it seems likely or at least possible that it has been done on a small scale for hundreds if not thousands of years. He was working with green turtles.

In *The Windward Road*, Archie Carr offers a compelling account of the identity of the Kemp's ridley and the entirely erroneous belief by some that the species might in fact be a hybrid, a cross between a hawksbill and a green.

Archie Carr's claim that "all sea turtles are endangered" in the long-term comes from a letter he wrote to Peter Scott of the IUCN on February 16, 1966. It is on file in the collection of Carr Papers, Series 2, box 22, held at the University of Florida's George A. Smathers Libraries. I became aware of the letter through Alison Rieser's wonderfully detailed 2012 book, *The Case of the Green Turtle: An Uncensored History of a Conservation Icon*, published by The Johns Hopkins University Press, Baltimore.

4: Releases

Dr. Elsa Galindo's explanation of the origin of the hawksbill turtle's infection is backed up by the scant available literature on sea turtle diseases. From the paper "Synopsis of infections in sea turtles caused by virus, bacteria and parasites: An ecological review," published by Alonzo Alfaro, Marianne Køie, and Kurt Buchmann at www.seaturtle.org /library/AlfaroA_2010_Synopsisofinfectionsinseaturtlescau.pdf, "In sea turtles, a virus may cause cellular damage that allows other pathogens (especially bacteria and fungi) to colonize unhealthy tissues. The reptile may clear the viral infection that initiated the disease process, and bacteria or fungus is often recovered from clinically ill animals."

I first thought about Jainism in the context of conservation after reading Ross Anderson's fantastic "A journey into the animal mind," an article about animal consciousness, published in the March 2019 edition of *The Atlantic*. Some of my examples of Jainist behaviors came from Anderson's article, backed up by other sources.

Sonia Shah's fascinating book, *The Fever: How Malaria Has Ruled Humankind for 500,000 Years*, describes the guilt felt by some Jains regarding the swatting of mosquitoes, even those that potentially carry malaria.

5: A Turtle Lost

Jeanne A. Mortimer (with a long string of coauthors, including Katia Ballorain, Carlos E. Diez, Nicole Esteban, Nancy FitzSimmons, Alexander R. Gaos, Graeme Hays, Christine A. Madden Hof, Michael P. Jensen, Michael Liles, Roderic Mast, Anne Meylan, Nicolas Pilcher, Jeffrey A. Seminoff, and Scott Whiting) called the hawksbill the most beautiful of sea turtles in her article, "Hawksbills: The most beautiful of sea turtles," published in the SWOT Report Number 17, June 16, 2022. SWOT stands for "State of the World's Sea Turtles," an organization that describes itself as an "ever-growing international group of scientists, conservationists, artists, and concerned citizens working together to achieve an otherwise unattainable common goal." Subscriptions to SWOT reports and SWOT memberships are free at https://www.seaturtlestatus.org, along with a link for donations.

I have seen hawksbill turtle shells in bars and restaurants throughout the world. Most recently, I saw one hanging, dust-covered, in a spare bedroom of a friend's house in the Netherlands. The friend inherited the shell from a relative who had spent time in the Dutch Indies, that is, in the colonies of the Netherlands that are now Indonesia. The friend's adult daughter thought the turtle was plastic until I pointed out the sutures holding the plastron to the carapace. For myself, as much as I value fossilized remains both as scientific curiosities and works of natural art, a preserved sea turtle carcass or shell hanging on my wall would only make me sad.

Although modern turtles have shells, early turtles did not. But even if the shell is not the defining characteristic of turtles for evolutionary biologists, it is for most people. Part of this book was written in the Netherlands, where I learned that the word for turtle is *schildpad*, literally a "shield toad" or a "shell toad."

Timelines of species appearances and extinctions, including those of turtles, are matters of debate, with different references often offering wildly different versions of the past. The twenty-four-hour timelines I have used to offer some perspective on the developing biosphere in deep time are based on various references. In all cases, I tried to use those references that seem to present the consensus view, or at least the mainstream view, of particular events in the history of life. If I have introduced errors, please forgive me. I was not there to witness the events in action and so I had no way to confirm the informed opinions of the many researchers who have devoted their careers to understanding the distant past.

Genetic comparisons between humans and other animals can be confusing. Genes make up only about 2 percent of DNA. When we say, for example, that we share about 90 percent of our genes with turtles, we are only taking into account 2 percent of our DNA. Another 8 percent or so of the rest of our ("our" here referring to both turtles and people) DNA regulates genes, basically turning them on or off. The rest of the DNA has other functions, or no functions at all; we do not really know. But still, if there is any doubt that life arose from a single common ancestor, an explanation for genetic similarity across species and even kingdoms is needed.

Nora Caplan-Bricker's beautiful article, "Long May They Reign," introduced me to people raising monarch butterflies. It was first published in *The Atavist* in 2020.

Nathanial Shaler's 1905 book, *Man and the Earth* (Duffield & Company, New York), focused on potential over exploitation of raw materials, including animals. "In this book," Shaler wrote, "I have endeavored to set forth certain reasons why there should be a change in the point of view from which we commonly regard the resources of the earth. As a teacher of Geology, I seen that there is a complete lack of understanding in our communities as to the duty we owe to our successors in their use of these limited resources. In this regard our conduct is like that of children who take the good that comes to them with no thought of the hereafter." The book is available from many sources. A 1910 edition is available digitally from the Library of Congress at https://www.loc.gov/item/40037810/.

The quoted description of breathing in turtles, referencing the need to breath without a flexible ribcage, came from the paper "Origin of the unique ventilatory apparatus of turtles," by Tyler Lyson, Emma Schachner, Jennifer Botha-Brink, Torsten Scheyer, Markus Lambertz, G. Bever, Bruce Rubidge, and Keven de Queiroz, published in *Nature Communications*, November 7, 2014.

The economic study from North Carolina used so-called Contingent Valuation Methods, in which survey respondents are asked about willingness to pay for various hypothetical actions. I have done Contingency Valuation Studies myself, and one of the problems with them is that people are far more willing to spend hypothetical money than real money. My impression is that people, if asked the right questions, would spend so much money on conservation that they would have no money left for little things like food and rent. In any case, the study mentioned in the text was "Ex ante willingness to pay with supply and demand uncertainty: Implications for valuing a sea turtle protection programme," by John Whitehead, published in 1992 in the journal *Applied Economics* (Volume 24, Issue 9, pages 981–988).

6: Rancho San Basilio

Ed Ricketts by some accounts was not at all happy with Steinbeck's portrayal of him as Doc in *Cannery Row* and *Sweet Thursday*.

Katherine L. Mansfield, Jeanette Wyneken, Warren P. Porter, and Jiangang Luo wrote of satellite tagging small loggerhead turtles in Florida in "First satellite tracks of neonate sea turtles redefine the 'lost years' oceanic niche," published in a 2014 edition of the *Proceedings of Royal Society B* (Volume 281, Number 1781). Mansfield and her colleagues, as well as others, have done similar work elsewhere, at least some of which was funded by Florida's sea turtle license plate program.

I once had the privilege of reviewing one of E. O. Wilson's books for the *New York Times*. The book was *Letters to a Young Scientist*, and I wrote the review in the form of a letter back to E. O. Wilson, calling it "A letter from a middle-aged scientist." At the time Professor Wilson was in the hospital, but he had his agent telephone me to convey his appreciation for the review and his delight in my interpretation of the book, and especially in my understanding of what he had hoped to accomplish with the book. I share this information because it suggested to me, in a very personal way, that E. O. Wilson was not only an accomplished person, he was considerate, and he seems to have gone through life with the instincts of a gentleman.

A series of Protected Planet Reports assess the size and other qualities of protected areas around the globe. They are published by the United Nations Environment Programme (UNEP) World Conservation Monitoring Centre (UNEP-WCMC) along with the International Union for the Conservation of Nature (IUCN). Citations often include a mention of support from the National Geographic Society. In fact, many people and many organizations, all working together, are responsible for these reports, and all concerned should be applauded for their efforts to inventory protected lands and waters. Such an effort requires diligence, a systematic approach, and a willingness to work past often confusing details in an ever-changing world to come up with something meaningful.

7: The Fishers

The *Science* paper describing dormant turtles was "Winter dormancy in sea turtles: Independent discovery and exploitation in the Gulf of California by two local cultures," by R. S. Felger, K. Cliffton, and P. J. Regal, published in the journal's January 23, 1976 issue (Volume 191, Number 4224, pages 283–285). Although I do not think the dormancy described in the paper has been substantiated by subsequent observations, it remains an interesting paper.

The E. O. Wilson quotes about "Anthropocene idealists" come from Wilson's 2016 book, *Half-Earth: Our Planet's Fight for Life* (Liveright).

The 2008 *Frontiers in Ecology and the Environment* paper, "Remembering the Gulf: Changes to the marine communities of the Sea of Cortez since the Steinbeck and Ricketts expedition of 1940," was authored by Raphael D. Sagarin, William F. Gilly, Charles H. Baxter, Nancy Burnett, and Jon Christensen (doi:10.1890/070067). The abstract ends with, "The changes we observed with historical perspective are in agreement with documented changes in ocean and coastal ecosystems around the world." In other words, ocean and coastal ecosystems around the globe have taken a beating. This is a scientific paper, and as such it is written in a passive, seemingly objective voice, making it is impossible to know if the end of the abstract struck the same emotional chord with the authors as it struck with me.

Aaron Hirsh's book, *Telling Our Way to the Sea of Cortez* (Farrar, Straus and Giroux, New York, 2013), offers readers an educational experience through a fictionalized account of one of the many classes he once taught through the Vermilion Sea Institute (or the Vermilion Sea Field Station). The station continues to operate today, educating children as well as young adults under the directorship of the energetic and dedicated Meghann McDonald. The world would be a better place if more educators shared the passions of Hirsh and McDonald.

Daniel Pauley's very short 1995 essay, "Anecdotes and the shifting baseline syndrome of fisheries," was published in *Trends in Ecology and Evolution* (Volume 10, number 10, page 430) and is readily available online. For such a short piece promoting what seems to me to be a very obvious but nevertheless important and often overlooked idea, the article has been extremely influential, perhaps because it brought a catchy name to an important idea.

8: Grupo Tortuguero

"To poach or not to poach an endangered species: Elucidating the economic and social drivers behind illegal sea turtle hunting in Baja California Sur, Mexico," by Agnese Mancini, Jesse Senko, Ricardo Borquez-Reyes, Juan Guzman Póo, Jeffrey A. Seminoff, and Volker Koch, was published in the academic journal *Human Ecology* in 2011, volume 39, pages 743–756.

A good source advocating a conservation mosaic approach is "The conservation mosaic approach to reduce corruption and the illicit sea turtle take and trade," by A. Alonso

Aguirre and Wallace Nichols, published in the *TNRC Practice Note* series in April 2020 and available online. The paper suggests the so-called "soft approach" will go beyond saving turtles to discouraging the kind of corruption that facilitates bribes and allows public officials to illegally consume turtle products without repercussions. Although Agnese Mancini, who I interviewed at Grupo Tortuguero's headquarters in La Paz, was not one of the coauthors of this paper, she was acknowledged for providing information and comments on a draft of the paper. This paper also provided estimates of the number of turtles consumed per week in Baja coastal settlements.

The 2022 article mentioned in the text, "The architecture of assisted colonisation in sea turtles: Building new populations in a biodiversity crisis," was written by Anna Barbanti, Janice Blumenthal, Annette Broderick, Brendan J. Godley, Alejandro Prat-Varela, Maria Turmo, Marta Pascual, and Carlos Carreras and published in the journal *Nature Communications*.

The article in *Yale Environment 360* that brought my attention to models indicating high extinction rates for poorly known species was "Lack of data may be hiding true extent of biodiversity loss," published August 9, 2022. The original research article describing the modeling study was written by Jan Borgelt, Martin Dorber, Marthe Høiberg, and Francesca Verones and published as "More than half of data deficient species predicted to be threatened by extinction" in the August 4, 2022, issue of *Communications Biology* (Volume 5, Number 679).

There are surprisingly few sources that attempt to compare various components of the living and nonliving worlds. I drew largely from the 2018 *Proceedings of the National Academy of Sciences* article, "The biomass distribution on Earth," by Yinon Bar-On, Rob Phillips, and Ron Milo (Volume 115, Number 25, pages 6506–6511). This is an excellent piece of scientific writing, and one of the few that contains a figure that could and should be printed on T-shirts (perhaps in a slightly simplified form). For information on the relative mass of stuff versus life, I drew from a 2018 *Global Environmental Change* article, "From resource extraction to outflows of wastes and emissions: The socioeconomic metabolism of the global economy, 1900–2015," by Fridolin Krausmann, Christian Lauk, Willi Haas, and Dominik Wiedenhofer (Volume 52, pages 131–140). I calculated the comparison of human and turtle biomass on my own, using estimated numbers and weights for both species.

9: Bahía de los Ángeles

Green turtles that survive to adulthood and avoid premature death can survive to an age of at least sixty years.

The seal (a ringed seal, *Phoca hispida*) that was wandering inland in the Alaskan Arctic was captured, treated for several months by the SeaLife Center in Seward, Alaska, fitted with a satellite tracking collar, and released on the coast close to where it was found. Its transmitter abruptly stopped sending signals, and for a time most of us involved believed that the seal had died, and in fact had probably been shot by one of the native hunters who retain and exercise the right to hunt marine mammals in the Alaskan Beaufort Sea. But several days later the transmitter suddenly started working again, showing that the animal had headed east, crossing into Canada. Its last signal came from somewhere close to the Mackenzie River delta. The collar, designed to fall off soon after the transmitter's battery was exhausted, was never recovered.

DDT remains in use today. It is produced in India. The Stockholm Convention on Persistent Organic Pollutants allows for the use of DDT to control *Anopholes* mosquitoes that spread malaria (despite evidence that many species and populations of *Anopholes* are becoming immune to DDT). The World Health Organization (WHO) supports the indoor use of DDT to control malaria in some countries, believing that the risk to birds is outweighed by the benefits to humans. And, in what to me is a rather shocking position, at least one agricultural trade association has suggested (in 2012) that Rachel Carson was wrong. Among other things, this group claimed that pesticides, by implication including DDT, allow greater food production per acre of land, which in turn protects habitat, and that, therefore, pesticides are good for wildlife. While I could understand an argument calling for the controlled use of pesticides as a necessary evil in a world attempting to feed eight billion humans and their livestock, I find it difficult not to break out in tearful laughter when I read something saying, in essence, that poisons are good for wildlife.

10: Puerto Peñasco

Geological information about Isla Ángel de la Guarda can be found in many sources, not all of which are consistent with one another. I relied on a widely circulated draft book chapter by Richard Brusca, called "A brief geological history of Northwestern Mexico." The chapter is intended to become part of a planned book, also by Brusca, called *A Natural History of the Sea of Cortez*. Brusca also summarized information about Gulf of California fisheries mentioned in the text.

I came across the description claiming that Isla Partida looks something like a barrel cactus in the outstanding book-length review, *The Record of Native People on Gulf of California Islands*, report number 201 from the Arizona State Museum Archaeological Series, written by Thomas Bowen in 2009. I cannot say enough good things about this report. On an island-by-island basis, the author provides summary information, often backed up by photographs and always with references, on the human history and prehistory of the islands. The report is available electronically free of charge at https://repository.arizona.edu/handle/10150/657631. No one should visit the islands of the Gulf of California without at least glancing through Bowen's report.

The histories of egg gathering and guano harvesting on the islands of the Gulf of California were brought to my attention by Conrad Bahre and Luis Bourillón's "Human impact in the Midriff Islands," a chapter in *A New Island Biogeography of the Sea of Cortez* (edited by Ted Case, Martin Cody, and Exequiel Ezcurra, Oxford University Press, 2000). The estimated number of Heermann's gulls and elegant terns on Isla Rasa came from the same book, in Enriqueta Velarde and Exequiel Ezcurra's chapter, "Breeding dynamics of Heermann's gulls."

Richard Nixon signed off on many environmental laws—the National Environmental Policy Act, the Clean Air Act Extension of 1970, the Marine Mammal Protection Act of 1972, the Endangered Species Act of 1973, the Safe Drinking Water Act of 1974, and others. He also belittled environmentalists. For example, he told Ford executives that environmentalists want to "go back and live like a bunch of damned animals" and that the underlying goal of their efforts was not so much one of protecting nature as it was one of "destroying the system." Nixon, pretty obviously, was not a straightforward or internally consistent man, but then few of us are.

The International Organization for Standardization already has guidelines in place for environmental labeling, under its ISO 14020 series. The standards were developed by a technical committee (or subcommittee) staffed by experts from around the globe. To my knowledge, the use of environmental labels is voluntary, although once a producer decides to use environmental labels certain regulations may apply in some jurisdictions. One obvious result of this is that environmentally harmful products remain unlabeled.

Elon Musk's tweet regarding the dangers of human population decline went viral, as many of his tweets have done, and articles about the tweet can be found easily through an online search. Most commentators suggested Musk's concerns were overblown and the slow population decline seen in some models is not likely to have a catastrophic impact on societies. Time will tell, but no doubt the human race will have weathered several more crises well before population declines meaningfully, and both me and Elon Musk will be long gone.

11: Endings

Cats are wonderful animals and can make beautiful pets, but when allowed to wander outside they kill birds and small mammals. According to the U.S. Fish and Wildlife Service, cats kill something like 2.5 billion birds each year in the United States. That is, according to their statistics, well over half of all wild birds killed by human activities or human infrastructure.

INDEX